SUSTAINABLE CAPITALISM

SUSTAINABLE CAPITALISM

Essential Work for the Anthropocene

EDITED BY
Inara Scott

THE UNIVERSITY OF UTAH PRESS
Salt Lake City

The Defiance House Man colophon is a registered trademark
of The University of Utah Press. It is based on a four-foot-tall
Ancient Puebloan pictograph (late PIII) near Glen Canyon, Utah.

LIBRARY OF CONGRESS CATALOGING-IN-PUBLICATION DATA
Names: Scott, Inara, editor.
Title: Sustainable capitalism : essential work for the Anthropocene /
edited by Inara Scott.
Identifiers: LCCN 2023049026
ISBN 9781647691752 (paperback)
ISBN 9781647691745 (hardcover)
ISBN 9781647691769 (ebook)
Subjects: LCSH: Capitalism--Social aspects.
Sustainability--Economic aspects.
Classification: LCC HB501 .S9597 2024 | DDC 338.9/27--dc23/eng/20240108
LC record available at https://lccn.loc.gov/2023049026

Errata and further information on this and other titles
available at UofUpress.com.
Printed and bound in the United States of America.

Contents

Introduction

This work starts from the essential observation that the United States, and the world as a whole, is on an unsustainable path. Sustainability can be defined in many ways, but by just about any definition, we are failing.

Consider first our physical environment. The Stockholm Resilience Center provides a helpful metric for assessing sustainability in the concept of planetary boundaries.[1] The planetary boundaries represent the limits of the processes that "regulate the stability and resilience of the Earth system."[2] Crossing these boundaries threatens to cause abrupt and irreversible change that threatens the ability of Earth to sustain human societies.[3] Studies suggest that we have exceeded five of the planetary boundaries.[4] Another key metric, the world's "carbon budget"—or amount of carbon that can be consumed while keeping the world within a target of limiting global warming to 1.5 degrees Celsius—will be exhausted in eleven years, based on 2021 emissions.[5] The U.S. continues to be one of the top emitters of carbon dioxide, both on a total and per capita basis,[6] and is historically the largest contributor to carbon emissions.[7]

Looking beyond a carbon and strictly environmental context, another metric that may be used for considering planetary sustainability is the Sustainable Development Goals (SDG) Index. This index ranks countries for their progress toward achievement of the United Nation's SDGs, which include environmental sustainability, social inclusion, and the elimination of poverty.[8] The United States ranks 31st on the index, well below most European countries, Japan, and Canada, but the U.S.'s failure to exercise leadership must be taken in the context that, across the board, the news is grim. The world is not only not on track to meet the 2030 targets, it is heading in the wrong direction on a number of key metrics, including income inequality and climate change.[9]

Sustainability is often defined to include social metrics, and these indices are also heading in the wrong direction. Wealth and income inequality in the United States have reached levels not seen since the 1920s.[10] Meanwhile, income inequality has only grown since the onset of the COVID-19 pandemic—in the U.S.[11] and across the world.[12] Not coincidentally, these crises of climate and economic inequality are mirrored by increasingly stark evidence of racial and social injustices and the systematic oppression of people of color and other marginalized groups. The murder of George Floyd ignited what many have called a "new era" of civil rights protests and urgent calls for racial justice in the United States,[13] while efforts toward environmental justice have taken on new importance as climate-fueled disasters fall disproportionately on marginalized communities.[14]

All of these elements of sustainability and reflections of our increasingly unsustainable trajectory are reflected in and may be tied to capitalism. Capitalism, and more specifically, an economic and social system built on growth and consumption, has been firmly blamed for climate change.[15] Capitalism has been linked to racism and disease.[16] Yet even as it may be blamed for these significant problems, capitalism may also facilitate the technological innovation and wealth generation necessary to lift people out of poverty, create conditions for improving health and welfare, and solve ecological crises.[17]

The explicit contradictions in these characterizations of capitalism raise essential questions as society hurtles toward and past planetary boundaries. Quite simply, we cannot shy away from the big questions embedded in the continued operation of a capitalist economy. To wit: Is capitalism incompatible with sustainability? Can a society that allows private businesses to operate for a profit exist and thrive within planetary boundaries? Can law and regulation further a more just and equitable society within the scope of what we call capitalism?

These questions are as complex as they are interdisciplinary, and as urgent as they are resistant to simple answers. They lie at the heart of this book and explain the wide diversity of topics and chapters you will find herein. While it may be tempting to consider capitalism from a unidimensional, economic lens, the variety of perspectives in this book illustrate that such a narrow focus is neither helpful nor accurate. Taking a multidimensional and contextual perspective, we realize American capitalism must be understood in the context of slavery and the commodification of labor. Environmental regulations must be designed to operate within a society in which wealth inequality can significantly impact democracy. We cannot address innovation and the promise of technology without considering how a neoliberal philosophy constrains our concepts of ethics and morality.

This work was a natural extension of the academic and professional circles I am lucky enough to move through. As a professor of environmental law and sustainable business, working within a business school, it is not uncommon to meet people who believe business and economic growth are incompatible with environmental protection; similarly, I talk to those who believe human well-being cannot be sustained or improved without economic growth. I hear from many students, popular media sources, and some academics that capitalism (that term being left deliberately undefined) is at the root of a multitude of society's ills. Yet I also hear from students, business owners, and colleagues—and have witnessed in my own work—how economic development can bring people out of poverty and improve their lives, and how innovation can be employed to solve enormous challenges.

This is no time for segmented, unilateral thinking. The scope and scale of our challenges is too great not to recognize the interdisciplinarity and complexity of the work ahead of us, if we want to sustain the physical environment and our social welfare.

While not promising to solve the sustainability crisis, this short but diverse set of chapters faces this complexity head-on. It starts with the premise that capitalism is not a god or a personified agent that controls a helpless society. Rather, it assumes that capitalism is a societal creation that is highly impacted by law, culture, and politics. While there are certain characteristics at the heart of this system—private property, markets, an economic division between capital and labor—much of it is subject to dispute, modification, and evolution. While some argue that the heart of capitalism will doom the enterprise (and Earth) to an unsustainable future, others see opportunities to constrain capitalism's worst impulses while harnessing its power for innovation and prosperity.

Then, it takes the perspective that sustainability must be viewed broadly. Like the variety of metrics mentioned earlier, it positions human rights, governance, labor relations, income equality, and socio-political relation-ships as crucial aspects of sustainability. While noting that humans cannot thrive without a healthy environment, it also acknowledges that a healthy environment is not enough for human sustainability. The sustainability of society, not just the physical environment, is at the heart of this book. With the grounding assumption that capitalism is a societal creation that reflects law, culture, and politics and with the intention to view sustainability broadly, this work seeks to bring together a variety of perspectives and scholarly views, including the history of capitalism, the uniquely American approach to capitalism, capitalism's risks and benefits, and what limits might be put on it to improve the sustainability of our human society.

It begins in Part I with an exploration of the foundations of capitalism. In Chapter 1, I review a range of popular, economic, and social understand-ings of capitalism, ultimately concluding that capitalism is impossible to define without reference to the society in which it develops. In Chapter 2, Dana Neacşu provides a discipline-based analysis of capitalism's founda-tions, considering a purely economic version; capitalism as the political economy of governance; capitalism informed by technological develop-ment; and capitalism as a complex system with legal, economic, political, and social facets. In Chapter 3, Robert Prentice examines the intersection of capitalism and democracy, and how wealth inequality can impact democ-racy in a capitalist economy. Dan Cahoy illustrates the potential power of capitalism to fuel innovation and growth within a sustainability frame-work in Chapter 4.

Part II examines U.S.-style capitalism, with its unique focus on glo-balism and individualism, and the foundational impact of slavery on the development of American capitalism. Using a comparative legal and ideo-logical lens, in Chapter 5 Gerlinde Berger-Walliser considers the unique American approach to capitalism in contrast to that of Western Europe. David Bernell offers a historical perspective of American capitalism and the growth of globalization in Chapter 6. In Chapter 7, Elizabeth Kennedy considers one specific and illustrative example of the connection between race and capitalism: the wealth gap experienced by Black Americans and how that gap developed through specific and targeted legal mechanisms. This chapter proposes a system of reparations and the Black radical tra-dition of collective resistance and cooperative economics as a viable and sustainable path forward.

Part III focuses on the unique relationship between capitalism and corporations, highlighting a central criticism of capitalism: the drive toward profit and growth. Ruth Jebe traces the historical development of the role of business in American society and how it reflects a unique focus on wealth maximization in Chapter 8. In Chapter 9, David Hess examines the ties between capitalism and human rights violations, and discusses how evolving regulation could lead to meaningful reform. Mark Kaswan considers the potential for cooperatives to change the way we view corporations and growth in Chapter 10. In Chapter 11, Ryan Katz-Rosene posits that capitalism cannot be separated from growth—a disastrous pairing that he argues may doom any long-term attempt at sustainability.

Part IV reviews some of the legal and regulatory mechanisms that undergird capitalism, particularly in the United States, and changes that may be made to these structures to rein in the threat capitalism poses to the environment and society. It asks what legal bumpers may be needed to reorient American capitalism away from the path it is currently on, and toward a consideration of long-term common good, protection of democracy, and promotion of broad stakeholder benefits. Liz Brown begins this part by describing efforts to improve sustainability through labor regulation (Chapter 12). Rajat Panwar and colleagues consider how corporate social responsibility efforts could be reframed to yield a positive social good in Chapter 13, and in Chapter 14, Victor Flatt and I consider how the use of "smart regulation" could enhance wealth creation while discouraging undesirable behavior like cheating and fraud. Finally, Christy Brekken (Chapter 15) offers a compelling view of the history and future of environmental law, arguing that, if capitalism is like an ecosystem, then "the conditions for sustainability must come from the legal and social governance systems that create the conditions for its evolution and maintenance," and ultimately, its impact on the environment.

The authors of this work—who come from law, forestry, political science, economics, and business—do not necessarily agree on what the future of capitalism will be. You will not find in these pages a singular answer to the question of whether capitalism is savior or foe. But you will find nuanced and important analyses of options and potential outcomes that should prove essential reading to anyone concerned about the path we are on, or how we might improve the lives of people around the globe.

Notes

1. Stockholm Resilience Centre, "The Nine Planetary Boundaries."
2. Stockholm Resilience Centre.
3. Stockholm Resilience Centre.
4. A study from August 2022 argues that the boundary for chemical pollution has been exceeded. Ian T. Cousins, et al., "Outside the Safe Operating Space of a New Planetary Boundary for Per- and Polyfluoroalkyl Substances (PFAS)," *Environmental Science & Technology* 56, no. 16 (2022). For information on the previous four boundaries, see Robert Monroe, "Earth Has Crossed Several 'Planetary Boundaries,' Threshold of Human-Induced Environmental Changes," UC San Diego Scripps Institution of Oceanography, January 15, 2015; European Environment Agency, "Status of the Nine Planetary Boundaries," December 5, 2019. Current research is investigating how to translate these planetary boundaries into economic metrics that investors can use to assess corporate sustainability. See Christoph Butz, et al., "Towards Defining an Environmental Investment Universe within Planetary Boundaries," *Sustainability Science* 13 (2018).
5. Pierre Friedlingstein, et al., "Global Carbon Budget 2021," *Earth System Science Data* 14, no. 4 (2022).
6. Union of Concerned Scientists, "Each Country's Share of CO2 Emissions," January 14, 2022.
7. Justin Gillis and Nadja Popovich, "The U.S. Is the Biggest Carbon Polluter in History. It Just Walked Away From the Paris Climate Deal," *New York Times*, June 1, 2017.
8. Jeffrey Sachs, "6 Ways America Can Get Back on Track with the UN Sustainable Development Goals, Columbia Climate School: Climate, Earth, and Society, September 21, 2018"; United Nations Department of Economic and Social Affairs, "Sustainable Development Goals."
9. United Nations Department of Economic and Social Affairs, *Global Sustainable Development Report 2019* (UNDESA, 2019), xx.
10. Drew DeSilver, "U.S. Income Inequality, on Rise for Decades, Is Now Highest Since 1928," Pew Research Center, December 5, 2013.
11. Alicia Adamczyk, "Inequality Has Been Building for Decades in the U.S., but Experts Say the Pandemic 'Ripped It Open,'" CNBC, October 26, 2020.
12. Patrick Henry, "Economic Inequality Has Deepened during the Pandemic. That Doesn't Mean It Can't Be Fixed," World Economic Forum, April 7, 2022.
13. Audra D. S. Burch, et al., "The Death of George Floyd Reignited a Movement. What Happens Now?," *New York Times*, April 20, 2021; Brakkton Booker, "George Floyd and the New Civil Rights Era," *Politico*, May 25, 2021.
14. EPA, "EPA Report Shows Disproportionate Impacts of Climate Change on Socially Vulnerable Populations in the United States," September 2, 2021; Glenn Thrush and Lisa Friedman, "Justice Dept. Tries to Shift Environmental Justice Efforts From Symbolic to Substantive," *New York Times*, May 12, 2022.
15. Lauren Pollock, "How Capitalism Is a Driving Force of Climate Change,"

People, Ideas, and Things Journal, 2020; George Monbiot, "Capitalism Is Killing the Planet—It's Time to Stop Buying into Our Own Destruction," *Guardian*, October 30, 2021; Naomi Klein, *This Changes Everything: Capitalism v. the Climate* (Simon & Schuster, 2014); Kate Aronoff, *Overheated: How Capitalism Broke the Planet—And How We Fight Back* (Bold Type Books, 2021).

16. Nancy Leong, "Racial Capitalism," *Harvard Law Review* 126, no. 8 (June 2013); Whitney N. Laster Pirtle, "Racial Capitalism: A Fundamental Cause of Novel Coronavirus (COVID-19) Pandemic Inequities in the United States," *Health Education & Behavior* 47, no. 4 (2020).

17. Andrew McAfee, *More from Less: The Surprising Story of How We Learned to Prosper Using Fewer Resources—and What Happens Next* (Scribner, 2019).

Part I

Foundations of Capitalism

Defining the Undefinable

Inara Scott

In the wake of the ongoing climate crisis[1] and skyrocketing income inequality,[2] a wave of scholars, popular press, and business leaders have called for a "reimagining" of capitalism,[3] and a reorientation of business around the welfare of all stakeholders.[4] Either because it is "good business"[5] or to reflect personal moral or ethical awakenings, CEOs and business leaders have been called upon to voluntarily transform capitalism to make it more sustainable, ethical, and equitable.

At the same time some business leaders and scholars imagine that a reconstituted form of capitalism can "save the world,"[6] others condemn capitalism as the root of societal problems. Naomi Klein, among others, holds capitalism responsible for climate change.[7] Many have drawn explicit ties between capitalism and racism and oppression, drawing a through-line from U.S. capitalism to slavery.[8] Others have suggested that capitalism has eroded freedom[9] and threatened democracy.[10] Among those aged 18–34, only 49% now hold a positive view of capitalism (compared to 46% who hold a negative view)—a decrease of almost twenty points in just two years. For those aged 18–24 (Gen-Z), 54% have a negative view.[11]

If capitalism had one tidy definition, one might be able to dig into these attitudes and views to determine whether capitalism ultimately is a force for creativity and entrepreneurship or a viral illness that infects social and economic relations. Indeed, the focus of this book—to investigate the connections between capitalism and possible solutions for the present unsustainable use of Earth's resources—clearly would benefit from some common understanding of what capitalism is. The problem, as this chapter will discuss, is that there simply is no such simple definition to be found. Capitalism is both economic characteristic and social phenomenon, both cause and effect. Popular understandings of the term include contradictory messages and beliefs. "[I]n capitalism, consumption is king,"[12] one article attempting to define capitalism tells readers. Others argue capitalism does not require growth.[13] Popular media articles suggest capitalism commoditizes relationships and love, furthering an epidemic of loneliness.[14] Others would attribute these negative outcomes to neoliberalism, not capitalism.[15] Many use capitalism to describe a fairly limited series of economic characteristics, while others point broadly to a variety of social arrangements (and social ills) that characterize the twenty-first century.

In this chapter, rather than picking a single definition and attempting to prove critics or proponents right (or wrong), I examine the most prominent definitions and uses of the term. To begin, I discuss the descriptive economic definition, which provides a useful starting point for most discussions of capitalism, though is ultimately unsatisfying in providing clarity about the term. I then review other ways in which the term is used or understood, including links that are commonly drawn between capitalism and freedom, capitalism and labor, capitalism and competition, and capitalism and neoliberalism. Finally, I offer an alternative to a simplistic definition of capitalism: a set of characteristics plus a related maxim that sees capitalism as a fundamentally incomplete term. Capitalism will always create contradictory understandings and experiences because capitalism does not exist in a vacuum—it absorbs, shapes, and is shaped by its social, economic, and political context. Just as we cannot define the shape of water without reference to the container in which it exists, we cannot define capitalism without reference to the society in which it operates.

Economic Definitions of Capitalism

In simplistic economic terms, capitalism may be defined as an economic system in which private individuals own the means of production (capital) and the price and availability of goods and services are set by forces of supply and demand, rather than by the government.[16] Other straightforward economic definitions propose that a capitalist economy has some of the following characteristics, at some level: private property, a system for defending contracts, individual access to markets and choice within those markets, and supportive government policies that further the use of capital and development of markets.[17]

Importantly, this approach to defining capitalism does not require purity or a singular approach to economic regulation. All of the functioning economies in the world today (including the United States) considered "capitalist" feature some form of government ownership of industry, significant government regulation of financial systems, and a mix of "free" markets and those markets in which supply and demand are more tightly controlled or the means of production are owned and operated by the government. Consider, for example, regulation of prescription drugs, municipal ownership of utilities, and the immense regulatory system for oversight of securities in the United States. "Free" markets in today's industrialized nations typically include significant government oversight of everything from product safety to energy production, and restrictions on contracting, corporate governance, and labor relations.

The obvious problem with this definition is its lack of clarity. Given the economic definition, one might argue as to whether Russia is capitalist. And how to explain or characterize China?[18] What about Sweden?[19] In response, many resort to discussing "mixed economies," and focusing on how complex, real-world economies combine elements of a market economy and a planned economy,[20] or by discussing "shades of capitalism" that highlight different types of government intervention.[21] Alternatively, we see references to state capitalism,[22] or the Nordic Model.[23] Dispensing with the term altogether, the Heritage Foundation ranks countries according to their degree of "economic freedom," which includes scales of "market freedom," "regulatory efficiency," and "government size."[24]

An alternative way to characterize capitalism is by discussing the economic assumptions that underlie a capitalist system. Perhaps one of the most common assumptions along these lines is that economic output and growth thrive in the absence of government regulation—thus the concept of a "free market" and the commonly held belief that regulation is bad for business. It is true that prominent capitalist theorists, including Milton Friedman and Frederich von Hayek, argue that capitalism requires markets free from government intervention. However, others, including John Maynard Keynes, have argued that capitalism requires strong government institutions to ensure competition.[25] And to be fair, few economists would argue against basic government structures and regulations to support the existence of markets and market activity. Most would support laws to enforce contracts, recognize and protect a variety of types of private property (including intellectual property, interest payments on debt, and contracts for provision of labor), and restrict monopolies and the restraint of trade.

Given this need for some government intervention to support free markets, capitalism cannot be fairly characterized by a system that thrives in the absence of regulation per se, but a system that thrives in the presence of strategic regulation to preserve market activity deemed favorable to the capitalist economy—or perhaps more cynically, to those in control of the capitalist economy. Thus, as some have noted, current banking and finance structures may be described as privatizing rewards, but socializing risks.[26] Or as one Twitter user put it, "i love how some people use 'capitalism' to refer to 'unregulated market competition' and some use it to mean 'collusion between government and big business' and those people argue with each other on this site and sometimes the same person uses both definitions simultaneously."[27]

As Mark Martinez argues in his book *The Myth of the Free Market*:

> Modern capitalist markets do not come to life simply because different parts of society are brought together and injected with money.... Rather, complex trade and investment patterns occur because capital—which is the lifeblood of capitalism—is made viable by government actions that fix and guard assets.... Injecting capital with life also includes guarding individual liberties and creating markets that support legal infrastructures so that creativity and investments pay off. It also means making sure that others in society don't have undue advantages or wield disproportionate power in markets. This prepares the conditions for market capitalism to exist and for entrepreneurs to prosper.

Finally, it is worth noting that these economic definitions of capitalism do not explicitly require a belief in the normative value of wealth maximization as an approach to governance, though that belief is certainly widespread. As will be discussed below, this belief actually derives from the neoliberal philosophy that emerged in the 1940s, and became a silent but powerful redefinition of what capitalism was and should be. Confronting this aspect of capitalist ideology may be essential to unpacking what is unsustainable about the current system, and what forms the basis of so many critiques of capitalism.

In the end, the economic definition of capitalism provides a helpful foundation for understanding major organizing concepts of today's complex state and global economic systems. It does not, however, capture the social, political, and governance aspects of capitalism.

Capital and Labor

One cannot talk about capitalism without addressing the systemic divide it creates between those who own the means of production and those who labor to produce goods. According to Karl Marx, political and economic societies evolved throughout history based on the struggle between classes of people—in the nineteenth century, those classes could be described as the capitalists (bourgeoisie) on one side and the workers (proletariat) on the other. Marx predicted that the struggle between these groups would culminate in a revolution by the proletariat and the creation of a communist system.[28] Marx's theories lurk beneath the surface of most understandings of how capitalism operates, whether expressed or implied.

As Marx described, in a capitalist system, the owner of capital profits by realizing a difference between the amount paid to workers and the amount charged for goods. This structure incentivizes the owners of capital to exploit workers by paying them as little as possible for their work, so they can realize a profit based on the difference between the price they charge for the commodity and the amount paid to the worker to produce it.[29] Marx also theorized that as the proletariat labored without control over the goods they produced, and with increasing distance from those products, they would ultimately become alienated from their work and from their own humanity.[30]

Importantly, whether Marx's analysis is "correct" on an economic basis is irrelevant; what is important is the sense of aggrievement by workers and the implicit belief that capitalism creates an unjust system whereby owners of capital profit at the expense of workers. Today, as inequality between low-paid workers and enormously wealthy capitalists rises, Marx's theories find particular resonance, evidenced by the legacy of the Occupy Wall Street movement[31] and the rising interest in democratic socialism in the United States.[32]

The relationships between capital and labor must also be examined in the context of race. Historian Caitlin Rosenthal, who has made an extensive study of the accounting methods used by U.S. slave owners, argues that "capitalism exists where capital (and through capital, power) is consolidated in such a way that labor can be highly commoditized."[33] For Rosenthal, one cannot separate an understanding of capitalism, particularly U.S. capitalism, from slavery. "Labor relations must be central to the history of capitalism, and a reconsideration of wage labor can lead us to a definition of capitalism that includes slavery."[34] Because ownership of capital has historically been centered in the hands of White, colonizing nations, and those classified as non-White have historically been subjugated as labor, scholars have further identified capitalism as being an explicit tool and extension of white supremacy and structural racism.[35]

Legal and financial structures, particularly tax structures and the role of equity and non-earned income in the U.S. economy, benefit and promote the holders of capital.[36] In the United States, an enormous wealth gap exists between Black and White Americans that can be directly tied to racist legal structures and direct action by racist governments that denied Black Americans the ability to accumulate capital.[37] Definitions of capitalism that do not include specific reference to the historic antagonism between capital and labor, the benefits that accrue to capital holders, and the racist history of the United States are missing something significant in understanding capitalism, its impacts on society, and popular understandings of the power imbalances it creates.

Capitalism and Democracy

An alternative to focusing on the economic characteristics of capitalism is to recognize that capitalism represents an economic structure embedded in a socio-political context. In his monograph *Capitalism*, for example, Bruce Smith characterizes capitalism as a system of governance, operating simultaneously with democracy, with each of these systems developing their authority from the government that is responsible for determining the structure of that authority and also defending and enforcing it.[38] In *Capitalism and Freedom*, Milton Friedman famously argued capitalism and democracy were necessarily intertwined: "[T]he kind of economic organization that provides economic freedom directly, namely, organization of economic activities through a largely free market and private enterprise, in short through competitive capitalism, is also a necessary though not a sufficient condition for political freedom."[39] Or put more directly, "only certain combinations of political and economic arrangements are possible, and that in particular, a society which is socialist cannot also be democratic."[40] Certainly many people believe that capitalism is synonymous with freedom, however that term is interpreted.

In recent years, the link between capitalism and democratic ideals has been significantly challenged. As economist Robert Reich notes, capitalism may be a precondition for democracy, but "democracy may not be essential to capitalism."[41] Indeed, in the twentieth and twenty-first centuries we have seen across the world the success of "authoritarian capitalism" that provides citizens with access to markets for goods and services, while restricting access to political democracy.[42] The fastest growing economies since the global economic collapse of 2008—China, Bangladesh, Cambodia, and Vietnam—have been authoritarian capitalist economies.[43]

The counterargument—that capitalism is incompatible with democracy, and in fact directly contributes to its demise—has emerged strongly during the twenty-first century.[44] The argument here is that if the accumulation of wealth and property can also foster an unequal distribution of political power, then capitalism will not strengthen democratic participation but will in fact hinder it.[45] In the United States, one can see an accumulation of wealth in the hands of a small number of private citizens and large corporations, both of which exercise a disproportionately loud voice in government.[46] When one mixes disproportionate access to power with an ethic that wealth maximization is good for society,[47] one must expect wealthy citizens and corporations to lobby for rules that will allow them to accumulate more power and more wealth, exacerbating and furthering levels of inequality.[48]

To view the operation of this principle, consider the formative government regulations that capitalists do support, such as a lower rate on income from capital gains versus earned income. In the United States, many argue that greater investment of capital will result in higher economic growth that will ultimately be beneficial to society; as a result, the government taxes capital gains at a lower rate relative to taxes on real income.[49] Yet the individuals who receive more of their wealth from unearned income also have a significant personal interest in maintaining this system. As long as those individuals who make the rules also stand to benefit from the rules, it is likely that what is considered "beneficial to society" will be influenced by what is beneficial to those in power.

The ability of some within society to exercise unequal power and therefore shape the rules of the game is not limited to capitalist economies. However, the combination of this potential with a widespread belief in the benefits of "free" markets and distaste for government regulation creates a system uniquely positioned for the growth of inequality. As long as those individuals who do not make the rules (and do not benefit from them) are also the laboring class, Marx's theories are unlikely to disappear.

Capitalism, Self-Interest, and Competition

Another understanding of capitalism views it as a socio-economic system that is driven by (and promoting of) competition and self-interest. In this view, the social and cultural aspects of capitalism, perhaps even more so than the economic aspects, must be considered for their enormous impact on society—for good and for bad.

Consider the social critiques that argue capitalism is to blame for repressive beauty standards,[50] or link capitalism to increasing mental health concerns, drug overdoses, and a rise in so-called "deaths of despair."[51] Each of these critiques focuses on the way in which capitalist economic systems depend on a human drive to accumulate individual rewards—i.e., to profit. This drive—which some call greed and others more benignly describe as self-interest—is arguably amplified by a capitalist structure that allows people to profit from human vulnerabilities. From a Marxist perspective, one can argue that capitalism reproduces and enhances class and individual conflict by embedding competition and a desire for profit into all social relationships: "capitalism [is] a system in which people are structurally inclined toward taking advantage of each other. . . . Profit, growth, and competition are systemic expressions of a culture in which self—and other—exploitation is normalized and institutionally protected."[52]

Self-interest is directly tied to competition, a drive to prevail over another to benefit one's self. Taking the opposing view to the Marxists, many believe this drive, which is often described as foundational to American values and the U.S. economy, is actually beneficial for society.[53] As the U.S. White House states: "when firms have to compete for customers, it leads to lower prices, higher quality goods and services, greater variety, and more innovation. . . . When firms compete to attract workers, they must increase compensation and improve working conditions."[54]

To this end, many economists and scholars argue that the drive toward profit and competition embedded in capitalist economies produces innovation and technological development that benefit society at large.[55] Extensive economic analyses have been undertaken to prove that capitalist economic systems do, in fact, benefit the people in those systems. These analyses focus on the rise of per capita incomes and the correlation between the rise of capitalism and the movement of millions of people out of poverty.[56] Proponents of capitalism also point to the way it drives entrepreneurship and innovation—they ask, would we have made it out of the COVID-19 pandemic with multiple vaccines were it not for capitalism?[57] In a time in which climate change is poised to ravage human societies, they also suggest capitalism's unique ability to spur technological innovation is essential and must be cultivated, rather than disparaged.[58]

This notion of innovation and creativity underlies definitions of capitalism such as the one below:

A predominantly capitalist economy . . . generally means a private ownership system marked by great openness to the new commercial ideas and the personal knowledge of private entrepreneurs and, further, by great pluralism in the private knowledge and idiosyncratic views among the wealth owners and financiers who select the ideas to which to provide capital and incentives for their development.[59]

Capitalism's focus on individual rights and the accumulation of individual benefit—embedded in a system of mutual, voluntary market transactions—has also been posited as a particular benefit to women. "[P]rogressive capitalism promotes the idea that no one is to be expected to sacrifice their interests with no expectation of benefit. Thus capitalism opposes the traditional, sexist ideal of womanly self-sacrifice."[60]

On the other hand, a core criticism of capitalism is that competition undermines the arts, creativity, and social connectedness by prioritizing the profits over creative expression and relationships. As one commentator put it, "capitalism kills culture.[61] The question that is answered differently in different societies is the extent to which various types of artistic or public service industries—including media, arts, and education—are subjected to open, competitive markets or supported by government funding.[62] Other industries may be excluded from markets for ethical reasons—for example, one cannot buy or sell organs in the United States.

Some industries, such as public utilities, are believed to operate more efficiently without competition, so competition is largely restricted and prices regulated by state agencies. Even among proponents of capitalism, debates wage over the extent to which certain types of regulation, such as antitrust laws, should preserve or promote competition, particularly when doing so would increase prices to consumers.[63]

The belief that competition and self-interest are positive traits that will result in the most beneficial ordering of society reaches its fullest expression in the pivotal ideological development of the twentieth century: neoliberalism.

Capitalism and Neoliberalism

Neoliberal economic theory views human behavior as motivated centrally by self-interest, and in particular, by economic self-interest.[64] Neoliberal theorists argue that wealth is the ultimate social good, so wealth maximization should be the driving goal of governance.[65] Unfettered market activity, competition, and profit, which are believed to produce the most wealth, should drive social outcomes, rather than government regulation or central planning.[66] "With its partner in globalisation, neoliberalism elevates the power of capital well above that of the nation-state, and above that of citizen democracy."[67]

The neoliberal ideology extends throughout society; thus, for example, the law and economics movement suggests that law should be driven by a central normative goal of efficiency, which can in turn be measured through economic output.[68] Under this theory, legal outcomes should be structured to promote economic efficiency and growth, rather than philosophical notions of justice or fairness. Gary Gerstle, who has made an extensive study of what he calls the neoliberal "political order," identifies three strands of political reform that accompanied the neoliberal ideology that arose in the United States in the postwar era:

> The first strategy of reform was to encase free markets in rules governing property and exchange and the circulation of money and credit. Encasement required strong government interventions in economic life, both domestically and internationally. The second strategy was to apply market principles ... to all areas of human endeavor. Some

neoliberals began extending market analysis into the private realm of family and morality, reimagining these spheres ... as behavior best understood in economic terms of inputs and outputs, investments and returns. The third strategy sought to recuperate the utopian promise of personal freedom embedded in classical liberalism. [69]

While research has generally discredited the theory that humans act consistently as wealth maximizers,[70] common approaches to governance today—particularly within the United States—seek out the goals of wealth maximization and economic growth, rather than human well-being.[71] Importantly—for sustainability purposes—the goal of neoliberal regulation in many capitalist societies—including most notably the United States—has been to maximize the ability of individuals in society to consume.[72] In the antitrust context, for example, the impact of the law and economics movement was to prioritize efficiency of production and redefine consumer welfare to focus narrowly on lower prices—even when that might result in less competition.[73] A review of Naomi Wolf's *Capitalism v. Climate* notes, "Klein's adversary is neoliberalism—the extreme capitalism that has birthed our era of extreme extraction."[74]

While capitalism and neoliberalism are today deeply entwined, it is essential to recall that this is a relatively recent phenomenon. Rising out of the postwar era, the neoliberal political order significantly changed the economic structure of the United States; as globalization and a neoliberal commitment to free trade across borders sent manufacturing jobs overseas, unions were decimated, industries (including telecom and Wall Street) were deregulated, and government spending dropped significantly as a percentage of GDP, recognizing a general agreement that it was the free market that should provide for Americans.[75] Economic inequality rose and job security for millions became a thing of the past.[76] Importantly, the cost of discretionary goods has fallen sharply, but the cost of housing, health care, and education has skyrocketed, leaving younger generations with an entirely different kind of future than previous ones—a future in which they cannot afford to buy a house or visit the doctor, but can afford a new cell phone or fast fashion.[77]

If neoliberalism can rise, it can also fall. The future of globalization, free trade, and a commitment to deregulation is difficult to predict, which proves the point—the neoliberal ideology, while clearly connected to the current form of capitalism, particularly U.S. capitalism, is not inseparable from it.

So What Is It? And Why Does It Matter?

Any discussion of whether capitalism can be made sustainable must begin with the task of defining the term capitalism. As a starting point, it is fair to describe capitalism as a system that includes some amount of private ownership of the means of production, access to markets for voluntary selection of goods and services, and competition among firms. Capitalist systems also tend to support individual liberties—at least with regard to the ability to consume products and services of one's choice. Finally, capitalist systems either implicitly or explicitly further the pursuit of self-interest, and focus on competition as a means of promoting economic growth.

While these characteristics tell us something important about capitalism, and may help ground a conversation, they fall short in failing to explicitly recognize the other aspects of capitalism that have been highlighted above. To address this, I offer the following addendum, based on the experience of actual capitalist economies and the common understandings of capitalism discussed above:

> *Understood as a set of economic, social, and political characteristics that appear in varying degrees in actual economies, "capitalism" is a fundamentally incomplete concept. Capitalist economies are actively managed through legal and regulatory structures to achieve desirable outcomes, and therefore always reflect the assumptions and beliefs of those in power about what those outcomes should be. Capitalism cannot be studied as an independent concept—it can only be understood in context.*

This may be the most important principle of any study of capitalism, and explains why scholars end up searching for descriptors to append to the term. Financial capitalism, regulatory capitalism, authoritarian capitalism, entrepreneurial capitalism, crony capitalism, and corporatism all attempt to provide rational understandings of an incomplete term.[78] These different flavors of capitalism explain the difference between the life experience of a steelworker living in Pennsylvania and one living in Russia, or a venture capitalist in California and one in China. A capitalist economy can curtail or celebrate political freedom. It can create vast inequality between capitalists and workers, or it can mediate the power differential and ensure a more equitable system of governance.

Rather than debating the viability and value of purely economic models that do not exist in practice, this qualified definition of capitalism tends toward a different use: an acknowledgment that global economies are a complex mix of regulated and unregulated markets, private and government-owned property, and regulatory structures to promote financial and social goals. Within this understanding, we are not bound to adopt or reject capitalism—we can deploy it as a targeted economic structure, for use in individual industries or markets to achieve desired outcomes. Similarly, and importantly, undesirable outcomes cannot solely be blamed on capitalism—we must acknowledge that they result from regulatory structures that do not prevent or worse, exacerbate, the harm we see.

When we can finally move away from debates over whether capitalism is good or bad, we can finally ask what tools we have to mitigate inequality, climate change, and racism, improve our collective well-being, and create a more sustainable world.

Notes

1. As John Kerry, U.S. climate envoy appointed in the early days of the Biden administration, noted, "The world is lagging behind the pace of change needed to avert catastrophic impacts from the climate crisis." Oliver Milman and Fiona Harvey, "John Kerry Commits US to Climate Crisis Fight but Warns World Is Way off Pace," *Guardian*, January 21, 2021, https://www.theguardian.com/us-news/2021/jan/21/john-kerry-climate-crisis-joe-biden-envoy.

2. Katherine Schaeffer, "6 Facts about Economic Inequality in the U.S.," Pew Research Center, February 7, 2020, https://www.pewresearch.org/short-reads/2020/02/07/6-facts-about-economic-inequality-in-the-u-s/. Inequality was rampant in the United States prior to the COVID-19 crisis, but the global pandemic sharpened the crisis. Greg Iacurci, "The Legacy of 2020: Riches for the Wealthy, Well Educated and Often White, Financial Pain for Others," CNBC, January 1, 2021; Nick Hanauer and David M. Rolf, "The Top 1% of Americans Have Taken $50 Trillion From the Bottom 90%—And That's Made the U.S. Less Secure," *Time*, September 14, 2020, https://time.com/5888024/50-trillion-income-inequality-america/.

3. Rebecca Henderson, *Reimagining Capitalism in a World on Fire* (PublicAffairs, 2021).

4. Business Roundtable, "Business Roundtable Redefines the Purposes of a Corporation to Promote 'An Economy that Serves all Americans,'" August 19, 2019, https://www.businessroundtable.org/business-roundtable-redefines-the-purpose-of-a-corporation-to-promote-an-economy-that-serves-all-americans.

5. Sustainable business leaders have argued for years that companies that take a "triple bottom line" approach to business success, balancing the interests of "people, planets, and profits," will be more successful and have higher returns over time than less sustainable businesses. See L. Hunter Lovins, "Climate Capitalism: The Business Case for Climate Protection," *Pace Environmental Law Review* 27, no. 3 (July 2010): 735–779, https://doi.org/10.58948/0738-6206.1650. Yet at the same time, the business literature has struggled to find straightforward data to support this assertion. "In fact, even the 'low hanging fruits' of CSR [corporate social responsibility], where a positive business case can be relatively easily established, including classic issues such as workplace safety, emissions reductions, or eco-efficiency, still remain subject to contestation and show strong variation across different contexts." Frank G. A. de Bakker et al., "The Elephant in the Room: The Nascent Research Agenda on Corporations, Social Responsibility, and Capitalism," *Business & Society* 57, no. 7 (September 2020): 1295–1302, https://doi.org/10.1177/0007650319898196.

6. As Rebecca Henderson puts it in the stirring introduction to her book, "[W]e have the opportunity to mobilize shared purpose at a global scale. . . . Join me. We have a world to save." Henderson, *Reimagining Capitalism in a World on Fire*, 6. The drive to change corporate behavior to achieve positive social ends is also in vogue in business schools. Geetha Bai, "Business schools should drive positive societal change, says AACSB's new CEO," *U2B*, September 7, 2022, https://u2b.com/2020/09/07/business-schools-societal-impact-aacsb-ceo/.

7. Naomi Klein, *This Changes Everything: Capitalism vs. the Climate* (Simon & Schuster, 2015). "As an increasingly globalised form of political economy, the capitalist drive to expand markets to maximize profits results in a perpetual treadmill of production and consumption. This treadmill is heavily reliant in turn on fossil fuels and other substances which then emit greenhouse gases — including nitrous oxide, methane, ozone, and chlorofluorocarbons." Hans A. Baer, "Global Capitalism and Climate Change," in *Handbook on International Political Economy*, ed. Ralph Petterman (World Scientific Publishing, 2012), 396.

8. Richard Delgado, "Rodrigo's Equation: Race, Capitalism, and the Search for Reform," *Wake Forest Law Review* 49 (2014): 87–120; Laura Pulido, "Flint, Environmental Racism, and Racial Capitalism," 1-16; Rosenthal, "Capitalism when Labor was Capital: Slavery, Power, and Price in Antebellum America," 296.

9. Katya Assaf, "Capitalism vs. Freedom," *N.Y.U. Review Of Law & Social Change* 38, no. 2 (2014): 201.

10. Robert B. Reich, "How Capitalism is Killing Democracy," *Foreign Policy*, October 12, 2009, https://foreignpolicy.com/2009/10/12/how-capitalism-is-killing-democracy/.

11. Laura Wronksi, "Axios | Momentive Poll: Capitalism and Socialism," *Axios*, 2021.

12. Kim Kelly, "What 'Capitalism' Is and How It Affects People," *TeenVogue*, August 25, 2020, https://www.teenvogue.com/story/what-capitalism-is.

13. Harry Saunders, "Does Capitalism Require Endless Growth? Marx and Malthus Reconsidered," *Breakthrough Institute*, June 21, 2016, https://thebreakthrough.org/index.php/journal/issue-6/does-capitalism-require-endless-growth.

14. Alexandra Jones, "Left Unchecked, Capitalism Will Ruin Human Relationships Forever," *Face*, March 2020.

15. George Monbiot, "Neoliberalism—The Ideology at the Root of All Our Problems," *Guardian*, April 15, 2016, https://www.theguardian.com/books/2016/apr/15/neoliberalism-ideology-problem-george-monbiot.

16. The Investopedia Team, "Capitalism," *Investopedia*, March 2023; Sarwat Jahan and Ahmed Saber Mahmud, "What Is Capitalism?," *Finance and Development* 52, no. 2 (June 2015), https://doi.org/10.5089/9781484371220.022.

17. Caitlin C. Rosenthal, "Capitalism when Labor was Capital: Slavery, Power, and Price in Antebellum America," *Capitalism: A Journal of History and Economics* 1, no. 2 (Spring 2020): 301, citing Larry Neal and Jeffrey G. Williamson, *The Cambridge History of Capitalism: Volume 1, The Rise of Capitalism: From Ancient Origins to 1848* (Cambridge University Press, 2015), 2–3.

18. Jude Blanchette and Scott Kennedy, *Chinese State Capitalism: Diagnosis and Prognosis* (Center for Strategic & International Studies, October 2021), 9 (describing Chinese system as "state capitalism").

19. See Deirdre Nansen McCloskey, "Sweden is Capitalist, *National Review*, May 20, 2019"; Nima Sanandaji, "Nordic Countries Aren't Actually Socialist," *Foreign Policy*, October 27, 2021.

20. Kimberly Amadeo, "What Is a Mixed Economy?," *Balance*, October 23, 2021, https://www.thebalancemoney.com/mixed-economy-definition-pros-cons-examples-3305594.

21. Jahan and Mahmud, "What Is Capitalism?"

22. Benjamin L. Liebman and Curtis J. Milhaupt, *Regulating the Visible Hand? The Institutional Implications of Chinese State Capitalism* (Oxford University Press, 2015).

23. Peter S. Goodman, "The Nordic Model May Be the Best Cushion Against Capitalism. Can It Survive Immigration?," *New York Times*, July 11, 2019, https://www.nytimes.com/2019/07/11/business/sweden-economy-immigration.html.

24. Terry Miller, Anthony B. Kim, and James M. Roberts, *2022 Index of Economic Freedom* (The Heritage Foundation, 2022).

25. Roger Backhouse and Bradley William Bateman, "Keynes and Capitalism," *History of Political Economy* (May 2009): 651; Daniel Indiviglio, "A Free Market Needs Free Contracts," *Atlantic*, January 20, 2010, https://www.theatlantic.com/business/archive/2010/01/a-free-market-needs-free-contracts/33861/.

26. Mariana Mazzucato, "We Socialize Bailouts. We Should Socialize Successes, Too," *New York Times*, July 12, 2020, https://www.nytimes.com/2020/07/01/opinion/inequality-goverment-bailout.html.

27. Max, @deepfates, "Status," Twitter, May 23, 2022, 8:43 a.m.

28. Karl Marx and Friedrich Engels, *The Communist Manifesto* (London: Verso: 2012), 14–21.

29. Geoff Boucher, *Understanding Marxism* (Routledge, 2014), 25.

30. Karl Marx, *Capital: A Critique of Political Economy* (Moscow, 1867), 411.

31. Courtney Kealy, "A Decade on, Occupy Wall Street's Legacy on Income Inequality," Al Jazeera, September 17, 2021, https://www.aljazeera.com/economy/2021/9/17/a-decade-on-occupy-wall-streets-legacy-on-income-inequality.

32. E.J. Dionne and William A. Galston, "Socialism: A Short Primer," *Brookings*, May 13, 2019, https://www.brookings.edu/blog/fixgov/2019/05/13/socialism-a-short-primer/.

33. Rosenthal, "Capitalism when Labor was Capital: Slavery, Power, and Price in Antebellum America," 301.

34. Rosenthal, "Capitalism when Labor was Capital: Slavery, Power, and Price in Antebellum America," 302.

35. Justin Leroy and Destin Jenkins, *Histories of Racial Capitalism* (Columbia University Press, 2021), 1. "Racial capitalism is not one of capitalism's varieties. . . . Rather . . . all capitalism, in material profitability and ideological coherence, is constitutive of racial capitalism."

36. John Rekenthaler, "Why the Rich Have Become Richer," *Morningstar*, December 29, 2022, https://www.morningstar.com/personal-finance/why-rich-have-become-richer; Frahad Manjoo, "Private Equity Doesn't Want You to Read This," *New York Times*, August 4, 2022, https://www.nytimes.com/2022/08/04/opinion/private-equity-lays-waste.html.

37. Kriston McIntosh, Emily Moss, Ryan Nunn, and Jay Shambaugh, "Examining the Black-White Wealth Gap," Brookings, February 27, 2022, https://www.brookings.edu/blog/up-front/2020/02/27/examining-the-black-white-wealth-gap/.

38. Bruce R. Scott, *Capitalism: Its Origins and Evolution as a System of Governance* (Springer, 2011), 12–13.

39. Friedman, *Capitalism and Freedom* (University of Chicago Press, 1962), 4.

40. Friedman, *Capitalism and Freedom*, 8.

41. Robert B. Reich, *Supercapitalism* (Vintage, 2008), 9.

42. Reich, *Supercapitalism*, 9; John Braithwaite, "Tempered Power, Variegated Capitalism, Law and Society," *Buffalo Law Review* 67 (2019): 555–57.

43. Braithwaite, "Tempered Power, Variegated Capitalism, Law and Society," 556.

44. Riad Kherdeen, "Democracy Is Incompatible with Capitalism," *Medium*, September 14, 2021.

45. "Capitalism and democracy can easily conflict in two situations: If the distribution and use of property rights lead to an accumulation of wealth large enough to hinder politics through capitalist pressure, and if democratic decisions are taken to massively limit the use of property rights." Wolfgang Merkel, "Is Capitalism Compatible with Democracy?," *Zeitschrift für Vergleichende Politikwissenschaft* 8 (July 2014), https://doi.org/10.1007/s12286-014-0199-4.

46. Joseph E. Stiglitz, "The American Economy is Rigged," *Scientific American*, November 1, 2018, https://www.scientificamerican.com/article/the-american-economy-is-rigged/. "Political scientists have documented the ways in which money influences politics in certain political systems, converting

higher economic inequality into greater political inequality. Political inequality, in its turn, gives rise to more economic inequality as the rich use their political power to shape the rules of the game in ways that favor them."

47. For more about the concept of shareholder primacy, see Chapter 8.

48. Sam Polk, "What's Wrong With Wall Street? A Culture That Breeds Greed," *PBS News Hour*, August 23, 2016, https://www.pbs.org/newshour/economy/whats-wrong-wall-street-culture-breeds-greed.

49. Robert Goulder, "The Capital Gains Tax Break: Great Idea or Big Mistake?," *Forbes*, November 16, 2021, https://www.forbes.com/sites/taxnotes/2021/11/16/the-capital-gains-tax-break-great-idea-or-big-mistake/?sh=4ad543123a02.

50. Jessica Defino, "How White Supremacy and Capitalism Influence Beauty Standards," *TeenVogue*, October 19, 2020, https://www.teenvogue.com/story/standard-issues-white-supremacy-capitalism-influence-beauty.

51. Anna Zeira, "Mental Health Challenges Related to Neoliberal Capitalism in the United States," *Community Mental Health Journal* 58 (2022), https://doi.org/10.1007/s10597-021-00840-7.

52. Elke Pirgmaier, "Consumption Corridors, Capitalism and Social Change," *Sustainability: Science, Practice and Policy* 16, no. 1 (2020), https://doi.org/10.1080/15487733.2020.1829846.

53. Adam Hayes, "What Are the Most Important Aspects of a Capitalist System?," *Investopedia*, 2022.

54. Heather Boushey and Helen Knudsen, "The Importance of Competition for the American Economy," The White House, July 9, 2021, https://www.whitehouse.gov/cea/written-materials/2021/07/09/the-importance-of-competition-for-the-american-economy/.

55. Rainer Zitelman, "The Driving Force Of Capitalism Is Empathy, Not Greed," *Forbes*, September 2, 2019, https://www.forbes.com/sites/rainerzitelmann/2019/09/02/the-driving-force-of-capitalism-is-empathy-not-greed/?sh=7c0d474b67aa.

56. Scherer, "The Dynamics of Capitalism" (HKS Faculty Research Working Paper Series No. RWP10-001, January 2010).

57. See Allysia Finley, "Capitalism is What Will Defeat COVID," *Wall Street Journal*, March 19, 2021, https://www.wsj.com/articles/capitalism-is-what-will-defeat-covid-11616192690.

58. See Thomas L. Friedman, "Want to Save the Earth? We Need a Lot More Elon Musks," *New York Times*, November 16, 2021, https://www.nytimes.com/2021/11/16/opinion/glasgow-climate-change.html.

59. Phelps, *Capitalism and Keynes: From the Treatise on Probability to The General Theory* (Center on Capitalism and Society, Columbia University, September 25, 2017), 1.

60. Ann E. Cudd, "Is Capitalism Good for Women?," *Journal of Business Ethics* 127 (May 2014): 761, https://doi.org/10.1007/s10551-014-2185-9.

61. Scott Timberg, "Book Publishing in Crisis: Capitalism Kills Culture," *Salon*, November 10, 2012, https://www.salon.com/2012/11/10/book_publishing_crisis_capitalism_kills_culture/.

62. See, e.g., Tyler Cowen, *How the United States Funds the Arts* (National Endowment for the Arts Office of Research and Analysis, 2004).

63. Maurice E. Stucke, "Is Competition Always Good?," *Journal of Antitrust Enforcement* 1, no. 1 (April 2013), https://doi.org/10.1093/jaenfo/jns008.

64. Assaf, "Capitalism v. Freedom."

65. "Economic theory is quick. . . . in asserting that the price people are willing to pay for a product or service is a good enough marketplace proxy for calculating [utility]. . . . Add to this the apparently reasonable assumption that consumers always prefer more to less, and it is a short step to concluding that continual income growth (and therefore output growth) is a decent proxy for ever-improving human welfare." Kate Raworth, *Doughnut Economics: Seven Ways to Think Like a 21st-Century Economist* (Chelsea Green Publishing, 2017), 31.

66. Monbiot, "Neoliberalism."

67. Lynelle Watts and David Hodgson, "Capitalism and Neoliberalism," in *Social Justice Theory and Practice for Social Work* (Critical and Philosophical Perspectives, 2019), 74–77.

68. Inara Scott, "Antitrust and Socially Responsible Collaboration: A Chilling Combination?," *American Business Law Journal* 53, no. 1 (October 2016); see also Eric M. Fink, "Post-Realism, or the Jurisprudential Logic of Late Capitalism," *Hastings Law Journal* 55 (2004): 936.

69. Gary Gerstle, *The Rise and Fall of the Neoliberal Order: America and the World in the Free Market Era* (Oxford University Press, 2022), 88.

70. Assaf, "Capitalism vs. Freedom," 208.

71. Raworth, *Doughnut Economics*, 31–35.

72. Delgado, "Rodrigo's Equation," 104–105; Daniel W. Bromley, *Possessive Individualism: A Crisis of Capitalism* (Oxford University Press, 2019).

73. Scott, "Antitrust and Socially Responsible Collaboration."

74. Rob Nixon, "Naomi Klein's 'This Changes Everything,'" *New York Times*, November 6, 2014, https://www.nytimes.com/2014/11/09/books/review/naomi-klein-this-changes-everything-review.html.

75. Gerstle, *The Rise and Fall of the Neoliberal Order*, 145–87.

76. Gerstle, *The Rise and Fall of the Neoliberal Order*, 230–31, 237–40.

77. James Manyika, et al., *The Social Contract in the 21st Century* (McKinsey Global Institute, February 2020).

78. David Levi-Faur, "The Rise of Regulatory Capitalism: The Global Diffusion of a New Order," *The Annals of the American Academy of Political and Social Science* 598 (2005); Stephen Moore and Tyler Grimm, "An Economy in Crisis: Law, Policy, and Morality During the Recession: Straw Man Capitalism and a New Path to Prosperity," *Harvard Journal of Law & Public Policy* 33, no. 2 (Spring 2010).

2

Essential Perspectives
Foundations of Capitalism

Dana Neacşu

Articulating a Working Definition of Capitalism. The Problem.

Capitalism is often referenced without a generally accepted definition. When authors describe it, their explanations are highly politicized, even when focused on its economic aspect. The absence of a generally accepted definition is further hampered by the reality of capitalism, by its historical and geopolitical variances, as well as social and economic disparities within the same region or country. Nevertheless, capitalism is conceptually different from what came before, but how? And more importantly, what is necessary for capitalism to continue? Is it the economic model? Is it the political and legal scaffolding? Is it the social structure? Is it the technical progress associated with capitalism? Is there a particular type of innovative culture associated with capitalism? In other words, what makes capitalism, capitalism?

Gertrude Stein's definition of a rose: "A rose is a rose is a rose,"[1] cannot suffice in a scientific work. To say "Capitalism is capitalism is capitalism" helps neither from an ontological nor epistemological perspective. Similarly, a workable definition cannot rely on empirical observations of the type: "I know it when I see it," implying that we all know capitalism when we go to the market and see it in action.

Conceptual ambiguities aside, capitalism stands on particular institutional foundations. These pillars are economic, legal, social, political, and cultural. In this chapter, I begin with a short historical overview of the birth of capitalism. I then turn to a brief discussion of the various explanatory perspectives of the meaning of capitalism, each of which yields a different understanding of the term. I conclude with an articulation of the essential nature of capitalism, and how that might be brought to bear on its ultimate sustainability.

Historical Perspective

To begin, capitalism represents a particular stage in human history. It built on existing legal institutions, cultural products, innovations, and social progress but emerged as something unique and different. The beginning of what we now consider capitalism may be traced to a period spanning the fourteenth to the sixteenth centuries in England.[2] After exploding to prominence in England, it reigns today as a global system, though a few geopolitical areas still negotiate its influence, such as regions under the so-called Taliban rule,[3] or the North Korean regime.[4] Japan made a dramatic jump to capitalism under American occupation after WWII,[5] and today socialist China is a capitalist success story.[6]

As the events of this period of development illustrate, capitalism has always been more than an economic system based on the pursuit of profit.[7] During the three-hundred-year period in which English capitalism replaced the previous English society, vast changes occurred in the country's social, economic, and legal institutions that were inseparable from the economic changes themselves. The transition to a new economic system prompted the only political revolution that country's history has known: The Glorious Revolution, which followed Oliver Cromwell's demise.[8] Socially, serfdom disappeared and the yeoman's relation to the land, waged labor, and the feudal lord became the socio-economic unit of agricultural production. Additionally, fugitive serfs found urban centers welcoming. There, they could participate in a public market space to earn a living as free agents selling their energy, time, and abilities to factory owners and producers, in exchange for a wage. This workforce market developed simultaneously with another market, where the labor-produced goods could be exchanged for money in order to be consumed. The exchange rate proved to include a profit for both the producer and the merchant, creating one of the essential aspects of the capitalist system.

In time, invested profit would become capital, a measure of prosperity and the stepping-stone for systemic progress.[9] The amount of capital produced would be driven by overproduction or underconsumption, which in turn would be based on demand for new goods and services.

Capitalism depends on accumulation by creating profit through investment, which, in turn, depends on new markets for these ever-complex cycles of production and exchange to take place. New markets may represent new physical or digital (metaverse) markets for the surplus of existing products or may refer to existing but expanded markets for new wants that are satisfied through new products. For instance, an older version of an iPhone (surplus) needs a new market while a newer version of an iPhone satisfies new wants of an existing market. Innovation and new wants go hand in hand as the unending way to ensure market expansion and profitability. New wants, conceptually created, imagined, and then sold to existing and potential consumers, produced a third market, a wants-production market. Culture, and especially, technology, drives this third market through technical innovation causing some to describe capitalism as informational.[10] It is focused on the method, and new wants are imagined—through "unilaterally claim[ing] human experience as free raw material for translation into behavioral data," and processing that data to "anticipate" what consumers will eventually purchase.[11] One thing remains constant: short-term profitability for investors.

Explanatory Perspectives

Conceptually, capitalism has been defined from a variety of angles, usually in a reductionist manner, in an attempt to find its essence. In this part, I explain how capitalism may be defined by reference to four explanatory perspectives: economic; political and legal; technological; and intersectional.

Accounts prior to Marx described capitalism as the emergence of "commercial society."[12] They reduced the definition of capitalism to a system of market-bound production, rooted in the belief that "private" and "public" denoted the independent realms of "economy" and, respectively, "politics."[13] Economy is presented as a realm organized into groups of participants based on ownership: owners of capital, partial owners, and destitute participants.[14] This perspective is not monolithic. Some emphasize and see capitalism emerging with the accumulation of capital based on the surplus value of unpaid labor,[15] and developing linearly until it reaches its monopolistic and imperialist phase defined by a hyperconcentration of capital, resources, and profit. For them, capitalism is a dynamic system whose goal is efficient capitalist production. A neoliberal vision of capitalism prioritizes self-regulating markets, which are believed to promote human progress through economic growth and efficiency (Milton Friedman and the Chicago School). Still others (Elinor Ostrom and the Bloomington School) regard capitalism not as a coherent system, but more as "mush" prone to particular political results in the name of particular economic solutions, including the decentralized self-organization of common-pool resources.[16]

Political scientists and legal scholars have noted that the political systems in which capitalism developed and continues to thrive tend to reinforce the power and stability of the successful participants in the marketplace. The structure of capital markets thus tends to consolidate the politically powerful. Given this symbiosis between economic wealth and political prominence, the definition of capitalism must encompass not only the economic system by which wealth is created, but also the political structure through which the economic system is constructed and refined. As David Grewal notes:

> Capitalism is not (or not merely) a socioeconomic system. It is a [political and] juridical regime. It is a form of the modern "rule of law." It is legitimated through constitutional ratification by an ultimate popular sovereign that then rules in theory, without in practice surrendering governmental administration to ongoing popular control. The effect of this regime is that emanation of commercial sociability we now call "the economy." It is produced as the outworking of legal rights and duties that offer special protections to asset-holders legitimated through a constitutional order.[17]

Capitalism is also equated with technological change, risk, and innovation. For example, as early as 1779, Alexander Hamilton's push for a privately owned central bank may be considered a significant financial innovation intended to stabilize the economic position of the United States. Yet, the very financial innovation Hamilton endorsed arguably promoted a particular socio-economic and political system that favored the emerging urban elites and their interests and led toward their monopolistic financial interests over small farmers and rural landowners.[18] Moreover, in its informational phase,[19] capitalism has come to fully rely on networked information technologies within business models that reflect and reproduce its defining economic and political power.

Finally, some authors explore capitalism as a complex, intersectional system with legal, economic, political, and social-cultural facets.[20] Capitalism relies on fundamental pillars absent which it could not exist. Thus, capitalism is more than a money-making machine for the benefit of a minority faction of our population and the globe. Otherwise, it would not be a potentially sustainable hypothesis.

The Economic Perspective

Even economically, capitalism is rarely defined. For instance, Adam Smith did not use the term in *The Wealth of Nations* (1776). Milton Friedman in *Capitalism and Freedom* (1962) qualified it as competitive, before defining it as "the organization of the bulk of economic activity through private enterprise operating in a free market ... a society dedicated to freedom and relying primarily on the market to organize economic activity."[21] When defined macro-economically, capitalism is described as production for exchange for profit,[22] or alternatively, a system for the administration of scarcity (the neoclassical perspective of supply and demand).[23] Mainstream economists use mathematical and statistical techniques to develop equilibrium models to analyze the interaction between macroeconomic variables.[24] In turn, banks rely on economic models when establishing interest rates in order to keep national economies growing at a relatively stable pace.

Neoliberal economics propose that markets will produce more wealth and be more efficient if left to operate with a minimum of government regulation. Perceived as conservative economics, despite their motto of laissez-faire, let it be, neoliberals promote going with the flow, the opposite of conserving the flow. Irony aside, they have had a major influence defining capitalism both academically and politically. A major representative of laissez-faire economics is the Austrian School of Friedrich August von Hayek, whose ideas are brilliantly explained in *The Road to Serfdom* (1944) and *The Constitution of Liberty* (1960). His work influenced prominent policymakers because it tolerated government action only to the extent it protected private firms and their ability to own and control the major economic resources of society.

Theoretically, Hayek took the responsibility of organizing the economy off the shoulders of the government and placed it squarely with each individual. Ironically, he does so by arguing that each individual knows only a small fraction of what is known collectively. For Hayek (interestingly, for Ostrom, too) decisions are best made by those with little local knowledge, rather than by those with comparably little central knowledge.

> To Hayek, the free market represented an adaptation to the "necessary" and "irremediable" ignorance that characterizes the human mind. Thanks to its decentralized structure, the free market allows us to use the tacit knowledge shared by all (and available to none in its entirety) in the most effective means.[25]

In America, the Chicago School incorporated Hayek's ideas, notably in the work of Milton Friedman, Ronald Coase, and George Stigler. The Chicago School promoted the ideology that society would flourish best with limited or no government intervention, allowing markets to allocate resources across classes and among people. Adherents could be found in law as well, notably reforming the field of antitrust law to focus on economic efficiency rather than elimination of monopolies.

In the last decade, it is hard to find a purely economic perspective, especially given the staggering income gap and the unprecedented accumulation of wealth, coupled with an unstoppable deterioration of our natural environment.[26] As put by Thomas Piketty in *Capital in the Twenty-First Century*, "modern economic growth and the diffusion of knowledge have made it possible to avoid the Marxist apocalypse,"[27] but there are other necessary fundamental components that cannot be forgotten.

Political and Legal Perspective

Scholars seem to agree that capitalism originated in Western Europe following the end of feudalism, in the modern era.[28] Thus, from its inception, capitalism has flourished in a particular type of self-reinforcing political system: a system that is relatively stable for the monied class, which trusts the markets and the banking system. In turn it further stabilizes and enhances the wealth of monied interests. The more successful capitalism becomes, the more it seeks to reinforce the political and economic stability of the ruling class, which become inextricable from each other.

For instance, in England, the ascent of Oliver Cromwell and his swift demise might be viewed as a result of the expansion of capitalism. To ensure its political and economic hegemony, the ruling class needed to escape suffocating monarchic authority for more reliable, parliamentarian methods of legal reform. Then, to preserve the ability to accumulate wealth and ensure economic growth, the ruling class needed to reject the chaos and violence Cromwell's leadership brought. Eventually, the Restoration produced these necessary changes, and England has not known any upheaval for the last five hundred years.[29]

A century later, the American colonies freed themselves from the English legal and political rule to create their own political and legal experiment. In the American capitalist experiment the goods market did not coexist with a market of free labor, but with a hybrid market, where some goods were the product of waged labor, while others were the product of free labor.[30] This political experiment proved to create historic wealth for a small ruling class of landowners. Less than a century later, arguably, the dispute over the future of this ruling class and the basis of their wealth (slavery) led to the Civil War and the greatest loss of human life in the history of the United States.[31]

That the U.S. capitalist experiment, which promoted a hybrid-labor market favoring slave labor to increase profit rates for a class of ruling elite, left political and legal scars is obvious in the fact that social unrest surfaces periodically; accordingly, periodically it requires reform to reproduce stability in the political economy of the nation. In 1964, Civil Rights legislation tried to fix some of those problems legally.[32] Most currently, the country is still facing its racist legacy, with increased demand for political and legal reform in the wake of racially charged police killings.[33] Everywhere, capitalism is cloaked in a political regime that calls for individual freedom, but only to the extent necessary to ensure individual agency as a market participant.

In France, the capitalist revolution had the swiftest change of its political and legal facets. The 1789 republic democracy replaced the French parliamentary monarchy. Within a decade though, it was replaced by a dictatorship, empire, and restoration, much like in England, a century earlier. What remained gained though was the inroads into capitalism, which required minimal individual agency ensuring market participation as labor provider and goods consumers.[34] Nevertheless, its colonial history aside, France remains one example of humane capitalism, where the political and legal establishments have curtailed unlimited capitalist profit.[35]

The Cultural-Legal Perspective—
Technological (Know-How) Capitalism

From the beginning, technology—broadly defined as the use of scientific knowledge to create new tools or solve practical problems—has been in part responsible for the appearance of capitalism.[36] Without technology, there would not have been economic growth in agricultural production, and without that growth, no change in the nature of rent—from rent in kind to rent in money. Without better tools and increased agricultural production, there would not have been an exodus of the workforce to cities. Without money, there would have been no ability to purchase the itinerant-peasant labor to produce new goods. Without technology, there would have been no geographical exploration and no production of new needs, demanding inventions for their satisfaction. Without technology, the race for unlimited profit could not have been sustained. More interestingly, if freely sold labor was one of the characteristics of the labor market and capitalism—with the exception of slave labor in the southern market of the United States—technology has made free labor, willingly provided for no economic exchange, into a new and reliable source of profit. Also riveting, technology has created a new market where free labor is willingly provided for corporate profit. Technology has also created a new currency: the digital market of free-of-charge labor.[37] People volunteer their work on digital spaces during their own "downtime," which assumes that there is a time when they sell their work for money, used afterward to purchase goods using algorithms each creates while consuming.

Overall, the operation of technology as a key agent in the ongoing evolution of the market for goods and services can be considered "technological capitalism." How we offer our own data so we become better targets of consumerism is one aspect of technological capitalism. Another aspect is financial innovation, mentioned earlier. Finally, technological capitalism is also about intangible assets such as computerized information, software and databases, and innovative property. Economic competition includes brand equity; firm-specific human capital; networks that join people and institutions; organizational know-how that increases enterprise efficiency; and advertising and marketing. Technology represents intangible assets, which comprise knowledge that has been introduced to the economic sphere. Historically innovation was about the creation of a new production technique or product. Here, technology is intrinsically valuable to capitalism because it creates both wants and ways to satisfy those wants. Technology has thus both an economic and a social dimension to the extent it creates new needs or wants to satisfy the population.[38]

Furthermore, like every other aspect of capitalism, technology can play an important role because of its legal "coding."[39] Technology as assetized knowledge brings intellectual rents because it is legal via the patent and the trademark system. Ironically, this legal system, which facilitates profit for technological innovation, also inhibits competition and free innovation: assetized knowledge exists because of the roles of legal monopoly. A patent gives a vaccine to one manufacturer. Another patent can be created for a different assetized knowledge. Each vaccine with its monopoly can inhibit innovation while it enhances private wealth, sometimes at the expense of the public if the underlying research was funded with government money.[40]

The race for assetized knowledge is becoming more complex each day. A handful of corporations control big data, which in turn produces innovation that the owners of big data now monopolize. Such intellectual monopoly causes not only misappropriation of economic results but also the possibility of finding solutions to the current crises based on the algorithms available to those with access to big data. This in turn describes technological capitalism—which defines both new ways of creating and satisfying wants, and with the advent of the metaverse, new markets.

As mentioned earlier, informational capitalism is its own concept. Scholars describe it as profit-maximizing, based on the accumulation of knowledge through higher levels of complexity in information processing.[41] The transformative importance of the sociotechnical shift to informationalism is viewed as an independent mode of production development and profit making, often through the monopolization of data collection.[42]

The Multifaceted, Intersectional, and Systemic Perspective: Marx and Capitalism

While it may be tempting to define it as such, capitalism is not just about private property or free marketplaces. Nor is it defined by reference to democracy or democratic ideals. Today, the democratic perspective seems outdated as capitalism seems to survive in such politically and legally inhospitable places as Russia or China. Russia is capitalist because it engages in imperialist wars of aggression[43] and values private property, though it is not a democracy relying on a periodical change of political leaders.[44] China is similarly living its capitalist dream[45] while governed by a single-party, autocratic political system. Profit is a defining element of every capitalist economy, and while technology ensures its success, it is the legal system that enables and protects private property, profit, and capital.[46] As noted earlier, a relatively stable political system is necessary for a flourishing capitalist market so wants can be imagined and satisfied (though capitalism has survived both world wars, as well as other atrocities).[47] In sum, it appears that capitalism is an economic, social, political, legal, and cultural system, with each element contributing in various degrees, with the winning formula appearing to be as dynamic as the system itself.

For Marx, capitalism represented a particular stage in human history. Capitalism was the production and reproduction of material life, of the means to survive physically, of ways to create new needs, which in combination with early social relationships provided the structure of the actual life processes. In *German Ideology*, Marx concluded:

> The production of life, both of one's own in labor and of fresh life in procreation, now appears as a double relationship: on the one hand as a natural, on the other as a social, relationship ... the multitude of productive forces accessible to man determines the nature of society, hence, that the "history of humanity" must always be studied in relation to the history of industry and exchange. . . . Thus it is quite obvious from the start that there exists a materialistic connection of men with one another, which is determined by their needs and their mode of production, and which is as old as men themselves.[48]

Marx defined capitalism also in terms of the conflict between that which was natural and that which was social.[49] Marx viewed the procreation of life both in terms of labor, social procreation, but also biologically. It had an inner duality, with facets coexisting and manifesting themselves differently in different societies. These facets contained some general assumptions about the nature of human existence; for example, that neither the natural nor the social had a greater or more fundamental significance than the other, however, each society promoted a particular solution and under capitalism, nature is not winning. In his *Economic and Philosophical Manuscripts* (1844), Marx wrote that the resolution of the conflict between man and nature, and between man and man, the true resolution of the conflict between existence and being, between freedom and necessity, between individual and species, would only be resolved with equanimity in a non-capitalist society. That prediction remains to be proven false, especially given the capitalist inertia to global, unprecedented environmental erosion.[50]

For Marx, capitalism represented the only society where the individual was able to manifest their humanity. For him, Man existed individually only as a result of the development of the productive power of labor. For him, Man existed individually only as a result of the development of the productive power of labor, and when "the social relations within the sphere of material life, between man and man, and between man and nature," have reached a particular level of development.[51] From a legal point of view, it is very interesting to note that the emerging forms of private property were crucial for the development of individuation. For instance, in the *Communist Manifesto*, the bourgeoisie, the vilified social exploiter, is presented as having played the most important part in history, because capitalists, at least in this early stage, are progressive and express human qualities of creativity and drive and inculcated others with those powers.[52]

Thus, capitalism for Marx is more than a mere mode of production. It is history, and it is a particular type of human interaction when Man quits pursuing his aims aimlessly, and "the realization of [his] essential powers [stop being] his whims."[53] Dangerously, perhaps, in Marx's capitalism, Man develops a conquering nature in a continuous manner within capitalist exploitation.

> Subjection of nature's forces to man, machinery, application of chemistry to industry and agriculture, steam navigation, railways, electric telegraphs, clearing of whole continents for cultivation, canalization of rivers, whole populations conjured out of the ground—what early century had even a presentiment that such productive forces slumbered in the lap of social labor?[54]

In this Marxian view, capitalism is rapacious and unethical, bent on destroying everything that stood in the path to profit, but it is more than that too. It made Man heroic to the extent Man subjugated nature. Today,

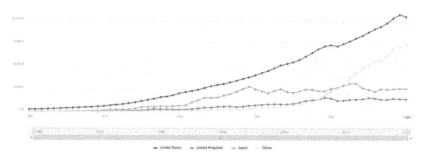

GDP growth annually (current U.S. dollars, 1960–2021). *Source: World Bank* (2022).

that heroic view is prevalent outside all Marxian narratives, and it is problematic for capitalist sustainability.

Perhaps, that explains its global reach: the combined economies of the United States, China, Japan, and the United Kingdom represent about half of the global economic output since 1960.[55]

In its quest for boundless profit, capitalism has reached most of the planet and is encroaching into the digital and outer space. The question becomes whether its endless capital/profit race is sustainable. Is short-term economic profit at all costs what capitalism is all about?

Sustainable Capitalism?

Capitalism, at least when it replaced the societies that preceded it, resulted in some fundamental freedoms afforded to individuals living in those societies. It provided additional prosperity and better living for those who freely sold their labor. Those who were able to purchase that labor, produced goods with the labor, and then exchanged those goods for capital particularly benefitted. "Freedom and prosperity, however, presupposes that human existence on this earth is possible at all," Felix Ekardt wrote recently.[56] The question remains about capitalism's ability to contain inequality. Does capitalism create the potential for global sustainability of lifestyles and economies? Efficiency proved to be a cornerstone of capitalist economies in their quest for profit, but long-term sustainability of resources and ecosystems plays no role in the classic approach to efficiency. Moreover, if consumption is the engine of capitalist economies in their search for profit, sustainable capitalism may be, simply, a contradiction in terms.

All the existing schools of thought described in this chapter contain one common element in their conceptualization of capitalism: global or local, capitalism relies on mobilizing and allocating access to resources and accordingly is responsible for the prosperity of societies. This competition against nature (the environment) sometimes happens within a particular public law system—governed by the laws of a particular state—or outside all public law systems within the private legal realms powerful law firms manufacture.[57] The legality of these private systems is assumed because of the supportive role played by international, non-governmental entities, such as the International Monetary Fund, even if these entities are neither democratic nor anti-monopolistic.[58]

Perhaps then the answer to sustainable capitalism becomes first and foremost an economic and legal question about the compatibility of capitalist competition with rules and regulatory decisions whose purpose is not unlimited profit for fewer monopolies, but the opposite. Sustainable capitalism seems to be about dismantling monopolies, changing corporate and individual expectations and their enabling behavior for the larger, societal purpose of common interest. To inquire if that is compatible with capitalism, we need to note that existing trends of capitalist conceptualization relying on traditional analytical tools of economics are not sufficient. In addition to their survey, this chapter endorses the role of sociology as well as political science, law, and economics to inquire about the viability of sustainable capitalism.

So, what is capitalism? Capitalism appeared as the most progressive system humanity had known; yet while pushing forward individual achievement and technological innovation, it risks to pitting human progress against planet Earth. Scholars need to correct the misperception that capitalism does not have a strong state backing. It does, only now, nationally and internationally governments need to refocus their capitalist subventions and limit profits in favor of social and environmental justice at the local, national, and planetary level. There is no individual progress without social progress, and there is no social progress without a planet. This planet.

Notes

1. Gertrude Stein, *Geography and Plays* (University of Wisconsin Press, 1993), 187.
2. Michael Tigar, *Rise of Capitalism* (Monthly Review Press, 2000), 286.

3. Whit Mason, ed., *The Rule of Law in Afghanistan: Missing in Inaction* (Cambridge University Press, 2011), 147–221.

4. Jieun Baek, *North Korea's Hidden Revolution* (Yale University Press, 2016), 1–44.

5. Minqi Li, *Profit, Accumulation, and Crisis in Capitalism* (Routledge, 2020), 57–70.

6. Li, 71–89.

7. Li, 1–18.

8. Charles K. Rowley and Bin Wu, *Britannia 1066–1884* (Springer, 2014), 100–107.

9. Karl Marx, *Capital: A Critical Analysis of Capitalist Production* (Berlin, 1867), 162–73.

10. Julie E. Cohen, *Between Truth and Power: The Legal Constructions of Informational Capitalism* (Oxford University Press, 2019), 170–201.

11. Shoshana Zuboff, *Age of Surveillance Capitalism* (PublicAffairs, 2019), 8.

12. Amy Kapczynski, "Law of Informational Capitalism," *Yale Law Journal* 129 (2020):1481.

13. Kapczynski, "Law of Informational Capitalism," 1481.

14. E. K. Hunt, *Property and Prophets: The Evolution of Economic Institutions and Ideologies* (Harper & Row, 1981), 15; E. K. Hunt and Mark Lautzenheiser, *History of Economic Thought: A Critical Perspective* (New York: M.E. Sharpe, Inc., 2011), 202.

15. Marx, *Capital: A Critical Analysis*, 156.

16. Elinor Ostrom, *Governing the Commons* (Cambridge University Press, 1990), 12–13.

17. David Singh Grewal, "Legal Constitution of Capitalism," in *After Piketty: The Agenda for Economics and Inequality*, ed. Heather Boushey, J. Bradford DeLong, and Marshall Steinbaum (Harvard University Press, 2017), 475.

18. William H. Janeway, *Doing Capitalism in the Innovation Economy* (Cambridge University Press, 2018), 1–10.

19. Cohen, *Between Truth and Power*, 170–201.

20. Bruce R. Scott, *Capitalism: Its Origins* (Springer, 2011), 427–580.

21. Friedman, *Capitalism and Freedom*, 13. The problem with competitive markets was that once a market was designated a "competitive market," it automatically became efficient. Efficient became competitive and vice-versa. "In that newly defined space . . . there is no need for regulation, no need for government intervention—because there the market will regulate itself." Always ignored was the massive government intervention, "the kind necessary to make possible a wheat pit at the Chicago Board of Trade." Harcourt, *Illusion of Free Markets*, 146.

22. Hunt and Lautzenheiser, *History of Economic Thought*, 202.

23. Luciano Vasapollo, *Crisis of Capitalism* (Brill, 2012), 55.

24. Sabrina Schneider and Thomas Clauß, "Business Models for Sustainability: Choices and Consequences," *Organization & Environment* 33, no. 3 (2019): 386.

25. Naomi Beck, *Hayek and the Evolution of Capitalism* (University of Chicago Press, 2018), 72.

26. Dana Neacșu, "The Aesthetic Ideology of *Juliana v. United States* and Its

Impact on Environmentally Engaged Citizenship," *Journal of Environmental Studies and Sciences* 21 (2021): 33.

27. Thomas Piketty, *Capital in the Twenty-First Century* (Belknap Press, 2017), 1.

28. Karl Polanyi, *The Great Transformation: The Political and Economic Origins of Our Time* (Beacon Press, 2001), 3–4; Ellen Meiksins Wood, *The Origin of Capitalism* (Monthly Review Press, 1999) 73–93; Grewal, "The Legal Constitution of Capitalism," 471–502; Kapczynski, "Law of Informational Capitalism," 1481.

29. Geoffrey Hodgson, "1688 and All That: Property Rights, the Glorious Revolution and the Rise of British Capitalism." *Journal of Institutional Economics* 13 (2017): 79–108.

30. Martin Ruef, *Between Slavery and Capitalism* (Princeton University Press, 2014), 21–49.

31. Phillip Shaw Paludan, *Victims: A True Story of the Civil War* (University of Tennessee Press, 2004), 59–62.

32. Hodgson, "1688 and All That," 79–108.

33. Joanna Lampe, *Congress and Police Reform: Current Law and Recent Proposals* (Congressional Research Service, 2020), 1.

34. William H. Sewell, "Connecting Capitalism to the French Revolution: The Parisian Promenade and the Origins of Civic Equality in Eighteenth-Century France," *Critical Historical Studies* 1 (2014): 7.

35. Piketty, *Twenty-First Century*, 13–14.

36. Marx, *Capital: A Critical Analysis*, 425–27, 524.

37. Marinus Ossewaarde and Wessel Reijers, "The Illusion of the Digital Commons: 'False Consciousness' in Online Alternative Economies," *Organization* 24, no. 5 (2017): 611.

38. Cecilia Rikap, *Capitalism, Power, and Innovation: Intellectual Monopoly Capitalism Uncovered* (Routledge, 2022), 45.

39. Katharina Pistor, *The Code of Capital: How the Law Creates Wealth and Inequality* (Princeton University Press, 2019), 1–23.

40. Peter S. Arno and Michael Henry Davis, "Why Don't We Enforce Existing Drug Price Controls? The Unrecognized and Unenforced Reasonable Pricing Requirements Imposed upon Patents Deriving in Whole or in Part from Federally Funded Research," *Tulane Law Review* 75 (2001): 632; Peter S. Arno, Dana Neacşu, and Kathryn Ardizzone, "March-In Rights Could Ensure Patient Access by Keeping Drug Prices in Check. They're under Attack," *Heath Affairs*, April 30, 2021.

41. Cohen, *Between Truth and Power*, 170–201.

42. Zuboff, *Age of Surveillance Capitalism*, 1–20.

43. Lynne Hartnett, "The Long History of Russian Imperialism Shaping Putin's War," *Washington Post*, March 2, 2022.

44. Dolgor Solongo, *Russian Capitalism and Money-Laundering* (United Nations, 2001).

45. Li, *Crisis in Capitalism*, 71–89.

46. Pistor, *The Code of Capital*, 205–34.

47. Torben Iversen and David Soskice, *Democracy and Prosperity: Reinventing*

Capitalism through a Turbulent Century (Princeton University Press, 2019), 257–78.

48. Karl Marx and Friedrich Engels, *The German Ideology*, trans. Tim Delaney and Bob Schwartz (Moscow: Progress Publishers, 1968), 10, accessed November 13, 2023.
49. Neacşu, *The Bourgeois Charm of Karl Marx & the Ideological Irony of American Jurisprudence* (Brill, 2020), 10–11.
50. Neacşu, "Aesthetic Ideology of *Juliana*."
51. Karl Marx, *Capital: A Critique of Political Economy*, vol. 1, trans. Samuel Moore and Edward Aveling, ed. Friedrich Engels (Moscow: Progress Publishers, 1887; reprint, New York: International Publishers, 1967), 336.
52. Karl Marx and Friedrich Engels, *The Communist Manifesto* (Workers' Educational Association, 1908), 11 ("The bourgeoisie, historically, has played a most revolutionary part").
53. Karl Marx, *Economic and Philosophic Manuscripts of 1844*, trans. Martin Milligan (Moscow: Progress Publishers, 1959), 54.
54. Marx and Engels, *The Communist Manifesto*, 14.
55. Li, *Crisis in Capitalism*, 2.
56. Felix Ekardt, *Sustainability: Transformation, Governance, Ethics, Law* (Springer, 2020), 3.
57. Pistor, *The Code of Capital*, 158–82.
58. Such positions might be reminiscent of the Chicago School, which did not promote anti-monopoly, but rather efficiency, in the application of antitrust law. Examples are provided by Bork and by Buchanan and Tullock, whose main idea is that antitrust should use economics in pursuit of economic efficiency. Robert Bork, *The Antitrust Paradox* (New York: Free Press, 1978), 421–25; James M. Buchanan and Gordon Tullock, *The Calculus of Consent* (University of Michigan Press, 1962), 213.

3

Democracy and Capitalism

Robert Prentice

Democracy and capitalism are, quite arguably, the best forms of govern-ment and economic organization that the world has seen. Even the imper-fect version of democracy practiced in the United States (e.g., originally lacking anything near universal suffrage) has long been a beacon to the world symbolizing freedom and self-determination. The American brand of capitalism also created and sustains the world's strongest economy (albeit one based on a historical foundation of slavery that proceeds at a great cost to the environment).[1]

Yet even as its economy has continued to grow, capitalism and democ-racy in the United States are failing to adequately advance broad public interests. Among other faults, the American brand of capitalism as cur-rently practiced produces huge economic inequality. The rich individuals and powerful corporations that enjoy great success in the economic arena often use their resources to also dominate in the political arena, advanc-ing their own economic interests at the expense of environmental quality and other public goods. This system that Professor Luigi Zingales calls a "Medici vicious circle"[2] and Nobel Prize winner George Stiglitz refers to as a "vicious downward spiral"[3] threatens the United States' economic vital-ity, political stability, and environmental well-being—and in doing so, may also threaten the planet as a whole.

Capitalism and Economic Inequality

Unfettered capitalism is generally effective at stimulating economic growth. Leaving key economic decisions in private hands, rather than in those of state planners, produces superior results, narrowly defined.[4] It also, at least as practiced in the United States, produces a large and growing inequality in income and wealth.

The Rise of Economic Inequality

In the late twentieth century and early twenty-first century, income inequality "exploded" in the U.S.[5] From 1977 to 2007, "the richest 10 percent appropriated three-quarters of the growth. The richest 1 percent absorbed nearly 60 percent of the total increase of U.S. national income."[6] Meanwhile, from 1980 to 2019, "the share of the nation's total household income going to the richest 1 percent more than doubled, while the earnings of the bottom 90 percent barely rose at all."[7]

Wealth inequality has also skyrocketed. Professors Saez and Zucman write:

> By any metric, the period from 1980 to 2020 has been an era of extraordinary wealth accumulation among the rich in the United States. Not only has wealth become more concentrated, wealth itself has been growing faster than income and output. In 1980, the ratio of aggregate household wealth to national income was 300 percent. In 2020, this ratio approaches 570 percent, the highest level ever recorded in the history of the United States.... In 1980, on average, members of the top 1 percent owned in wealth the equivalent of 60 years of average U.S. income. In 2020, ... they own 200 years of average U.S. income in wealth.[8]

Jeff Bezos, Bill Gates, and Warren Buffett together are worth more than the entire bottom half of America's 330 million population.[9] These are staggering disparities, but may even understate the true state of affairs because wealthy individuals are able to access tax evasion devices that are not available to others.[10] Such inequalities are opposed by the great majority of Americans, Republican and Democratic voters alike, but they persist and increase nonetheless.[11] Jeff Bezos and Elon Musk can afford to race to outer space while 40 percent of Americans would struggle to raise just $400 in an emergency.[12] Although federal assistance temporarily reduced the income gap during the first 18 months of the COVID-19 pandemic, the wealth gap continued to grow.[13] In February 2022, U.S. wealth inequality was the highest since World War II.[14]

The reasons for the rising level of income and wealth inequality are not completely clear. Experts have compiled lists of suspects, most of which are largely consequences of our current form of capitalism. Factors that suppress wage increases and wealth accumulation by workers include, among many others: the diminution of unions, which reduces the power of workers to advocate for themselves;[15] automation[16] and globalization,[17] which tend to reduce both the number of jobs and the wages of (especially) unskilled workers; the fact that the federal minimum wage hasn't been raised since 2009;[18] the greatly reduced progressivity of the American tax system;[19] restrictive covenants often required even of unskilled workers that retard wage increases;[20] and private equity funds' purchasing of huge numbers of homes, which has made it more difficult for individuals to buy houses (which provide the most common avenue for ordinary people to create intergenerational wealth).[21]

A variety of factors have led to the rapid increase of the income and wealth of the already wealthy and powerful. They include increased economic concentration that enables large corporations to gain even larger profits;[22] huge increases in CEO salaries relative to the wages of their firms' average workers;[23] virtual elimination of the estate tax;[24] significant reduction in the effective tax rate for corporations;[25] an increase in the ability of wealthy individuals to hide income and wealth from tax collectors;[26] the continued underfunding of the IRS, which limits its ability to enforce tax liabilities;[27] and, of course, the 2017 Tax Cuts and Jobs Act's reduction in tax rates for corporations and individuals (which carried outsized benefits for the wealthy).[28]

Economic and Social Impact of Inequality

After studying the extreme economic inequality in the United States, economist Thomas Piketty found it "hard to imagine an economy and society that can continue functioning indefinitely with such extreme divergence between social groups."[29] A recent Organization for Economic Co-operation and Development (OECD) report concluded that inequality hampers economic growth, limits investment opportunities for large swaths of society, reduces social cohesion and social mobility, damages human capital development, and inflicts a range of other destructive impacts.[30]

This should not be surprising. Fukuyama argues that "[t]he greatest economic efficiency [is] not necessarily achieved by rational, self-interested individuals, but rather by groups of individuals who, because of a preexisting moral community, are able to work together effectively."[31] Egregious economic inequality undermines trust and thereby damages such moral communities. Trust promotes economic growth by reducing transaction costs.[32] An International Monetary Fund study found a sharp decline in trust and other indicators of social capital in the United States over the past forty years and traced the decline substantially (44 percent) to growing economic inequality.[33]

All this inequality would not be as great a cause for concern if those at the bottom had a realistic opportunity to improve their economic status, but merit does not reliably predict individual success in America's current version of capitalism. The percentage of people who will make more money than their parents has dropped from 90 percent in 1970 to 50 percent today.[34] Only 8 percent of people in the top quartile of income had a father in the bottom quartile.[35] The most important predictor of people's economic success in life is the family into which they were born.[36] Winning the genetic lottery by being born into a well-to-do American family carries significant advantages in terms of quality health care, good schools, successful role models, beneficial social and economic connections, and so much more.[37]

At the end of the day, Americans must now "ask the age-old question of whether there are in fact two tracks in the market economy, one for the very rich and one for everyone else."[38] Most developed nations use taxes, subsidies, and other public policy actions to reduce economic inequality within their borders. Properly implemented, government programs can level the economic playing field and thereby strengthen social capital.[39] Such redistributive policies, especially progressive taxation, are hallmarks of modern democracies.[40]

However, by combining low tax rates with relatively stingy government benefits, the United States "has done less well by its poor than a number of other affluent nations."[41] U.S. policies reduce income equality "noticeably less than they do in other advanced economies."[42] Existing inequalities indicate that in the United States these policy tools are used too little to help the needy and too much "to raise the welfare of more influential pressure groups."[43] The second part of this chapter explores why.

Democracy and Economic Inequality

The essence of democracy is political equality, with all citizens having an equal opportunity to have their voices heard in the shaping of public policy. Political equality is a "polestar" of democratic theory.[44] Unfortunately, as it currently operates in the United States, effective access to democracy is largely dominated by wealthy individuals and corporations and serves their interests not exclusively, but excessively.[45] As Robert Reich notes, "[w]ealth and power have become one and the same."[46] The wealthy families and major corporations that often pay few to no taxes are unlikely to forfeit these and other advantages; America's current version of democracy affords them the means and mechanisms to avoid doing so. This part describes three examples of the pathways by which economic inequality fuels democratic inequality: campaign contributions, lobbying, and dark money.

Campaign Contributions

While the best-funded candidate does not always win, the better-funded U.S. House or Senate candidate prevails 85 percent of the time.[47] Any candidate for office would prefer to be the one with more money to spend rather than the opponent with less, and large corporations and wealthy individuals dominate campaign giving. In 2016, corporations donated $3.4 billion to presidential and congressional races while labor unions contributed only $213 million.[48] A recent sample of board members and CEOs of Fortune 500 companies found that 80 percent also reported making campaign contributions.[49]

Increasingly, campaign contributions come largely from a relatively small coterie of millionaires and billionaires. In the 2016 election cycle, fewer than 25,000 people (one one-hundredth of 1 percent of Americans) made 40 percent of total campaign contributions.[50] In 1980, the top individual contributor gave only $1.94 million (in 2020 dollars),[51] while in 2020, Sheldon and Miriam Adelson alone gave 112 times that amount ($218 million) to Republican candidates. Michael Bloomberg gave $152 million to Democratic candidates, including, of course, himself.[52]

Politicians have become increasingly reliant on these wealthy individual donors,[53] which is why megadonors to successful presidential campaigns are often rewarded with ambassadorships or other sinecures. "Nearly 80 percent of those who collected more than $500,000 for Obama [in the 2008 election] took 'key administrative posts,' as defined by the White House."[54]

These rich individuals are also rewarded with access to policymakers. Wealthy liberal donor Peter Buttenwieser admitted: "I am close to a number of senators and see them on a very consistent basis. I understand that the unusual access I have correlates to the millions of dollars I have given to political party committees, and I do not delude myself into feeling otherwise."[55] The late Democratic senator Paul Simon admitted as much: "[If] there were twenty phone calls waiting for me, nineteen of them names I did not recognize and the twentieth someone I recognized as a $1,000 donor to my campaign, that is the one person I would call."[56]

All this culminates in policy results that tend to favor the preferences of wealthy individuals. There is, of course, no mathematically direct connection between money and influence: making twice as big a donation does not guarantee twice the influence on the candidate's votes. Indeed, it doesn't guarantee any influence at all. Nonetheless, political scientists Gilens and Page found, after studying 1,779 policy issues, that "economic elites and organized groups representing business interests have substantial independent impacts on U.S. government policy, while average citizens and mass-based interest groups have little or no independent influence."[57] A longitudinal study by political scientist Larry Bartels regarding senators' votes on a variety of important issues found that the views of the wealthiest constituents were given the greatest weight while "the views of constituents in the bottom third of income distribution received no weight at all in the voting decisions of their senators."[58]

Lobbying

Corporations devote more resources to lobbying than to campaign contributions, again vastly outspending unions—$3 billion to $48 million annually in Washington, DC.[59] Like campaign contributions, lobbying buys access. Former congressman Mick Mulvaney confirms: "We had a hierarchy in my office in Congress. If you're a lobbyist who never gave us money, I didn't talk to you. If you're a lobbyist who gave us money, I might talk to you."[60] Lobbying can be beneficial, as lobbyists can educate elected officials regarding the nuances of the issues that face them. Unfortunately, in lobbying, studies show that who you know often counts more than what you know.[61]

Corporations regularly reward members of Congress and government regulators with jobs as lobbyists, a form of bribery that occurs in plain sight. "In the 1970s, only about 3 percent of retiring members of Congress later became Washington lobbyists. In recent years, fully half of all retiring senators and 42 percent of retiring representatives have turned to lobbying, regardless of party affiliation."[62] Around and around the influence flows.

As Congress debated President Biden's $3.5 trillion infrastructure bill in fall 2021, large pharmaceutical companies sent 1500 or so lobbyists to Capitol Hill (three for each senator and representative) to battle the forces attempting to reduce the price of pharmaceuticals to consumers. According to Nobel Prize winner Angus Deaton and his co-author Anne Case, this was just more of the same: "The opioid epidemic did not happen in other countries both because [unlike the United States] they had not destroyed their working class and because their pharmaceutical companies are better controlled and their governments are less easily influenced by corporations seeking profits."[63]

As an example of the returns lobbying can provide, JPMorgan Chase's net income in 2018 was $30.7 billion, about half of which came from tax savings flowing from the 2017 Tax Cuts and Jobs Act.[64] Morgan's CEO Jamie Dimon lobbied fiercely for the cuts, as did the Business Roundtable, which he headed. As did the Kochs, America's second richest family, who have pocketed up to $4 billion in tax savings each year since the law passed.[65]

Economists such as New York University's Thomas Philippon and the University of Chicago's Luigi Zingales agree that the biggest problem with capitalism today is not too much competition, but too little, and that the key cause is corporate influence over politics wielded to shelter firms from competition. Philippon's 2019 book illustrates that in recent years competition has declined in most sectors of our economy and that this decline "is explained largely by policy choices, influenced by lobbying and campaign contributions"[66] aimed at raising entry barriers and weakening antitrust law enforcement.[67] The lack of competition causes "lower wages, lower investment, lower productivity, lower growth, and more inequality."[68]

Zingales and Rajan agree that capitalism's biggest problem is a lack of competition and that this stems from corporate political power. They note that "[s]mall, well-focused groups can sway government policies toward their interests at the expense of the public."[69] In the United States, corporations spend more on lobbying and campaign contributions than their European counterparts and are much more likely to be successful in influencing political decisions.[70]

Zingales emphasizes that "to detect the power of corporations we need to look at output, not inputs."[71] He gives several examples, including a dropped Federal Trade Commission (FTC) investigation into Google following 427 visits by Google employees and associated entities to the Obama White House.[72] He also notes a study by Brown and Huang, showing that

> the share price of companies whose executives visited the White House from 2009–2015 increased an extra 1 percent in the following two months. It might not seem very much, until you discover that during Obama's presidency, the chairman and chief executive officer of Honeywell International visited the White House 30 times, while the head of General Electric visited 22 times.[73]

Dark Money

Wealthy individuals and large corporations also engage in various other forms of influence-buying to advance their political aims. Some donate openly to controversial causes that they support, as billionaire George Soros donates to Black Lives Matter. Often, they are not so open. In 2018, liberal-leaning nonprofit the Sixteen Thirty Fund stole a page from rich conservatives' playbook, funneling huge amounts of "dark money" (money not easily traced to the real donors) to left-leaning causes.[74] In 2020, Democrats may have pulled in more dark money than Republicans who initiated use of the tactic.[75]

The rich and powerful may also secretly fund centers to produce "research" that they and their political allies can use to advance their interests, as Big Tobacco did when it knowingly funded inaccurate and misleading research regarding the cancer-causing properties of tobacco.[76] Wealthy Americans may also secretly fund organizations that then spawn what appear to be organic political movements, as the Kochs did in setting up Americans for Prosperity which, in turn, gave birth to the Tea Party movement.[77]

Big corporations and wealthy individuals obviously do not always get their way, no matter how much they donate to political campaigns or how much effort they put into lobbying. It would further be a mistake to assume that all rich individuals have the same electoral views or political priorities, or that all corporations are on the same page regarding all issues of government-business interactions. Many left-leaning millionaires strongly support governmental actions to reduce inequality.

It would be accurate to conclude that, in the great scheme of things, self-interest drives rich and powerful individuals and corporate entities alike, and that they tend to do very well in the political arena, in part because of a structural advantage that allows them to act less aggressively (or take fewer risks) and yet achieve desirable outcomes. As Page and Gilens point out, "[t]he many 'veto points' in our complex political system (that is, the many opportunities for one or another political actor to thwart policy change) are used [by corporations, interest groups, and wealthy individuals] to prevent the enactment of policies that most Americans want."[78]

The great advantage that the rich and powerful enjoy in politics would not be as worrisome if they shared the same views as the majority of Americans. However, wealthy individuals' views differ "significantly from those of middle-class and poor people,"[79] especially on policy issues that would mitigate economic inequality such as spending on public schools, raising the minimum wage, and protecting Social Security and Medicare.

The Republican Party's leaders consistently advance the interests of the well-off and the well-connected.[80] Democrats' official policy platforms represent the views of the less-wealthy better than Republicans,[81] and generally support reducing inequality.[82] However, Democrats' commitment fades in and out over time (for example, the party was very pro-business during the Clinton years),[83] and defections by a minority of Democrats often thwart the aspirations of the majority. Moreover, Democrats' actions often fail to match their rhetoric and some studies suggest they, like Republicans, vote for the interests of their most prosperous constituents over the less affluent.[84] Professor Bonica and colleagues observed: "While it is difficult to gauge the effect of the Democrat's [sic] reliance on contributions from the wealthy, it does likely preclude a strong focus on redistributive policies."[85] Reich asserts:

Why haven't Democrats fought harder to reverse the power shift? . . . It was because Clinton, Obama, and most congressional Democrats sought the votes of the suburban swing voters—so-called soccer moms in the 1990s and affluent politically independent professionals in the

2000s—who supposedly determine electoral outcomes, and turned their backs on the working class. They also drank from the same campaign funding trough as the Republicans—big corporations, Wall Street, and the very wealthy.[86]

Like rich individuals, corporations have different priorities than the common citizen. Kent Greenfield says: "The reason why corporate political speech is so corrosive to democracy is that the benefits and prerogatives of the corporate form are marshaled to bolster the speech of a tiny sliver of the financial and managerial elite. The fact that corporations speak is not itself a problem; whom they speak for is."[87]

Deaton and Case use the pharmaceutical industry and the health care industry as examples of how the "Medici circle" can corrupt:

> The benefits of free-market capitalism are often rightly noted.... But the American medical system, including the pharmaceutical industry, is nothing like a free market. The existence of moneymaking corporations does not imply competitive markets. Instead, these highly regulated corporations are largely concerned with seeking protective regulation from government and government agencies to protect their profits and limit competition in a way that would be impossible in a free market.[88]

These differing priorities mostly lean toward expanding rather than closing the existing economic gap. Rich individuals' priorities typically include maintenance and expansion of their own wealth. They often use their influence to reduce their income taxes,[89] preserve the capital gains tax break,[90] and virtually eliminate the estate tax.[91] Large corporations similarly use their political power to protect themselves from competition,[92] prevent the minimum wage from being raised,[93] preserve the carried interest tax break for private equity firms and others,[94] and ensure that they do not incur costs in the battle against climate change.[95]

Climate Change and Sustainability

Theoretically, a wealthy democracy such as the United States should be a leader in promoting sustainability and fighting climate change. The United States has far more economic resources to devote to saving the environment than any other nation.[96] Because U.S. citizens enjoy freedom of the press, freedom of speech, freedom of association, and the right to vote, Rodger Payne has suggested that they should be substantially more effective than counterparts in less democratic nations in informing themselves about the perils of climate change, advocating for policies to fight climate change, forming pro-environmental organizations, and voting into office pro-sustainability political candidates.[97]

In contrast, in autocracies, the small ruling elite is able to block out all these freedoms and generally will have control over the most polluting industries and benefit from their operations. These elites will have little interest in mitigating climate change because their political power and wealth will shield them from its worst impacts.[98] Indeed, studies show that generally democracies are more environmentally responsible than autocracies.[99]

Unfortunately, the United States has not led the way in advancing sustainability and fighting climate change. Inequality is an important reason for this failure because it exacerbates climate problems. Evidence indicates that "even among similarly affluent countries, the ecological footprint in more equitable countries tends to be much smaller than in more inequitable countries."[100] Many studies document the negative impact of income inequality, as exists in the United States, on environmental policies and outcomes around the world.[101]

In the United States, as in autocracies, the benefits of environmental pollution tend to flow to the top of the income ladder, enriching the owners of the polluting industries (including corporate titans and smaller shareholders of both political persuasions) while the burdens of pollution tend to settle upon those in the poorer economic strata.[102] These effects could be mitigated by policy changes as they have been in some Scandinavian countries,[103] but this largely hasn't happened in the United States.

Certainly, some of the wealthiest and most powerful U.S. citizens and corporations are sustainability proponents.[104] In general, however, corporations are too much motivated by the short-term profit imperative, the need to hit financial targets as often as every quarter to the exclusion of long-run considerations.[105] Individuals are subject to the psychological phenomenon known as "the tangible and the abstract," which causes them to respond much more strongly to concerns of the here-and-now than concerns of the future.[106] Moreover, like the leaders of autocracies, they assume that they have the resources to protect themselves from most of the adverse effects of climate change.[107]

Notwithstanding Payne's predictions, freedom of the press and freedom of speech have not enabled the U.S. populace to adequately inform itself of the dangers of climate change. And the rights to assemble and to vote have been significantly neutralized by voting restrictions, gerrymandering, dark money, and the like, all of which make action to address sustainability and climate-change problems less likely. Much of this may be traced to inequality. As Eric Neumayer notes: "in as much as concentrated economic power also allows a greater influence on political decision-making, greater inequality will also bias political decision-making against environmental protection."[108]

Harvard's Nancy Krieger similarly argues:

> In the case of the United States (US), an extremely wealthy and powerful political minority has been spending lavishly to change the rules of the game to undermine the democratic majority, thereby making it increasingly difficult to protect people's health and have a thriving democracy. Key tactics include . . . [p]olitical gerrymandering [and] . . . voter suppression. In all cases, these political stratagems are linked by the desire to weaken or eliminate regulations that crimp the ever-growing concentration of power and wealth, orchestrated and funded especially but not exclusively by those with a financial stake in the fossil fuel and petrochemical industries and energy markets.[109]

Thus, the billionaire Koch family and their company's Koch Foundation funded think tanks and university-affiliated centers for the purpose of spreading environmental disinformation and fueling environmental skepticism,[110] drafted anti-environmental model laws for state legislators to put their names on, worked hand-in-hand with climate change-denier politicians,[111] lobbied vigorously against any environmental regulation,[112] and made lavish campaign contributions to conservative candidates for political office who would resist environmental regulation.[113] It has been estimated that the Kochs have spent more than a billion dollars (much of it well disguised) on their political causes, which tend to align almost perfectly with their economic well-being.[114]

ExxonMobil was well aware for decades of the damage fossil fuels were doing to the environment. It planned its own future based on this knowledge. Nevertheless, like the Kochs, ExxonMobil used lobbying activities, campaign contributions, and dark money to muddy the scientific consensus, spread disinformation, and recruit conservative politicians to spout the industry line.[115] The energy industry spent more than two billion dollars to resist climate-change legislation just in the first decade of this century.[116]

Like Big Tobacco, the Kochs, ExxonMobil, and other fossil fuel companies and wealthy conservative donors have enjoyed great success for a long time by undermining the scientific consensus on climate change. Because of this, the United States has overinvested in fossil fuels and underinvested in green technology to the long-term detriment of both our environment and our economy.

In a rational world, the beliefs of the general populace would mirror those of the large majority of climate scientists who know that climate change is real and extremely dangerous.[117] Although the factors mentioned above have kept the percentages of Republicans who have believed in climate change dangerously low, the evidence has become so overwhelming that today a majority of both parties in a recent poll agreed that climate change is happening—89 percent of Democrats and 57 percent of Republicans.[118] Even some fossil fuel companies, such as Shell, now openly admit that climate change is real and largely caused by human activity.[119]

Notwithstanding the fact that two-thirds of Americans had come to believe that government should do more to remedy climate change,[120] President Biden's efforts to act were stymied through the first eighteen months of his administration by opposition from all Senate Republicans and two Democrats.[121] Finally, after relentless negotiation, Biden induced the reluctant Democrats to vote for the Inflation Reduction Act (IRA). Vice President Kamala Harris cast the deciding vote, and in August 2022, the U.S. government took its first truly meaningful action to remedy climate change. This was a significant and in many ways surprising victory for pro-environmental forces.

However, the IRA's environmental provisions were far from perfect. The monetary commitment was much smaller than originally envisioned, and to gain approval, Democrats had to make major concessions to the fossil fuel industry, which continues to lobby and make campaign contributions designed to expand rather than contract its impact on the environment.[122] Even if it has the intended impact, which is optimistic, the law will not produce enough improvement to meet the U.S. commitment made in the Paris Agreement, which in itself is not enough to ensure climate stability.[123]

Worse still, because no Republican senators voted for the law and the vast majority of Republic representatives also opposed it, the IRA's climate provisions could be largely repealed with a small shift in the 2024 elections.[124] As political scientist Jacob Grumbach notes, "extremely wealthy individuals in an era of high economic inequality" increasingly find their views in the minority and have therefore worked diligently to tweak the rules of the democratic game to their advantage.[125] As conservative views on the environment have lost support among the general public, Republicans have responded by undermining democratic conventions. Political scientist Pippa Norris notes they have

> capitalized on institutional features of U.S. elections . . . including the extreme decentralization of electoral administration to partisan officials with minimal federal regulation, partisan gerrymandering of districts, overrepresentation of rural states in the U.S. Senate and Electoral College, partisan appointments in the judiciary, primary elections rallying the faithful in the base but excluding the less mobilized moderate independents, the role of money from rich donors in elections and campaigns, and so forth.[126]

Importantly, the Supreme Court, now packed with conservatives (another long-term project of the Kochs and other wealthy individuals and entities),[127] seems poised to drastically limit Congress's ability to regulate under the Commerce Clause, which threatens the viability of environmental laws such as the IRA.[128] This conservative majority has already overturned a century's worth of administrative law to block any meaningful climate change action by the EPA in West Virginia v. EPA[129] by inventing a "major question" doctrine. In that case and others, the Court's conservative justices have signaled a desire to do their best to neuter administrative agencies' ability to implement the IRA's climate provisions (and other laws) by overturning decades-old doctrines such as the ability of Congress to delegate authority to administrative agencies,[130] and the Chevron doctrine requiring deference to administrative agencies' expertise.[131]

Conclusion

Although most Americans believe the government should be taking stronger action to fight climate change, efforts to do so face an extremely uncertain future because, in part, a group of individuals and corporations have garnered an outsized share of the country's wealth and have used that to influence the political system in order to thwart the majority's desires. Economist Robert Ayres has rightly warned that if America's hypercompetitive winner-take-all capitalism and its resultant inequalities go too far, "[o]ur liberal democracy will be replaced by illiberal plutocracy or something much worse,"[132] and the odds that the U.S. will take the necessary actions to thwart disastrous climate change will be greatly diminished.

Notes

1. Katya Assaf Zakharov, "Capitalism vs. Freedom," *New York University Review of Law and Social Change* 38 (2013): 1–68. Assaf Zakharov argues that American capitalism is associated with the freedom of individuals to pursue personal economic goals but not with the freedom to pursue collective and non-pecuniary interests such as a clean environment.
2. Luigi Zingales, "Toward a Political Theory of the Firm," *Journal of Economic Perspectives* 31, no. 3 (2017): 119–20. The Medici family motto was purportedly: "Money to get power. Power to protect money."
3. Joseph Stiglitz, *The Price of Inequality* (W. W. Norton & Company, 2012), xi. The economic inequality "is cause and consequence of the failure of the political system, and it contributes to the instability of our economic system, which in turn contributes to increased inequality—a vicious downward spiral"; Ray Dalio, "Why and How Capitalism Needs to Be Reformed (Parts 1 & 2)," *LinkedIn*, April 5, 2019. Billionaire investor Ray Dalio calls this situation "self-reinforcing spirals up for the haves and down for the have-nots."
4. John Mackey and Rajendra Sisodia, *Conscious Capitalism: Liberating the Heroic Spirit of Business* (Harvard Business Press, 2013), 11–12.
5. Thomas Piketty, *Capital in the Twenty-First Century* (Belknap Press, 2017), 294.
6. Piketty, 297.
7. Robert Reich, *The System: Who Rigged It and How We Fix It* (Knopf, 2020), 15.
8. Emmanuel Saez and Gabriel Zucman, "The Rise of Income and Wealth Inequality in America: Evidence from Distributional Macroeconomic Accounts," *Journal of Economic Perspectives* 34, no. 4 (2020): 11.
9. Joseph E. Stiglitz, *People, Power, and Profits: Progressive Capitalism for an Age of Discontent* (W. W. Norton & Company, 2019), 5.
10. Gabriel Zucman, "Global Wealth Inequality," *Annual Review of Economics* 11 (2019): 134.
11. Murad Antia, "Wealth Inequality Is Far Worse than People Guess," *Tampa Bay Times*, October 2, 2021.
12. Federal Reserve Board, "Survey of Consumer Finances," Board of Governors of the Federal Reserve System, February 25, 2022.
13. David Leonhardt, "America's Cash Glut," *New York Times*, October 18, 2021;

Chuck Collins, "U.S. Billionaires Are Now $2.1 Trillion Richer than before the Pandemic," *Nation of Change*, October 23, 2021.

14. Peter Coy, "Wealth Inequality Is the Highest since World War II," *New York Times*, February 2, 2022.

15. Stiglitz, *People, Power, and Profits*, 66–67.

16. Sungki Hong and Hannah G. Shell, "The Impact of Automation on Inequality," *Economic Synopses* 29 (2018): 2.

17. Kevin Phillips, *Wealth and Democracy: A Political History of the American Rich* (New York: Broadway Books, 2002), 264.

18. Stiglitz, *People, Power, and Profits*, 86.

19. Shigehiro Oishi, Kostadin Kushlev, and Ulrich Schimmack, "Progressive Taxation, Income Inequality, and Happiness," *American Psychologist* 73, no. 2 (2018): 165.

20. Evan Starr, "Are Noncompetes Holding Down Wages?" (Brookings Institution Press, 2021), 127.

21. Claudia Irizarry Aponte, "When Private Equity Came Knocking, Bronx Renters Were Given Two Options: Buy or Get Out," *City*, February 23, 2022; Sheelah Kolhatkar, "What Happens When Investment Firms Acquire Trailer Parks," *New Yorker*, March 8, 2021.

22. Thomas Philippon, *The Great Reversal: How America Gave Up on Free Markets* (Belknap Press, October 2019), 54.

23. William Greider, *The Soul of Capitalism: Opening Paths to a Moral Economy* (Simon & Schuster, September 2004), 65.

24. Paul L. Caron and James R. Repetti, "Occupy the Tax Code: Using the Estate Tax to Reduce Inequality and Spur Economic Growth," *Pepperdine Law Review* 40, no. 5 (2013): 1256.

25. Stiglitz, *People, Power, and Profits*, 206.

26. James Alm, "Tax Evasion, Technology, and Inequality," *Economics of Governance* 22 (2021): 321.

27. Leandra Lederman, "The IRS, Politics, and Income Inequality," *Tax Notes* 150, no. 11 (2016).

28. Stiglitz, *People, Power, and Profits*, 206.

29. Piketty, *Capital in the Twenty-First Century*, 297.

30. Organization for Economic Cooperation and Development, *In it Together: Why Less Inequality Benefits All* (Organization for Economic Cooperation and Development, May 2015), 11, 19.

31. Francis Fukuyama, *Trust: Human Nature and the Reconstitution of Social Order* (Free Press, 1996), 21.

32. Frank B. Cross and Robert Prentice, *Law and Corporate Finance* (Edward Elgar Publishing, July 2007), 28–29.

33. Eric D. Gould and Alexander Hijzen, *Growing Apart, Losing Trust? The Impact of Inequality on Social Capital* (International Monetary Fund Working Paper 16/176, August 2016), 8.

34. Dalio, "Why and How Capitalism Needs to Be Reformed (Parts 1 & 2)."

35. Robert Ayres, *On Capitalism and Inequality: Progress and Poverty Revisited* (Springer, 2020), 210.

36. Fabian T. Pfeffer and Robert F. Schoeni, "How Wealth Inequality Shapes Our Future," *The Russell Sage Foundation Journal of the Social Sciences* 2, no. 6 (October 2016): 15–16.

37. Lane Kenworthy, *Social Democratic Capitalism* (Oxford University Press, 2019), 141.

38. Raghuram Rajan and Luigi Zingales, *Saving Capitalism from the Capitalists: Unleashing the Power of Financial Markets to Create Wealth and Spread Opportunity* (Princeton University Press, 2020), 280–81.

39. Bo Rothstein, "Social Capital in the Social Democratic Welfare State," *Politics & Society* 29, no. 2 (2021): 208.

40. Laura Seelkopf and Hanna Lierse, "Democracy and the Global Spread of Progressive Taxation," *Global Social Policy* 20, no. 2 (2020): 192.

41. Kenworthy, *Social Democratic Capitalism*, 121.

42. Steven Pearlstein, *Can American Capitalism Survive? Why Greed Is Not Good, Opportunity Is Not Equal, and Fairness Won't Make Us Poor* (St. Martin's Press, 2018), 82.

43. Daniel A. Farber and Philip P. Frickey, *Law and Public Choice: A Critical Introduction* (University of Chicago Press, 1991), 14–15.

44. Robert. A Dahl, *A Preface to Democratic Theory* (University of Chicago Press, 1956), 34–35.

45. Robert Reich, "A Free Market Manifesto That Changed the World, Reconsidered," *New York Times*, September 14, 2020; Randall G. Holcombe, "Capitalism, Cronyism, and Inequality," in *Capitalism and Inequality*, ed. G. P. Manish and Stephen C. Miller (New York: Routledge, 2020), 9.

46. Reich, *The System: Who Rigged It and How We Fix It*, 10.

47. Timothy K. Kuhner, *Capitalism v. Democracy: Money in Politics and the Free Market Constitution* (Stanford University Press, 2014), 199; Alex Blumberg, "Senator by Day, Telemarketer by Night," *National Public Radio*, March 30, 2012.

48. Reich, *The System: Who Rigged It and How We Fix It*, 16.

49. Adam Bonica et al., "Why Hasn't Democracy Slowed Rising Inequality?," *Journal of Economic Perspectives* 27, no. 3 (Summer 2003): 113.

50. Reich, *The System: Who Rigged It and How We Fix It*, 16.

51. Bonica et al., "Why Hasn't Democracy Slowed Rising Inequality?," 112.

52. OpenSecrets.Org., "Top Individual Contributors: All Federal Contributions," 2022.

53. Bonica et al., "Why Hasn't Democracy Slowed Rising Inequality?," 113.

54. Kuhner, *Capitalism v. Democracy: Money in Politics and the Free Market Constitution*, quoting Jake Tapper and Kirit Radia, "Report: Nearly 80% of Obama's Top Bundlers Given 'Key Administrative Posts,'" ABC News, June 15, 2011.

55. Peter L. Buttenwieser, "Why I Participate in a Corrupt System," in *Inside the Campaign Finance Battle: Court Testimony on the New Reforms*, ed. Anthony Corrado, Thomas E. Mann, and Trevor Potter (Brookings Institution Press, 2003), 311.

56. Paul Simon, "How the Senate Was Corrupted by Soft Money," in *Inside the Campaign Finance Battle: Court Testimony on the New Reforms*, ed. Anthony

Corrado, Thomas E. Mann, and Trevor Potter (Brookings Institution Press, 2003), 318.

57.   Martin Gilens and Benjamin I. Page, "Testing Theories of American Politics: Elites, Interest Groups, and Average Citizens," *Perspectives on Politics* 12, no. 3 (2014): 565.

58.   Larry Bartels, *Unequal Democracy: The Political Economy of the New Gilded Age* (Princeton University Press, 2015), 254; see also Martin Gilens, *Affluence & Influence: Economic Inequality and Political Power in America* (Princeton University Press, 2012), 5.

59.   Reich, *The System: Who Rigged It and How We Fix It*, 56.

60.   Philippon, *The Great Reversal*, 189.

61.   Marianne Bertrand et al., "Is It Whom You Know or What You Know? An Empirical Assessment of the Lobbying Process," *American Economic Review* 104, no. 12 (2014).

62.   Reich, *The System: Who Rigged It and How We Fix It*, 59.

63.   Anne Case and Angus Deaton, *Deaths of Despair and the Future of Capitalism* (Princeton University Press, 2020), 126.

64.   Reich, *The System: Who Rigged It and How We Fix It*, 26.

65.   Reich, *The System: Who Rigged It and How We Fix It*, 143.

66.   Philippon, *The Great Reversal*, 9.

67.   Amy Klobuchar, *Antitrust: Taking on Monopoly Power from the Gilded Age to the Digital Age* (Knopf, 2021), 176.

68.   Philippon, *The Great Reversal*, 9.

69.   Rajan and Zingales, *Saving Capitalism from the Capitalists*, 171.

70.   Philippon, *The Great Reversal*, 148.

71.   Zingales, "Toward a Political Theory of the Firm," 123.

72.   Zingales, "Toward a Political Theory of the Firm," 123.

73.   Zingales, "Toward a Political Theory of the Firm," 123.

74.   Scott Bland and Maggie Severns, "Documents Reveal Massive 'Dark-Money' Group Boosted Democrats in 2018," *Politico*, November 19, 2019.

75.   Ken Vogel and Shane Goldmacher, "Democrats Decried Dark Money. Then They Won with It in 2020," *New York Times*, January 29, 2022.

76.   David Michaels, *The Triumph of Doubt: Dark Money and the Science of Deception* (Oxford University Press, 2020), 185.

77.   Michaels, *The Triumph of Doubt*, 190, 192; Henrik M. Schatzinger and Steven E. Martin, *Game Changers: How Dark Money and Super PACS Are Transforming U.S. Campaigns* (Oxford University Press, 2020), 61.

78.   Benjamin Page and Martin Gilens, *Democracy in America? What Has Gone Wrong and What We Can Do About It* (Oxford University Press, 2017), 3.

79.   Bartels, *Unequal Democracy: The Political Economy of the New Gilded Age*, 273.

80.   Bartels, *Unequal Democracy*, 269–70.

81.   Mads Andreas Elkjær and Michael Baggesen Klitgaard, "Economic Inequality and Political Responsiveness: A Systematic Review," *Perspectives on Politics* 1 (October 2021).

82.   Bartels, *Unequal Democracy*, 270.

83. Bonica et al., "Why Hasn't Democracy Slowed Rising Inequality?," 107.
84. Case and Deaton, *Deaths of Despair*, 13. "Analysis by political scientists of voting patterns . . . [indicates] both Democratic and Republican lawmakers consistently vote for the interests of their more prosperous constituents with little attention to the interests of others."
85. Bonica et al., "Why Hasn't Democracy Slowed Rising Inequality?," 113.
86. Reich, *The System: Who Rigged It and How We Fix It*, 163.
87. Kent Greenfield, "A New Strategy to Fight Citizens United," *Huffington Post*, November 14, 2012.
88. Case and Deaton, *Deaths of Despair*, 130.
89. Reich, *The System: Who Rigged It and How We Fix It*, 142.
90. Albert Hunt, "Washington's Oldest Contact Sport: Lobbyists Scrum to Dilute or Kill Democrats' Tax Bill," *The Hill*, September 19, 2021.
91. Reich, *The System: Who Rigged It and How We Fix It*, 144; "the estate tax is so tiny that only 0.2 percent of estates were subject to it in 2017."
92. Philippon, *The Great Reversal*, 24: ". . . we see a lot of lobbying aimed at restricting competition and little advocacy to protect it."
93. Reich, *The System: Who Rigged It and How We Fix It*, 27.
94. Christina Wilkie, "Lobbyists Shielded Carried Interest from Biden's Tax Hikes, Top White House Economist Says," *CNBC*, September 30, 2021.
95. Paul Krugman, "Corporate America Is Lobbying for Climate Disaster," *New York Times*, September 2, 2021.
96. Caleb Silver, "The Top 25 Economies in the World," *Investopedia*, September 20, 2023.
97. Rodger A. Payne, "Freedom and the Environment," *Journal of Democracy* 6, no. 3 (July 1995): 42.
98. Eric Neumayer, "Sustainability and Inequality in Human Development," 8–9.
99. Michèle B. Bättig and Thomas Bernauer, "National Institutions and Global Public Goods: Are Democracies More Cooperative in Climate Change Policy?," *International Organization* 63, no. 2 (2009): 281; Thomas Bernauer and Vally Koubi, "Effects of Political Institutions on Air Quality," *Ecological Economics* 68, no. 5 (2009): 1355.
100. S. Nazrul Islam, "Inequality and Environmental Sustainability" (Department of Economic & Social Affairs Working Paper No. 145, August 2015), 4.
101. James K. Boyce et al., "Power Distribution, the Environment, and Public Health: A State-Level Analysis," *Ecological Economics* 29, no. 1 (April 1999): 127; Tim G. Holland et al., "A Cross-National Analysis of How Economic Inequality Predicts Biodiversity Loss," *Conservation Biology* 23, no. 5 (October 2009):1304; Gary Koop and Lise Tole, "Deforestation, Distribution, and Development," *Global Environmental Change* 11, no. 3 (October 2001): 193; Elisabetta Magnani, "The Environmental Kuznets Curve, Environmental Protection Policy and Income Distribution," *Ecological Economics* 32, no. 3 (March 2000): 431; Gregory M. Mikkelson et al., "Economic Inequality Predicts Biodiversity Loss," *PLoS ONE* 2, no. 5 (2007): e444; Neumayer, "Sustainability and Inequality in Human Development," 10; Marina

Vornovytskyy and James K. Boyce, "Economic Inequality and Environmental Quality: Evidence of Pollution in Russia" (working paper, University of Massachusetts Political Economy Research Institute, February 2021), 1.
102. James Boyce, "Inequality and Environmental Protection," 138.
103. Rachel Hellman, "Denmark Shines, U.S. Lags in Latest Climate Protection Rankings," *U.S. News & World Report*, February 28, 2022.
104. Katherine Burton, "George Soros Commits $1 Billion to Start Global University to Fight Climate Change," *Financial Post*, January 23, 2020.
105. Lynne Dallas, "Short-Termism, the Financial Crisis, and Corporate Governance," *Journal of Corporation Law* 37 (2011): 267.
106. Cara Biasucci and Robert Prentice, *Behavioral Ethics in Practice: Why We Sometimes Make the Wrong Decisions* (Routledge, 2020), 113.
107. Frances Stewart, "Sustainability and Inequality," *Development* 57, no. 3 (December 2014): 352.
108. Neumayer, "Sustainability and Inequality in Human Development," 10.
109. Nancy Krieger, "Climate Crisis, Health Equity, and Democratic Governance: The Need to Act Together," *Journal of Public Health Policy* 41 (2020) (emphasis added).
110. Ronald C. Kramer, *Carbon Criminals, Climate Crimes* (Rutgers University Press, 2020), 23, 97–98; Nancy MacLean, *Democracy in Chains: The Deep History of the Radical Right's Stealth Plan for America* (Viking, 2017), 216–17; Shawn Lawrence Otto, *The War on Science: Who's Waging It, Why It Matters, What We Can Do about It* (Milkweed Editions, 2016), 84.
111. Coral Davenport and Eric Lipton, "The Pruitt Emails: E.P.A. Chief Was Arm in Arm with Industry," *New York Times*, February 22, 2017.
112. Christopher Leonard, *Kochland: The Secret History of Koch Industries and Corporate Power in America* (Simon & Schuster, 2019), 549–61.
113. Schatzinger and Martin, *Game Changers: How Dark Money and Super PACS Are Transforming U.S. Campaigns*, 73–74; Joseph Zeballos-Roig, "How the Koch Brothers Used Their Massive Fortune to Power a Conservative Crusade that Reshaped American Politics," *Insider*, November 13, 2020; Jane Mayer, *Dark Money: The Hidden History of the Billionaires Behind the Rise of the Radical Right* (Doubleday, 2016), 204.
114. Jeff Nesbit, *Poison Tea: How Big Oil and Big Tobacco Invented the Tea Party and Captured the GOP* (Thomas Dunne Books, 2016), 9.
115. John Cook et al., *America Misled: How the Fossil Fuel Industry Deliberately Misled Americans About Climate Change* (Fairfax, VA: George Mason University Center for Climate Change Communication, 2019), 3; Kramer, *Carbon Criminals, Climate Crimes*, 66–82; Chris Mooney, *The Republican War on Science* (Basic Books, 2005), 82.
116. Otto, *The War on Science*, 295.
117. Cook et al., "Consensus on Consensus: A Synthesis of Consensus Estimates on Human-Caused Global Warming."
118. Zoe Strozewski, "10 Percent of Americans Don't Believe in Climate Change, 15 Percent Unsure: Poll," *Newsweek*, October 26, 2021.

119. Justin Worland, "The Reason Fossil Fuel Companies Are Finally Reckoning with Climate Change," *Time*, January 16, 2020.
120. Alec Tyson and Brian Kennedy, "Two-Thirds of Americans Think Government Should Do More on Climate," *Pew Research Center*, June 23, 2020.
121. Sylvan Lane, "Manchin to Oppose Biden Fed Pick over Climate Stances," *The Hill*, March 14, 2022; Oliver Milman, "'He's a Villain': Joe Manchin Attracts Global Anger over Climate Crisis," *Guardian*, January. 26, 2020.
122. Emily Cochrane and Lisa Friedman, "What's in the Climate, Tax and Health Care Package," *New York Times*, August 7, 2022.
123. Cliff Majersik and Alex Dews, "What the Inflation Reduction Act Does and Doesn't Do for Climate and Equity," *MIT Institute for Market Transformation*, August 10, 2022.
124. David Rosner, "The Inflation Reduction Act's Climate Provisions: A Pleasant Surprise," *Milbank Quarterly*, August 25, 2022.
125. Thomas B. Edsall, "The Republican Strategists Who Have Carefully Planned All of This," *New York Times*, April 12, 2023.
126. Edsall, "The Republican Strategists Who Have Carefully Planned All of This."
127. Anne Nelson, *Shadow Network: Media, Money, and the Secret Hub of the Radical Right* (Bloomsbury Publishing, 2019), 143.
128. Erwin Chemerinsky, *Worse Than Nothing: The Dangerous Fallacy of Originalism* (Yale University Press, 2022), 193.
129. *West Virginia v. Environmental Protection Agency, 142 S.Ct. 2587 (2022).*
130. Peter J. Wallison, "Only the Supreme Court Can Effectively Restrain the Administrative State," *National Review*, December 1, 2020.
131. *American Hospital Association v. Becerra, 142 S.Ct. 1896 (2022).*
132. Ayres, *On Capitalism and Inequality: Progress and Poverty Revisited* (Springer, 2020), v.

4

The Techno-Optimist Case for Addressing Sustainability and Its Grounding in Capitalist (Market) Incentives

Daniel R. Cahoy

The effort to create a more sustainable society touches on many facets of the environment, public policy, and social responsibility. We seek solutions to the negative impacts of climate change, a lack of access to medicines, environmentally friendly sources of energy that will permit continued economic progress, and sufficient food to feed a world of ten billion people. Many say that a conservation-based approach that restores humanity to a more natural state is the best path. But to others, the only way out of our predicaments is the way we got in: technology.

A "techno-optimist" mindset views sustainability issues largely as problems that can be solved through invention and investment.[1] Such an advocate might argue that we can continue our economic progress if we utilize new or emergent technologies like bioengineered medicines, genetically modified foods, alternative energy sources, and carbon scrubbing and capture systems. In other words, we can innovate our way out of crises as we have since the beginning of the industrial revolution. In the modern world, the economic system that has proven most likely to generate effective innovation is based on private investment, ownership, and individual need—in other words, capitalism. Although government and community investment in solutions is a necessary cohort, techno-optimism for addressing sustainability challenges seems inherently premised on capitalism.[2]

Is techno-optimism a realistic strategy for creating a more sustainable world? This chapter will first create a working definition of techno-optimism, acknowledging that it can be subject to varying perspectives and political and ideological capture. It will consider the contrast in a mindset that prioritizes technology development versus one that focuses on conservation and reduction. Next, it will explore the connection between technology incentives and capitalism, looking particularly to increasingly harmonized legal systems that have created a broader-than-ever base for innovation. Finally, it will consider evidence that technology-based solutions are more than a distraction or palliative in the contexts of disease, food security, climate change, and energy production. It concludes that, although the hope for technological solutions for overwhelming global sustainability challenges can tend toward Pollyannaish thinking, the drive to invent around problems should be encouraged and policy must be adopted in response.

Techno-Optimist Thinking Versus Eco-Pessimism

The idea of techno-optimism is essentially that technology can have a positive effect on society and that through technological innovation, the world will get better and problems can be solved.[3] The trendy phrasing has received recent attention, finding promotion and acclaim in the works of entrepreneur and XPRIZE founder Peter Diamandis and Harvard psychologist Steven Pinker.[4] Regardless, techno-optimism has roots in the economic theories of scholars such as Robert Solow, who won the Nobel Prize in 1987 for his groundbreaking work demonstrating that economic growth requires technological progress in addition to labor and capital.[5] Techno-optimism has been used to justify the barrier-breaking mindset of Silicon Valley that was believed to play a central role in improving human relationships and understanding through increasingly more capable electronic systems.[6] It also undergirds a great deal of investment in biotechnology and medicine under the presumption that previously immutable conditions might be treated or re-written by technologies like CRISPR/Cas9 gene editing.[7] It is the calling card of the venture capitalist and inspires entrepreneurs and inventors to seek new solutions to seemingly intractable problems.

Interestingly, techno-optimism is recovering from a low point in the last decade. Around 2010, many technology analysts and writers suggested that true innovation had largely stalled and that businesses and consumers had settled for slickly marketed regurgitations of existing products.[8] However, the flurry of important innovations in recent years, like truly marketable electric cars, technologies to enable remote work, and amazingly adaptable vaccines, have provided some hope that true technological progress is alive and well.[9] Perhaps when the world is truly in need, new technologies can actually be created to solve problems.

Beyond the trends, one can look at techno-optimism as another iteration of a basic belief in the ability of humans to employ scientific and mathematical knowledge to overcome the challenges of the natural world. It is premised on the idea that the environment is ultimately understandable and the underlying forces that impact the human condition can, through careful study using the scientific method, be unlocked.[10] This information can then be used by humans to substantially alter their environment and impact—even determine—their ability to survive and thrive. One might reasonably assume that any natural science-based problem, whether it be climate, disease, or the availability of critical resources, can be confronted with scientific information and potentially solved (or at least addressed). Human suffering and the increased decline of humanity's viability are not only not preordained, but science-based thinking suggests that we can apply our knowledge to make the world better, no matter how dire a current issue appears to be.

One can argue that science-based thinking is in many ways contrary to the more spiritual branches of philosophies of ecology, conservation, and nature in balance. Scholars have pointed out that some conservation movements have almost religious overtones in their belief that environmental stewardship is a sacred responsibility that involves the rejection of technology.[11] The antidote to unthinking modern consumption and excess is restraint and the pursuit of harmony with nature—what one might call "reduction-based thinking" or "eco-pessimism." An excellent framing of the inherent conflict between reduction and technology is provided in Charles C. Mann's *The Wizard and the Profit*, which contrasts the belief that food and planetary resources can support a finite population with the fact that technology seems to enable ever-greater growth.[12] Of course, anti-technology movements can be traced back at least to the British Luddites of over two hundred years ago,[13] and the reasons for techno-skepticism are broad, varied, and not always related to the environment. In fact, even the Luddites were not anti-technology per se, but rather were raising concerns with how poorly workers were treated when technology was introduced. But at the very least, those who question the power of science and technology to resolve sustainability issues are more likely to conclude that a humanist perspective is required, and even that perspective may have limited effect against technology-driven harms.

To be sure, this is not to suggest that all conservation or reduction-based thinking is anti-science. In fact, much depends on a scientific understanding to operationalize techniques and determine what forms of conservation will have an impact on sustainability challenges.[14] A great example of the positive impact of science-based reduction can be viewed in the improved air quality in countries that undertook an effort to reduce or eliminate the use of chlorofluorocarbons (CFCs) and attached an economic value to pollution with sulfur dioxide.[15] The result has been a reduction in acid rain and ozone depletion.

Beyond the relative discount of science, some aspects of eco-pessimism are grounded in the idea that there is a limit to the "carrying capacity" of Earth.[16] No matter what technology is employed, only so many people can be sustained on the planet, the theory posits. If we do not use our intellect to self-limit our expansion and impact, we will eventually destroy our ecosystem and make Earth uninhabitable. It is a caution frequently illustrated in the context of other animal ecosystems, and we could be destined to join those past populations in growing and consuming ourselves to extinction if changes are not made.

In the end, one can argue that the complaint against techno-optimism is not an opposition to technology per se, but rather the optimism.[17] In other words, the aspect of conservation or reduction-based thinking that tends to conflict with techno-optimism is the belief that solutions that allow continued growth and production will necessarily fail to serve as a full counter to the world's sustainability challenges. Technological solutions are, for the most part, limited, untested, and not an appropriate vessel for global faith.

On the other hand, even if one believes that techno-optimist strategies can have net positive effects, one must accept that this approach has problems as well. It can be an approach accompanied by inherent disparities because, fundamentally, technological development is expensive. If technology provides a solution, it is reasonable to assume that it will not be equally available to all those in need, at least at the outset.[18] Perhaps no better example exists than vaccines developed in the wake of the COVID-19 pandemic. The wealthiest and most developed nations clearly had an advantage supporting vaccine innovation, and it is not surprising that they secured the earliest and most broad-based access.[19] As a result, the world's most vulnerable populations generally lagged in vaccine access for a substantial time after the treatments first became available.

The philosophical counter to the inherent inequity of technology-based solutions is that they at least have the potential to diffuse to all populations if the right factors exist.[20] Considering again the example of medical treatment, the World Health Organization's list of essential medicines is largely populated by drugs that were at one point patented and otherwise restricted to those who could afford monopoly rents. These medicines are, for the most part, now available to anyone with basic production facilities as "generic" compounds, yielding lower prices and greater access.[21] Conversely, one might argue that restrictive, conservation-based mindsets frequently privilege the wealthy who can afford the fruits of lower production activity. Thus, eco-pessimistic strategies are not necessarily more equitable.

In addition to disparities and inequities, another argument against techno-optimism is that it is often based on solutions to a specific problem that may not reflect the entire ecosystem in play. For example, wind and solar power are generated from inexhaustible sources of clean energy and seem (from a simplistic view) to be a perfect replacement to traditional, polluting sources. However, both wind and solar require the construction of complex energy capture devices like windmills and photovoltaic panels, which has an impact on energy and materials.[22] Both also require energy storage systems to compete with the easy startup availability of fossil-fueled power plants. Energy transmission also has an impact that may not be entirely green, particularly when it leads to catastrophic wildfires. To seriously support a techno-optimist approach, such limitations must be taken into account. In some cases, the broader view of limitations may render a particular technological solution ineffective as a sustainable alternative.

In the end, even a techno-optimist cannot claim that the embrace of technology is a savior without impact or cost. The essential question is whether it is a savior at all, or merely just a substitution with different sets of problems in combination with false hope and complacency.

Techno-Optimism as a Capitalistic Endeavor

The human spirit for invention and problem-solving is indomitable, and there is no doubt that new ideas for alleviating sustainability issues will arise no matter what the support structure looks like. However, there is also little question that the environment can be shaped and even enhanced by law and regulation.[23] That is the premise of innovation prize and protection systems (for example, legal protections for intellectual property) that extend back at least six hundred years.[24] Through law and regulation, the technological environment can be shaped and enhanced by the state. Importantly, for the most part, these interventions simply allow private actors to realize an advantage from investment, rather than directly stimulating a particular type or process of innovation.

Thanks to private investment-oriented legal and regulatory structures in place, modern technology development is now fundamentally capitalist. Although it is true that direct government innovation can exist, typically the resulting innovation is then commercialized in the private sector. We depend on private firms to risk their own capital in research and commercialization to ensure that the optimal amount and design of innovation takes place. Government can place its thumb on the scales to direct information through rights systems, but funding, regulation, and recent investment have been overwhelmingly private.[25] Moreover, it is unlikely that the current level of innovative activity would be as high without substantial private investment.

There are many reasons that justify turning innovation over to the private market. The most important is, of course, choice. There has long been a perceived gap in the government's ability to deliver final products that meet the needs and desires of consumers. When the market links private choice with product research and development, it is far more likely that aligned activity will be profitable for the firm and generate interest. In the context of sustainability, if there is a business case for environmental, social, or governance activities, companies will respond.

Indeed, as market interest has emerged in sustainability-related products, private investment has followed. Perhaps the most prominent current example is electric cars. Electricity in personal mobility has existed essentially as long as gasoline, but consumer interest was low due to the convenience of fossil fuel infrastructure and relative cost and inconvenience of electric charging infrastructure.[26] The market remained extremely niche until a few firms, particularly Tesla, innovated high-range cars that were also attractive, bringing in new consumers. Purchase incentives also rose contemporaneously, complementing the attraction of technological advance.[27] By 2021, Tesla was the most valuable car company in the world, and most other manufacturers announced plans to essentially convert to producing only electric cars in the future.[28] Private investment, company innovation, and individual interest produced a seismic technological shift that was fueled by a capitalist system.

Of course, one might argue that a state-directed innovation system could have achieved success similar to that of Western firms like Tesla if sufficient funds were expended. In fact, it is not unreasonable to wonder if a state-run system might be more successful because it is not burdened by the need to attract investor buy-in. A natural experiment of sorts exists in this context, as the Chinese government has been pouring substantial funds into electric vehicle research and development in pursuit of creating a domestic industry. From at least 2015 through 2021, China was estimated to have spent approximately $100 billion in government funding and subsidies to develop electric cars.[29] The results to date have been less than impressive. Globally, Chinese companies have produced no serious competitor to Tesla and have not created technology that approaches its advances. As of 2021, Tesla was the most successful electric car company in China.[30]

The connection between the legal framework for innovation and the interest of private investors is essential for explaining the success of the innovation environment. Fundamentally, legal systems throughout the world, including command and control economies, treat innovation as something to be privately owned, protecting innovators against rote copyists and free riders. In some systems, like the United States, patent, copyright, and trade secret rights have the attributes of personal property (though with some limitation on full constitutional protection). By offering such rights, countries openly promote a capitalistic approach to innovation.[31]

Although capitalist-based innovation is the most important form that exists today in most of the world's largest economies, this has not always been the case. Prior to the Second World War, most basic research and development (outside of the military) was funded by industry or universities.[32] After the war, the United States, in particular, funneled massive amounts of government funding into basic science.[33] As a result, the government became the most important source of research support, and this was a trend that lasted until relatively recently. Beginning around 1980, industry spending in the United States overtook that of the federal government.[34] Today, approximately 72 percent of basic and applied research, along with development funding, comes from private industry.[35] Shrinking federal government budgets for research suggest this trend will continue in the future.

Despite the increase in industry funding, government support for research and deployment remains strong and important, particularly for areas without clear commercial applications. In particular, state-controlled innovation is a viable method for identifying technology-based solutions for sustainability problems. It would therefore be incorrect to suggest that innovation is entirely a capitalistic endeavor; the shared role for government, universities, and industry going forward is clear. Yet it is also true that the current level of innovation would be impossible without the investment of firm-controlled property and capital. For that reason, the link between capitalism and innovation cannot be ignored and is an essential aspect of the techno-optimism framework. If technology can save us, capitalist inputs are an axiomatic part of the equation.

Is There Evidence That We Can Invent Our Way Out of Sustainability Problems?

In the abstract, it is easy to claim that technology is either the solution for or the cause of environmental and social harm. A debate at such a high level is not incredibly helpful for anything other than making general philosophical points. Thankfully, because the debate has taken place for some time, we do have some specific contexts that can be considered to determine whether techno-optimism is warranted. At the very least, reviewing specific examples may provide some perspective for determining how to balance technology and retrenchment.

In discussing specific sustainability contexts, it is useful to survey a diverse set because technology solutions may not be equally advantageous for all concerns. Some problems lend themselves to science, whereas others are more defined by social or governance issues that require supplemental or alternate approaches. In the end, an all-or-nothing approach to relying on technology is unlikely to be the final conclusion. Rather, we will adopt a mix of solutions in most cases that will provide the maximum benefit.

Energy Production and Climate Change

Perhaps the most substantial and dire sustainability problem facing the world is the negative impact of climate change; it remains the grand challenge of our time. The accumulation of greenhouse gasses since the industrial revolution has permanently altered our environment. As a result, Earth is undeniably heating up in most parts of the world, and at least experiencing disruptive weather patterns in others. According to NASA's Goddard Institute for Space Studies, the average global temperature of Earth has increased 1.1° Celsius since 1880.[36] The oceans are rising, polar ice is melting, wildfires are increasingly devastating, and arid portions of the globe are becoming less habitable with each passing year.

At this point, the opportunity to entirely avoid or largely reverse climate change has effectively passed; the focus now is on limiting future temperature increases. At the 2021 United Nations Climate Change Conference (COP26), the attending countries agreed on several initiatives with the goal of limiting global warming to 1.5° Celsius.[37] Although this increase will have dramatic effects, they will be far less catastrophic than those that will occur if global temperatures reach the 4.4° increase some predict by 2100 without amelioration.[38]

Thankfully, despite some historical reluctance to acknowledge the problem, there is a relative global consensus among governments and businesses that combating climate change is an important objective. According to the Governance and Accountability Institute, approximately 92 percent of companies in the S&P 500 published sustainability or ESG (environmental, social, and governance) reports in 2020.[39] Businesses highlight environmental concerns as the "E" in ESG reporting and investing. Some argue that these efforts are largely greenwashing. However, the increased attention has, without a doubt, led to a proliferation of pledges for addressing global warming.[40]

For years, the eco-pessimist focus on reduction has been the default plan for mitigating global warming. Limiting carbon output through less travel, energy use, and consumption is potentially effective if enacted on a large enough scale. Unfortunately, the limited scale to date has been a problem, particularly in view of the increasing greenhouse gas emissions from developing areas of the world. Despite efforts to control emissions, the global production of CO_2 continues to increase.[41] There was a slight downturn at the beginning of the pandemic, and some initial hope that the recovery could redirect us to a more "sustainable" path.[42] Unfortunately, those hopes were quickly frustrated by the 6 percent CO_2 increased in 2021.

An intermediate approach that might be positioned for success is the substitution of more eco-friendly materials, products, and energy systems in the pursuit of lower carbon lifestyles. Such a strategy would arguably permit people to maintain the same standard of living and level of wealth with a lessened environmental impact. For example, Beyond Burgers are often lauded for tasting like beef, but with significantly less environmental impact. More broadly, energy sources that are sufficiently less polluting, like natural gas, can help to hold down carbon output. According to the U.S. Energy Information Administration, U.S. carbon output related to energy production has actually declined since 2000, largely due to the substitution of natural gas for more polluting energy sources like coal.[43]

Of course, the substitution proposition often involves tradeoffs that are not possible for every consumer. Some products may be more expensive than their less environmentally friendly counterparts. As a result, the most vulnerable populations may have the least access. There are efforts to coordinate financing for decarbonization initiatives across the world. Among the most prominent is the Glasgow Financial Alliance for Net Zero (GFANZ) that developed in the wake of COP26. The Alliance articulates seventeen investment opportunities that are intended to provide a roadmap for financial institutions, including wind-based generation in the EU and U.S. and "green steel" in Asia.[44] However, even with financing, it is possible that some initiatives may cause other environmental or social impacts that may balance out the advantages. Electric cars use rare earth minerals in the manufacture of electronics and magnets, and extracting such minerals leads to significant waste products (some of which are even radioactive).[45]

In any case, transition technologies and holding patterns are not enough to have the desired impact on global temperatures. According to the Intergovernmental Panel on Climate Change (IPCC), in order to achieve the desired 1.5° Celsius peak, the world must do more than simply restrict the output of current systems.[46] The true climate techno-optimist expects something more. This hopeful person believes that we can employ technology to remove carbon from the atmosphere, thus pausing or even reversing climate impacts. Taken to its limits, this view suggests that the absolute peak, whether it is 1.5° or 2°, may not be critical because greenhouse gasses can be removed at some point in the future. Arguably, if there is a serious possibility of carbon removal, education and conservation mindsets are less necessary as well.

In fact, there are proposals for removing carbon from the atmosphere on a large scale. One of the most ambitious is "direct air capture" technology, which aims to actually pull carbon out of the air and sequester it (likely underground in rock formations).[47] As the concentration of CO_2 in the atmosphere is relatively low (even at its most problematic), carbon capture technology requires large plants and a significant amount of electricity.[48] The power must also be produced through renewable sources if net removal is to result. Another process is to capture carbon in biomass (essentially all of the carbon in a plant is pulled from the atmosphere), and then use that biomass for electricity. If this "bioenergy" is coupled with a system to capture and sequester the carbon produced when it is burned for energy, a net zero emission is the result.

Even more extreme is a concept known as geoengineering, or more specifically, solar geoengineering. Related to the initial heating of the sun's rays, this would involve actually modifying the atmosphere, at least temporarily, to reflect more sunlight. Scientists have proposed using sulfite particles similar to those released from volcanic activity that block sunlight and lower global temperatures for a few years.[49] Another proposal involves "brightening" clouds to reflect more sunlight.[50] Ocean geoengineering has also been proposed, a form of which would induce the growth of phytoplankton that would absorb CO_2 similar to the way that land-based plants do.[51]

Currently, it is unclear that carbon capture can be employed on the scale necessary to significantly reduce or zero out emissions. Additional technological advances are necessary to establish that it can be environmentally effective and economically feasible. Geoengineering is perceived as radical planetary alteration, with unknown consequences. Altering Earth's air or water on a global scale reasonably frightens people and is unlikely to garner sufficient support absent an absolute emergency.

This example demonstrates how techno-optimism must be constrained with some appreciation of the risks and the potential for failure. For the foreseeable future, a techno-optimist approach must be coupled with an eco-pessimist mindset that limits and reduces carbon output where possible. Both approaches must be intertwined in the context of energy and climate change. Total faith in technology as a savior would seem unwarranted and dangerous.

Clean Water

The availability of water resources is an issue that obviously touches on climate change (temperature increases mean more stress on supplies), but it is also an essential consumptive product for health and sanitation. Moreover, it is not enough to say that we need sufficient water—that water must also be in a form available for human use. If one subtracts the amount of global water consisting of ocean, and then also takes out that which is polluted or inaccessible, what is left over is not inexhaustibly abundant.

Another issue with water availability is that it is inherently a geographically diverse phenomenon. Within the same country, it is possible for some regions to suffer from drought and others to have relatively abundant resources. Importantly, water scarcity has a greater impact in much of the developing world than in the United States. As climate change progresses, it is likely that countries like India and China will be impacted more than the U.S. and most European countries.[52] In part, this is a result of increasing populations in addition to the inherent geographical challenges. Water availability is therefore an equity issue in addition to a generic welfare concern, and maintaining and delivering water supplies is likely to be one of the most challenging global sustainability goals and constraints in coming decades.[53]

The obvious solution to water scarcity is to reduce use and conserve. In other words, the eco-pessimist view that we must preserve what we have is not only the historic solution, but also an important strategy for the future. One important manifestation of water conservation is limiting municipal use though devices like low-flow showers and toilets and eliminating grass lawns and car washing.[54] However, globally, most water is used in industrial or agricultural applications.[55] Serious conservation can only be achieved with more efficient irrigation, less pollution of existing supplies, and better water management for industry.

A compromise between lower use and creating new water resources is making better use of water that has already been captured. When drinkable water has been used in some manner and disposed of in sewage systems, the effort and energy needed for purification is lost. It is possible to recover much of this effort through a practice called "potable reuse."[56] Wastewater can be cleaned and retuned to drinkable water systems. Technology can play a role in improving the efficiency of this purification process through the use of cheaper and more effective membranes for filtering.[57] Alternatively, where regulations do not permit so-called "direct potable reuse," the waste-water can be returned to resources like reservoirs or streams for natural filtering before being pulled into municipal systems.

But can we use technology to create more usable water, essentially alleviating the shortage directly? Optimists place a great deal of hope in the potential for ocean desalinization. Since most of the world's water is unusable for drinking or farming due to its salinity, technologies to remove the salt and make the water potable are in great demand. Desalination technologies have existed for a long time and are currently in use in many countries like Saudi Arabia and Israel, but only recently have they become viable on a large scale.[58] Two technologies of current interest are reverse osmosis filtering and seawater vaporization to condense to freshwater.[59] Due to the significant amount of energy required, the primary limitation is cost. Additionally, waste from desalination is generally an extremely salty brine that can harm sea life if returned without treatment. So far, the cost of desalination has limited its use, and progress on better technologies has been slow. Even if this techno-optimist solution seems apparent and theoretically within reach, it will likely not be practical on a large scale for many years. A more eco-pessimist approach to water is reasonable for the foreseeable future.

Food Production

The earth's population continues to increase while the resources neces-sary to support humanity are practically finite. Inevitably, it seems that we must reach a point where the number of people on the planet exceeds our ability to sustain them. Although we have become extremely efficient in producing and delivering calories to more and more people, some required amount surely exceeds the availability of arable land. Some wonder if we can realistically expect to provide enough food to a population that is pre-dicted to eventually number 9.7 billion by 2050.[60]

Complicating the food capacity problem is the impact of climate change. Agricultural experts expect that the theoretical maximum of food production will be pushed downward by change that will make previously productive land more arid.[61] In particular, equatorial growing regions may become so hot that the crops that millions depend on for food will no longer be viable. Additionally, climate change may foment related disasters like harsher storms, insect invasions, and plant disease.[62] It is possible that the world's ability to produce food in the hotter future will be so reduced that even the current population of 7.8 billion people would suffer increased hunger.

Global conflict is another challenge to food access. A recent example is the Russian invasion of Ukraine; the war has exposed just how fragile the world's food resources are, even beyond climate as a factor. In just a few months, the war disrupted Ukraine's role as an essential global producer of crops like wheat and sunflower seeds. Russia's role as a global supplier has also been disrupted. Those who suffer include not only those in the conflict zone, but also populations in many smaller countries that depend on imported grain from the warring nations. For example, Eritrea, Armenia, and Mongolia get over 90 percent of their wheat from either Russia or the Ukraine.[63] When a significant growing region is attacked and supply chains are severed, it can impact the entire world.

Whether global population growth will outstrip the earth's ability to feed humanity has long been an issue for economists and international policymakers. In 1798, English economist Thomas Malthus theorized that rising living standards would allow populations to quickly exceed the planet's ability to feed them.[64] Later scholars have predicted the same outcome, reframed slightly to acknowledge the food production increase in the twentieth century.[65] This is essentially an eco-pessimist view; if birthrates are not significantly limited, we will eat ourselves into a humanitarian or ecological disaster. Although some still argue that population management is a critical element of maintaining access to food, most academics and policymakers now consider this view to be a distraction.[66] The most important current limitation perspective is advocating a shift to less land- and energy-intense food sources, particularly reducing animal farming for meat due to its outsized impact.[67]

Thankfully, food production has not remained static. In fact, agricultural science—beginning in Indigenous communities hundreds of years ago—has repeatedly facilitated greater food production that has staved off global starvation.[68] According to the U.S. Department of Agriculture (USDA), crop production tripled between 1948 and 2017.[69] It is not going too far to say that, thanks to the so-called "green revolution," hunger as a persistent and unavoidable plague has been tamed.

Challenges to feeding the world in the future are daunting and the need may exceed how much more can be done. Without a doubt, avoiding scarcity and famine will require the earth to produce a level of human consumable calories that exceeds what is currently possible. According to the World Resources Institute (using Food and Agriculture Organization (FAO) data), there is a 56 percent "food gap" between what was produced in 2010 versus what is necessary for 2050.[70] Farming more land is not sufficient to meet our needs. Is it realistic to continue to assume that we can figure out technological solutions to address food availability, or do we need to return to reduction and conservation philosophies that previously gained favor?

The reductionist perspective would first suggest that we need to move away from inefficient sources of calories, particularly meat. Most of the future population growth will come from developing countries, and if, as predicted, those countries progressively move toward a greater percentage of meat consumption, food supplies will be stressed.[71] Thus, vegetarianism or even veganism should be promoted. Reducing food waste is also an important option, which could be achieved with better storage and, frankly, more portion control.[72]

However, simply changing consumption strategies is unlikely to address the coming shortfall. The truth is, absent a punctuated catastrophe, we seem unable to dramatically alter our consumptive habits. Most agricultural experts point to the need for technological advances to satisfy future demand. The FAO specifically points to the need for more research and development expenditures to produce the agricultural technology that can feed nine billion people.[73] Crops that are genetically resistant to drought and disease are certainly likely to be important. In addition, better and more efficient farming techniques that waste less water or require less fertilizer can increase the productivity of existing farmland. Methods to expand agricultural land without destroying the environment through shared land use that preserves biodiversity must also be on the table.

This is not to say that technological advance in agriculture is an easy option with universal agreement. Some resist changes to foods or techniques that have been a part of cultures for hundreds of years. One of the most controversial innovations in this area is, not surprisingly, genetically modified crops. Although the resistance is precautionary and not deeply embedded in available science, many reject the use of genetically modified foods as a risky and unwarranted manipulation of the natural world.[74] Additionally, agricultural technology can be costly and lower income populations may not be able to afford new seed varieties and farming systems. It is possible that governments and agricultural conglomerates could ameliorate some of the expense by using price discrimination between the developed and developing world, like that used with pharmaceuticals.

In the context of food security, techno-optimism would seem to be a necessary characteristic. We cannot limit or reform our way to fully feeding the world. The good news is that agricultural technology has space for progress, and it seems possible that we can do more with what we have available in the world. Faith in technology to blunt hunger does not appear to be such a dramatic stretch.

Access to Medicines

The issue of medical treatment availability is interesting as an aspect of sustainability in that it combines both environment and social factors. To a great extent, the lack of adequate medical care is a problem of economics. The cost of health care continues to rise, and the more vulnerable members of society often face difficulty in obtaining necessary treatments. The high cost of effective treatments as well as preventive care also reduces overall lifespan and time free of medical burden. The combination of the two is known as a disability adjusted life year (DALY). Cost barriers are a factor in all countries.[75] The United States is, of course, famous for favoring health care funding through employer programs, leading to significant inequities based on the ability to pay for care; on the other hand, nations with national health care systems must ration care based on what the system can sustain.[76] Still, developing and least developed nations may not even have sufficient wealth to provide effective care to any but the privileged few.

In addition to cost, there is an increasing appreciation of the fact that our impact on the environment can create health problems. Air and water pollution is an obvious context for concern, but another suite of medical concerns stems from the rise in zoonotic disease that can be connected to travel (particularly international air travel) and land development.[77] For example, research suggests expansive development into previously unmarred areas of nature has unleashed new diseases, including particularly virulent forms of hemorrhagic fevers like Ebola, and possibly COVID-19.[78] It could be argued that reducing our constant societal expansion and population growth is a more efficient means of combating disease than reliance on the scientific community's ability to find the next vaccine or treatment.

One could surmise that techno-optimism is more than just an aspiration when it comes to disease; it is a forgone requirement and the only possible path forward. Future health and technological advances appear necessarily intertwined. Is there an alternative to medical access that could even plausibly achieve the same health outcomes? The answer would at first appear to be "obviously not." However, ameliorations have been proposed that might reduce the instances of illness or sickness requiring medication. Arguably, by changing lifestyle and activities and promoting a return to a simpler existence, the need for technological solutions to medical unsustainability might be minimized.

For personal health, the less technology-dependent route could involve changes to diet and exercise that eliminate the conditions requiring or leading to illness. Conditions that might be impacted include obesity and the related problems of heart disease and diabetes.[79] Additionally, some suggest that more intractable diseases like Alzheimer's, arthritis, and osteoporosis might be addressed by leading a life less defined by processed foods, sugars, grains, or animal products.[80] Studies also indicate that the over-use of technology solutions, like antibiotics or pain medications, may actually create a host of new problems that then require novel medical solutions in a vicious circle of progress and pain.[81] Alternatively, if one leads a healthy life, one might avoid the need for medical treatment.

Despite the attractive simplicity of this argument, there is at best conflicting evidence that such modifications can truly make differences that substantially impact human disease. So many factors impact even seemingly cause-related conditions like weight gain that replacing technology or deemphasizing it seems unlikely. Moreover, in environments where the disease burden is high, it is technology that has allowed the most vulnerable populations to actually change their future, become more productive, and lift their societies out of poverty.[82] In the context of personal health, technology provides the most optimistic future outcome.

The anti-technology or anti-development rationale fails in the context of pandemic disease prevention as well. Based on the increasing human life span, it is very difficult to argue that medical technologies have done significantly more harm than good in addressing the random harm of unexpected death from disease.[83] Development provides societies with the wealth to at least start addressing the conditions of poverty that lead to the spread of disease.

Given the difficulty of modifying human behavior (and the advantages of continuing our current tack in terms of wealth and knowledge development), access to medicines seems to be the sustainability issue most tied to technology. In this case, society is likely to continue funding and favoring advances in medicines as a means to achieve a better future.

Conclusions

An in-depth consideration of specific sustainability issues makes clear that simply modifying human behavior is not enough to face the enormity of our current challenges; technology must play a role. Thankfully, technology has demonstrated its effectiveness in many areas of sustainability, and it is reasonable to assume that our ability to use science and engineering to modify or enhance natural processes can help ameliorate the impact of various sustainability challenges. It therefore is critical to adopt sustainability policies that support research and development into sustainability solutions.

However, two important caveats have been revealed by this challenge-specific review. First, technology may not be able to fully reverse the harm to the planet we have caused to date (or will cause in the future). To the extent that full techno-optimism suggests no matter what we do, we can think and invent our way back to a desirable point in time is simply unrealistic. The changes to Earth from the impact of human populations and human activities mean that technology will be able to help us adapt, but not avoid change. A techno-optimist who declares "Who cares? We'll figure it out later" is not living in reality.

Second, technology must work in concert with reduction and conservation. Techno-optimists and eco-pessimists both play an important role in achieving sustainability goals. Simply relying on technological fixes can create an incentive to continually increase consumption and global stress; technology will never keep pace if we do not also reframe our expectations for consumption. Already, we see that collaboration in many contexts, such as the surprising adoption of electric cars, the ease with which people use water bottles instead of single-use plastics, and even disease protocols to accompany technology-based medical treatments. In the future, we should all strive to play both roles.

Notes

1. James E. Krier and Clayton P. Gillette, "The Un-Easy Case for Technological Optimism," *Michigan Law Review* 84 (1985).
2. Peter Newell and Matthew Paterson, *Climate Capitalism* (Cambridge University Press, 2010).
3. Krier and Gillette, "The Un-Easy Case for Technological Optimism."
4. Peter Diamandis and Steven Kotler, *Abundance: The Future is Better Than You Think* (Free Press, 2012); Pinker, *Enlightenment Now: The Case for Reason, Science, Humanism and Progress* (Viking, 2018).
5. Robert M. Solow, "Technical Change and the Aggregate Production Function," *Review of Economics and Statistics* 39, no. 3 (August 1957).
6. Margaret O'Mara, "The Church of Techno-Optimism," *New York Times*, September 28, 2019.
7. Bill Alpert, "With Rare Speed, Gene Editing Emerges as Biotech's New Cutting Edge," *Barron's*, January 14, 2021.
8. Tyler Cowen, *The Great Stagnation: How America Ate All the Low-Hanging Fruit of Modern History, Got Sick, and Will (Eventually) Feel Better* (Dutton, 2011).
9. David Rotman, "Are you Ready To Be a Techno-Optimist Again?," *MIT Technology Review*, February 24, 2021.
10. David Wootton, *The Invention of Science* (Harper Perennial, 2016).
11. Bron Taylor, "Religion and Environmentalism in America and Beyond," in *The Oxford Handbook on Religion and Ecology*, ed. Roger S. Gottlieb (Cambridge: Oxford University Press, 2006), 588–612.
12. Charles C. Mann, *The Wizard and the Prophet* (Penguin Random House, 2019).
13. Brian J. Bailey, *The Luddite Rebellion* (Sutton Pub Ltd, 1998).
14. Peter Kareiva and Michelle Marvier, "What is Conservation Science?," *BioScience* 62, no. 11 (November 2012).
15. Richard Schmalensee and Robert N. Stavins, "The SO_2 Allowance Trading System: The Ironic History of a Grand Policy Experiment," *Journal of Economic Perspectives* 27, no. 1 (Winter 2013).
16. Cowen, *The Great Stagnation*.
17. Michael Huesemann and Joyce Huesemann, *Techno-Fix: Why Technology Won't Save Us Or the Environment* (New Society Publishers, 2011).
18. Huesemann and Huesemann, *Techno-Fix*.
19. Keith Collins and Josh Holder, "See How Rich Countries Got to the Front of the Vaccine Line," *New York Times*, March 1, 2021.
20. James. W. Dearing and Jeffrey G. Cox, "Diffusion of Innovations Theory, Principles, and Practice," *Health Affairs* 37, no. 2 (2018).
21. Amir Attaran, "How Do Patents and Economic Policies Affect Access to Essential Medicines in Developing Countries?," *Health Affairs* 23, no. 3 (2004).
22. National Renewable Energy Laboratory, "Life Cycle Assessment Harmonization," 2023.
23. William S. Landes and Richard A. Posner, *The Economic Structure of Intellectual Property Law* (Harvard University Press, 2003).
24. Suzanne Scotchmer, *Innovation and Incentives* (MIT Press, 2004).

25. National Science Foundation (NSF), "U.S. R&D Increased by $62 Billion in 2019 to $667 Billion; Estimate for 2020 Indicates a Further Rise to $708 Billion," National Science Foundation, June 1, 2022.

26. United States Department Of Energy, "The History of the Electric Car," energy.gov, September 15, 2014.

27. Hardman, et al., "The Effectiveness of Financial Purchase Incentives for Battery Electric Vehicles—A Review of the Evidence," *Renewable and Sustainable Energy Reviews*, vol. 80 (2017).

28. Rebecca Elliott, "Tesla Surpasses $1 Trillion in Market Value as Hertz Orders 100,000 Vehicles," *Wall Street Journal*, October 25, 2021.

29. Michael Schuman, "The Electric-Car Lesson that China is Serving Up for America," *Atlantic*, May 21, 2021.

30. Schuman, "The Electric-Car Lesson that China is Serving Up for America."

31. Landes and Posner, *The Economic Structure of Intellectual Property Law*.

32. National Science Foundation, "U.S. R&D Increased by $62 Billion in 2019 to $667 Billion."

33. David C. Mowery, et al., *Ivory Tower and Industrial Innovation* (Stanford University Press, 2014).

34. National Science Foundation, "U.S. R&D Increased by $62 Billion in 2019 to $667 Billion."

35. National Science Foundation, "U.S. R&D Increased by $62 Billion in 2019 to $667 Billion."

36. National Aeronautics and Space Administration (NASA), "GISS Surface Temperature Analysis (GISTEMP v4)," 2023.

37. United Nations Framework Convention on Climate Change (UNFCCC), *Glasgow Climate Pact*, Decision -/CP.26, November 13, 2021.

38. Intergovernmental Panel on Climate Change (IPCC), "Summary for Policymakers" (IPCC, 2021).

39. Governance and Accountability Institute, "Sustainability Reporting in Focus" (2022).

40. Net Zero Tracker, "Companies," 2023, https://zerotracker.net/#companies-table.

41. International Energy Agency, *Global Energy Review: CO2 Emissions in 2021* (March 2022).

42. International Energy Agency, *Global Energy Review: CO2 Emissions in 2021*.

43. United States Energy Information Administration, *U.S. Energy-Related Carbon Dioxide Emissions, 2020* (2021).

44. Glasgow Financial Alliance for Net Zero, "Financing Roadmaps: Exploring Investment Opportunity Roadmaps" (2021).

45. International Energy Agency, *The Role of Critical Minerals in Clean Energy Transitions* (2021).

46. Intergovernmental Panel on Climate Change, "Summary for Policymakers."

47. International Energy Agency, "About CCUS" (2021).

48. International Energy Agency, "Direct Air Capture" (September 2022).

49. National Academies of Sciences, et al., *Reflecting Sunlight: Recommendations for Solar Geoengineering Research and Research Governance* (Washington, DC: The National Academies Press, 2021).

50. National Academies of Sciences, et al., *Reflecting Sunlight*.

51. National Academies of Sciences, *A Research Strategy for Ocean-based Carbon Dioxide Removal and Sequestration* (Washington, DC: The National Academies Press, 2022).

52. Chunyang He, et al., "Future Global Urban Water Scarcity and Potential Solutions," *Nature Communications* 12, no. 4667 (2021).

53. See, e.g., United Nations Sustainable Development Goals, "Goal 6: Ensure access to water and sanitation for all," in *The Sustainable Development Goals Report 2022*, ed. United Nations (2022).

54. United States Environmental Protection Agency (EPA), "Water Management Plans and Best Practices at the EPA," March 31, 2023.

55. United Nations Food and Agriculture Organization (FAO), *The State of the World's Land and Water Resources for Food and Agriculture—Systems at Breaking Point* (United Nations, 2021).

56. Jacques Leslie, "Where Water is Scarce, Communities Turn to Reusing Wastewater," *Yale Environment 360*, May 1, 2018.

57. Will Henley, "The New Water Technologies that Could Save the Planet," *Guardian*, July 22, 2013.

58. Henry Fountain, "The World Can Make More Water from the Sea, but at What Cost?," *New York Times*, October 25, 2019.

59. National Research Council, *Review of the Desalination and Water Purification Technology Roadmap* (Washington, DC: The National Academies Press, 2004).

60. United Nations Food and Agriculture Organization, *The Importance of Ukraine and the Russian Federation for Global Agricultural Markets and the Risks Associated with the Current Conflict* (United Nations, March 2022).

61. Deepak K. Ray, et al., "Climate Change Has Likely Already Affected Global Food Production," *PLoS ONE* 14, no. 5 (2014).

62. S. Chakraborty and A. C. Newton, "Climate Change, Plant Diseases and Food Security: An Overview," *Plant Pathology* 60, no. 1 (February 2011).

63. United Nations Food and Agriculture Organization, *The Importance of Ukraine and the Russian Federation for Global Agricultural Markets and the Risks Associated with the Current Conflict*.

64. Thomas Robert Malthus, *An Essay of the Principle of Population* (London: J. Johnson, 1798).

65. Paul R. Ehrlich, *The Population Bomb* (Sierra Club/Ballantine Books, 1968).

66. Mann, *The Wizard and the Prophet*.

67. José Graziano Da Silva, "Feeding the World Sustainably," *UN Chronicle* XLIX, no. 1 & 2 (June 2012).

68. Mann, *The Wizard and the Prophet*.

69. Eric Njuki, "A Look at Agricultural Productivity Growth in the United States, 1948–2017," United States Department of Agriculture, March 5, 2020.

70. Tim Searchinger, et al., *Creating a Sustainable Food Future* (World Resources Institute, July 2019).

71. Graziano Da Silva, "Feeding the World Sustainably."

72. Graziano Da Silva, "Feeding the World Sustainably."

73. United Nations Food and Agriculture Organization, *The Future of Food and Agriculture—Trends and Challenges* (Rome, 2017).
74. United Nations Food and Agriculture Organization, *The Future of Food and Agriculture*.
75. United Nations Secretary-General's High-Level Panel on Access to Medicines, *Promoting Innovation and Access to Health Technologies* (United Nations Secretary General's High-Level Panel on Access to Medicines, September 2016).
76. Ezra Klein, "In the UK's Health System, Rationing Isn't a Dirty Word," *Vox*, January 28, 2020.
77. Amy McDermott, "Climate Change Hastens Disease Spread Across the Globe," *PNAS* 119, no. 7 (February 2022).
78. Jeff Tollefson, "Why Deforestation and Extinctions Make Pandemics More Likely," *Nature*, August 7, 2020.
79. Taheri S., et al., "Effect of Intensive Lifestyle Intervention on Bodyweight and Glycaemia in Early Type 2 Diabetes (DIADEM-I): An Open-label, Parallel-group, Randomized Controlled Trial," *Lancet Diabetes & Endocrinology*, October 8, 2020.
80. Mark A. Lawrence and Phillip I. Baker, "Ultra-Processed Food and Adverse Health Outcomes," *BMJ*, 2019; Megan Brooks, "Highly Processed Foods are Bad for Older Brains, Study Says," *WebMD*, August 15, 2022.
81. C. Lee Ventola, "The Antibiotic Resistance Crisis," *Pharmacy and Therapeutics* 40, no. 4 (April 2015).
82. United Nations Secretary General, *Synthesis Report: The Road to Dignity by 2030: Ending Poverty, Transforming All Lives and Protecting the Planet* (United Nations, December 2014).
83. World Health Organization, *World Health Statistics 2022: Monitoring Health for the SDGs, Sustainable Development Goals* (2022).

5

Comparative Capitalism
Contrasting American and European Systems

Gerlinde Berger-Walliser

Contrary to what its title may suggest, this chapter is not a treatise on the history of capitalism in the United States. Our goal is to identify unique features of American capitalism as they relate to sustainability and to contrast them with what we will call European capitalism.[1] Why Europe? According to the 2020 Environmental Performance Index (EPI), a worldwide ranking of countries on their environmental health and vitality of their ecosystems, European countries occupy the top eleven spots, followed by Japan, while the United States ranks at number 24 out of 180 countries surveyed.[2] While the EPI ranks countries, European companies—especially those in Northern Europe—also top the list in so-called ESG (Environmental, Social, and Governance) performance, featuring the Netherlands as the world's most sustainable stock market, followed by France, Sweden, and Finland. The United States ranks 13th out of 48 on ESG practices in a 2021 ranking by Morningstar.[3]

Rankings like these, though not without flaws,[4] suggest that the economies of Europe and Japan, while arguably growth-oriented modern capitalist economies, are more sustainable than their American counterpart. While this chapter does not attempt to prove the truth of this supposition, the observation does highlight the value of studying the institutional variance between and among these countries. Accordingly, the following sections examine differences in the socio-economic systems of the United States, (Continental) Europe, and (though only marginally) Japan.[5] We discuss how legal, political, and societal structures have supported the development of more sustainable capitalist economies in these regions, while the United States has been lagging. The corporate governance paradigm, examined in depth in other chapters of this book, is approached from a distinctively comparative perspective. As we analyze the interdependence between stakeholder thinking, governance, and sustainability, we include other aspects of the political and regulatory business environment that may explain why, even in an era of international convergence of corporate governance regimes, more sustainable economies have developed in European capitalist countries than in the United States.

Comparative Capitalism and Sustainability

We begin by establishing an analytic frame for this chapter. As has been widely noted, in the wake of the collapse of state socialism in the 1990s, capitalism became the main organizing principle of economic life in developed as well as developing economies around the world, even in so-called state-capitalist economies such as China.[6] With that, a new research stream interested in the differences between various expressions of modern, or knowledge-oriented capitalism emerged in the socio-economic academic literature. This so-called Comparative Capitalism, or Varieties of Capitalism (CC or VoC) literature sought to explain the relative merits of varying models of capitalism, mostly in terms of economic success.[7] While economic success may not seem directly relevant to the sustainable capitalism discussion in this book, the comparative analysis of national institutions based on socio-economic criteria partially explains the interdependency between certain features of Anglo-American capitalism, European capitalism, and their effects on sustainability.

   Sustainability is understood here in a broad sense, not limited to environmental sustainability, but encompassing the effects of business on social equity, human and economic health, the communities in which businesses operate, and protection of individual (human) rights, in line with the Brundtland Report.[8] In short, this report, which was commissioned by the United Nations and published in 1987—a cornerstone of the corporate sustainability debate ever since—defines sustainability as "meeting the needs of the present without compromising the ability of future generations to meet their own needs."[9] In this sense, sustainability builds on two basic elements: long-term orientation and "looking out for others"; in other words, stakeholderism. The following sections provide examples as to why and to what degree European capitalism, and the legal system that supports it, embodies these virtues while American capitalism, at least historically, has had difficulties embracing the concept.

Development and Features of American Capitalism

In *American Business History: A Very Short Introduction*, Walter Friedman identifies four key factors that allowed for American businesses to prosper: growth-friendly policymaking, business-friendly financial institutions, the professionalization of the managerial class, and the inventiveness and dynamism of entrepreneurs.[10] Capitalism in the United States, he posits, was further aided by the sheer physical size of the United States, allowing for market specialization according to geographic regions, but also enabling another American ideal: actual, individual ownership of real property as a means of production. Property was considered a natural right in many state constitutions. But more importantly, it gave landowners influence among legislators—contributing to an individualistic ideal embodied in early American Capitalism.[11]

As capitalism progressed and more people were able to afford property, the gap between societies' classes began to shift. People no longer only grew food to feed themselves; with land, people had the capacity and capital to produce commodities. Gradually, a more entrepreneurial mindset emerged. While states historically granted organizations' charters to fulfill a special public purpose, such as operating a school or building bridges, the nineteenth century marks the rise of "general incorporation."[12] General incorporation meant that any firm that met certain statutory incorporation requirements could seek incorporation independent from its purpose, thereby ending state favoritism and democratizing incorporation. Initially, these laws were still quite restrictive. However, with technological progress in the late 1800s, companies grew into bigger and more complicated structures. As a consequence of the federal political system, states started to compete by attracting incorporations with increasingly business-friendly corporate laws.[13]

As American industries moved away from a capitalist elite, a new phenomenon emerged in the twentieth century: equity-based corporate finance. Corporations evolved from closely held private firms controlled by their managing owners to larger public corporations owned by share-holders and operated by managers.[14] With this shift came a need to pro-tect dispersed shareholders that neither had the ability nor interest in controlling firm policy from self-dealing corporate directors. At the same time, as firms grew in size and power, many hoped corporations would use that power to aid society and perform functions that had once been performed by government, including the provision of welfare benefits.[15] While some adopted the view that managers owed a duty to society, others advocated for a broad fiduciary duty for managers to act in the interest of the corporation's shareholders based on the shareholders' property rights. Ultimately, the ideals of individualism, independence, and natural prop-erty rights left little room for stakeholder interests. Under the emerging American governance regime, it fell upon shareholder-owners to keep pro-fessional management in check.[16] It is the property-rights based fiduciary relationship between corporate directors and shareholders that explains why the idea of shareholder primacy runs deep in American capitalism.

In the twenty-first century, another characteristic of American capital-ism developed: short-termism and shareholder activism. With the opening of international capital markets along with privatization of national enter-prises and pensions, wealthy and powerful institutional investors appeared and pressured corporate managers to put shareholder wealth maximiza-tion over long-term corporate strategy—with sometimes devastating con-sequences for the firms that they owned.[17] However, while institutional investors at the beginning of this century may have been responsible for extremely unsustainable business practices, this group is more recently driving the ESG movement in corporate America by specifically seeking socially responsible investment (SRI) opportunities.[18]

State-defined Status Categories vs. Voluntary Transactions

According to at least one author in the CC literature, a defining feature of European capitalism is the prominence of "state-defined and state-protected status categories," or what we might call a status system.[19] In a status system, virtually all economic transactions and actors associated with them are governed by state-defined rules, procedures, and certifica-tions as opposed to transactions, limited only by general criminal or civil legal rules, economic, and moral concerns.

To be clear, state-defined rules related to status categories are not synonymous with legal rules or regulated versus unregulated markets. The common law of contracts, environmental laws, taxation, competition, and antitrust laws all shape transactions in any economy founded on the rule of law independent from the importance of status categories. According to the German political sociologist Offe, "[t]he measure of the strength of the status component of a capitalist economic system is the degree to which partners to contracts are endowed with non-negotiable entitlements and duties, as well as the degree to which obligations to third parties not immediately involved in economic transaction are stipulated and enforced by law."[20] He illustrates the distinction with the example of the American wage system compared to pay structures in continental European countries. Typically, in the United States, "you get paid for what you actually do, while in Europe you get paid for what you can do according to some certificate obtained through formal training."[21]

Country-specific differences aside, formal training, firm hierarchy, and certifications are indeed essential for getting and progressing in a job in most European countries.[22] In Germany, for example, if a person aspires to become a plumber, they cannot simply work under the supervision of an experienced plumber to receive training on the job until they have gained enough experience to serve clients on their own. To be able to work independently, they will need to participate in an apprenticeship program that leads to certification as a licensed plumber. Even if there are no laws requiring such certification outside of heavy regulated industries such as the medical profession, in Europe, there is a social expectation that a professional has received formal, job-specific training that makes them an expert in their field. In France, a server in a high-end restaurant will not be a student earning money three nights a week, but a highly trained professional who earns a living wage in a full-time job with social benefits and regular working hours.

While professional success in the United States is determined by how the individual performs in the "free" market, a successful career in Europe largely depends on training and the obtention of a degree or seniority in a company—in other words, a certain professional "status."[23] This preference makes switching careers as well as re-organization in European companies difficult, while a more volatile American labor market has been linked to a more adaptable workforce and innovation-friendly corporate environments.[24] However, the professional status system comes with other advantages, such as a highly skilled workforce, long-term stability, and job security, that are characteristic of the European and Japanese labor market. The emphasis on stability and loyalty is further exemplified by the stark contrast between the American concept of employment-at-will, which permits either the employer or employee to terminate the employment relationship at any time, with or without cause, versus strong labor protection laws in most European countries.[25]

While liberal capitalist societies are often associated with short-term economic goals driven by individual cost and price considerations, status regimes are based on the individual's belonging to a larger group. Inherent in this approach is "a stronger readiness to look out for others" and to act in the collective interest of the entire group.[26] As Offe points out, linguistic differences illustrate how deeply the status approach runs in European culture. In German terms, a worker belongs to their company's "Belegschaft," a French or Spanish artisan is part of the "artisanat," and a lawyer admitted to the German bar joins the "Anwaltschaft." Suffixes such as the French "-at," the Spanish "-ado," or the German "-schaft" indicate belonging to a socio-economic collectivity, for which the English language barely provides an equivalent.[27] In English, we use "-ship," as in membership, and "-ry" as in judiciary, to indicate an individual's belonging to a certain group. However, these terms lack the collective status connotation akin to the aforementioned French, Spanish, or German suffixes.[28] Probably the most accurate English translation for the German "-schaft" is "-hood," like in brotherhood or neighborhood. While these terms do connate community and social belonging, they are rarely used in professional settings in English. Nobody would translate the German term "Belegschaft" with "employee" or "company-hood." The English language uses words such as "personnel" or "workforce" instead, terms that bear no collective or status connotation but rather evoke a sense of subordination to corporate interests.

Third-party Rights

Closely related to the status paradigm, and yet another signal for a society's readiness to "look out for others," including future generations, is the degree to which a society provides legal protection or procedural rights to third parties not immediately involved in an economic transaction. In the CC literature this is often illustrated by trade unionism.[29] In some countries, such as Japan, trade unions primarily exist on the company level, while trade unions in Europe are organized in relation to industry sectors, skill, or educational level.[30] The former advocate for wage increases or working conditions for a small percentage of workers in a single firm with company-specific concerns. On the other hand, European sector unions negotiate for employees in a multitude of companies spanning all sizes and occupations whose only common characteristic is that they happen to be part of the same industry, and who—like in Germany and France—do not necessarily need to be union members. In this respect, sector unions often represent different interests and concerns that might not always align or have broader political, civil, and social implications for society. In the United States, trade unions that are industry based but without institutionalized relations to employers tend to secure the narrow interest of their members rather than advancing the development of a welfare state.[31]

Attention to the interests of others runs even deeper in European legal institutions than the previous example suggests. It can be further exemplified by the German contract law concept of "Vertrag mit Schutzwirkung für Dritte" (contract with protective effects for third parties). While a third-party beneficiary claim under the Anglo-American common law of contracts usually requires intention by the parties to make the third party a beneficiary of the contractual obligations, the German concept provides contractual rights and duties to outsiders if they "are so closely involved with the performance of the contract that they need its protection."[32] It has been suggested in the German legal literature to use the concept, for example, in the realm of corporate human rights litigation when there is no direct relationship between the victim and the corporate defendant in a lawsuit.[33] This scenario arises, for example, when a mistreated worker in a supplier's or independent subsidiary's factory wants to sue the legally independent parent company that ultimately profits from the abuse. Litigants in the United States struggle to find a cause of action in such cases.[34]

Human rights, as well as environmental litigation, also provide examples of the inability of the American legal system to protect third party rights through procedural means. Victims in such cases often do not have the financial or other means to bring cases before courts, leaving this task to non-governmental organizations (NGOs). In the United States, an NGO's ability to pursue litigation is heavily impeded by procedural rules that require plaintiffs to be personally affected by the defendant's actions in order to have "standing" before the court. For that purpose, according to the United States Supreme Court, "standing only as representatives of the public interest" is not enough.[35] In contrast, in the Netherlands in 2019, several NGOs successfully brought a case against Royal Dutch Shell arguing that Shell's negligence toward climate change and greenhouse gas emissions endangered Dutch citizens.[36] Similarly, recently enacted laws in France and Germany that impose obligations on companies to monitor their supply chains for human rights violations allow trade unions, NGOs, and, in the case of the French law, "any interested party," to bring suit.[37] These laws not only exemplify the state-protected status categories described by the CC research above, but are examples of the growing tendency in numerous capitalist societies to regulate stakeholder interests, or what long has been regarded as voluntary corporate social responsibility.[38]

Stakeholder, Shareholders, and Corporate Governance Regimes

As an embodiment of individualism and natural property rights, the predominant view in the United States is that shareholders "own" the corporation. Therefore, it is upon them to control the actions of corporate management through voting or, if necessary, to bring shareholder lawsuits against corporate directors that are far less viable in many continental European jurisdictions.[39] Moreover, corporate governance and fiduciary duty in the United States has evolved to strongly favor the prioritization of shareholder profits above—or to the exclusion of—any other concerns. This regime, discussed in depth in Chapter 8, is generally known as "shareholder primacy."

In contrast, the corporate government regimes of European capitalist economies are said to embody a stakeholder approach. Stakeholder theory was introduced by R. Edward Freeman[40] as a normative model for effective management.[41] Originally a management theory, it was later adopted by legal scholars who positioned it against the shareholder primacy norm and argued that corporations had both a social and profit-driven mission in society.[42]

The contrasting approach to corporate governance in the United States and in Europe has been attributed in part to differences in corporate ownership structure, which in turn can be traced back to the diverse history of economic development in both regions. Unlike the dispersed ownership model that emerged in the United States at the beginning of the twentieth century, in German and French companies, it was, and to a certain degree still is, common that individual or small groups of shareholders, including families or the government, own large blocks of shares.[43] This tradition explains why courts and legislators in Germany and France were concerned that large shareholders with sometimes competing interests would interfere with the proper management of the company and public-economic interests more broadly. It led to protection of the enterprise and its stakeholders against majority shareholders in German and French corporate governance rules, while the American rules emphasize protection of disperse shareholders against self-interested dealings of powerful management.[44] The German system of co-determination (formal representation of employees on the corporate board of directors) is another expression of stakeholderism in European corporate governance. The highest German court, in a decision that challenged the 1976 German codetermination act, went as far as to declare that "ownership of stock was subject to social restrictions."[45] Combined with broad protection of the environment in the German constitution,[46] stakeholder orientation becomes a basic feature of German corporate governance.

The stakeholder-shareholder divide is often positioned at the heart of the corporate governance discussion around sustainability. It seems reasonable to assume that governance structures that take stakeholder interests into account are more likely to adopt sustainable policies than those that focus on shareholder interests. As evidenced by the recent movement towards ESG investment, it is nevertheless possible that shareholder and stakeholder interests can be made to align or that shareholders can act as guardians of greater societal interests. Nevertheless, the fiduciary duty that corporate law in the United States has instilled upon corporate management has shaped existing corporate governance structures and the corporate purpose debate in the United States.

Other elements of American capitalism that are typically associated with short-termism or individualism are also far less developed in Europe. For example, stock-based incentive compensation that potentially could induce managers to adopt short-term profit maximizing strategies is less common and much lower in continental European countries. Historically, hostile take-overs were uncustomary in Germany, France, or Japan, and even today, attempts are often abandoned under political pressure or the influence of worker's campaigns.[47] Creditors receive far greater protection under European and Japanese corporate governance rules, which not only require corporations to maintain robust capital, but also provide restrictions for dividend distribution.[48] Finally, the role of banks as creditors in corporate financing historically has been greater in these economies, especially in Germany and Japan where banks often have long-standing relationships to the companies they finance. However, the importance of institutional investors has risen significantly in these countries starting in the 1990s, and revisions to corporate governance rules and practice reflect this development.[49]

Convergence and Future Trends

As the previous section has shown, we need to acknowledge that under the influence of globalization of financial markets, the differences in corporate governance regimes are dissipating. An important factor in the rapprochement of corporate governance rules in Europe is the fact that European Union member states are united in a common market. In the European Union, for decades, economic policy has been coordinated between British liberal and continental coordinated market economies, leading to a greater influence of U.K. style rules on European corporate governance, and vice-versa, while the influence of American law on Japanese corporate governance is undeniable.[50] Still, distinct historical political and economic developments, combined with cultural values that run deep in national institutions, help explain continued diversity in capitalism, even within the European Union.[51] After the British exit from the European Union, the European socio-economic landscape is prone to change once again.[52] These fundamental features shape national variations in capitalism at the more granular level, and, as the previous sections have illustrated, have and continue to play a role in how receptive a country's economy is to sustainable public and corporate policies. Institutional differences also determine who the driving forces behind sustainable initiatives are. In Europe, it might be governments or corporate directors who spearhead sustainable development, while institutional investors may have a bigger role to play in American sustainable capitalism.

Notes

1. Clause Offe, "The European Model of 'Social' Capitalism: Can It Survive European Integration?," *Journal of Political Philosophy* 11, no. 4 (2003): 437–46. In economic terms, capitalism can be classified with various degrees of granularity ranging from industry-sector classification, over national economies to the broad distinction between liberal (meaning Anglo-American) versus regulated (Western European and Japanese) market economies. It is the latter categorization that forms the basis for this chapter's analysis.

2. Yale Center for Environmental Policy & Law, "About the EPI," 2023.

3. Valerio Baselli, "Mapping ESG Practices and Carbon Risk in 48 Countries' Stock Markets," *Morningstar*, April 12, 2022.

4. Critics point to the fact that while the United States and European countries have made progress on domestic de-carbonization, in recent years, consumption-based emissions have increased rather than decreased. Brad Plumer, "You've Heard of Outsourced Jobs, but Outsourced Pollution? It's Real, and Tough to Tally Up," *New York Times*, September 4, 2018.

5. Cynthia A. Williams and John M. Conley, "An Emerging Third Way?—The Erosion of the Anglo-American Shareholder Value Construct," *Cornell International Law Journal* 38, no. 2 (2005): 511–23. The UK economy, while historically assimilated with liberal Anglo-American capitalism, has tried to pursue a "third way" by combining strong shareholder protection with sustainability policies since the early 2000s.

6. Offe, "The European Model of 'Social' Capitalism," 437–48.

7. Bruno Amable, *The Diversity of Modern Capitalism* (New York: Oxford University Press, 2003), 74–115; Gregory Jackson and Richard Deeg, "How Many Varieties of Capitalism? Comparing the Comparative Institutional Analyses of Capitalist Diversity," MPIfG Discussion Paper No. 06/2, April 2006, 30–37. Within the CC literature, various "waves," mostly in reaction to historical political events, have been identified. Andreas Nölke, "Economic Causes of the Eurozone Crisis: The Analytical Contribution of Comparative Capitalism," *Socio-Economic Review* 14, no. 1 (2016): 145–47. Early research has focused on the differences between the Anglo-American liberal market economy and coordinated market economies of Continental Europe and Japan. Peter A. Hall and David Soskice, *Varieties of Capitalism* (Oxford University Press, 2001), 1–45. CC literature in the 2010s evolved around European integration, growth models, and finally, after the United Kingdom's exit from the European Union and as nationalist movements emerged in many European countries, transitioned to the study of European disintegration. Martin Höpner and Armin Schäfer, "A New Phase of European Integration: Organised Capitalisms in Post-Ricardian Europe," *West European Politics* 33, no. 2 (2010): 349–61; Alison Johnston and Aidan Regan, "Introduction: Is the European Union Capable of Integrating Diverse Models of Capitalism?," *New Political Economy* 23, no. 2 (2018): 15155; Lucio Baccaro and Jonas Pontusson, "European Growth Models Before and After the Great Recession," in *Growth and Welfare in Advanced*

Capitalist Economies: How Have Growth Regimes Evolved?, ed. Anke Hassel and Bruno Palier (Oxford University Press, 2020), 180–95; Ben Clift and Sean McDaniel, "Capitalist Convergence? European (dis?)Integration and the Post-crash Restructuring of French and European Capitalisms," *New Political Economy* 26, no. 1 (2021): 4–5, 12–14.

8. UN World Commission on Environment and Development, *Our Common Future* (Oxford University Press, 1987).

9. UN World Commission on Environment and Development, *Our Common Future.*

10. Walter A. Friedman, *American Business History: A Very Short Introduction* (Oxford University Press, 2020), 135–49.

11. Geoffrey D. Korff, "Reviving the Forgotten American Dream," *Penn State Law Review* 113, no. 417 (2008): 420–32.

12. Harwell Wells, "The Modernization of Corporation Law, 1920–1940," *University of Pennsylvania Journal of Business Law* 11, no. 3 (2009): 581–602.

13. Wells, 589–602.

14. See Chapter 8, this volume.

15. Wells, "The Modernization of Corporation Law," 610–12.

16. Jackson and Deeg, "How Many Varieties?," 9, 15–17.

17. Jackson and Deeg, "How Many Varieties?," 28–29.

18. Dorothy S. Lund, "Corporate Finance for Social Good," *Columbia Law Review* 121, No. 5 (June 2021): 1633–44.

19. Offe, "The European Model of 'Social' Capitalism," 441–46.

20. Offe, "The European Model of 'Social' Capitalism," 442.

21. Offe, "The European Model of 'Social' Capitalism," 443.

22. Marc Maurice, François Sellier, and Jean-Jacques Silvestre, *The Social Foundations of Industrial Power: A Comparison of France and Germany*, trans. Arthur Goldhammer (MIT Press, June 1986), 19–34.

23. Offe, "The European Model of 'Social' Capitalism," 443–46.

24. Amable, *The Diversity of Modern Capitalism*, 200–210.

25. Carol Daugherty Rasnic, "Die Kundigung, Licenciement, Recesso Dal Contrato, 'Firing', or 'Sacking': Comparing European and American Laws on Management Prerogatives and Discretion in Termination Decisions," *Indiana International and Comparative Law Review* 18, no. 1 (2008): 37–52, 66–72.

26. Offe, "The European Model of 'Social' Capitalism," 442–45.

27. Offe, "The European Model of 'Social' Capitalism," 443.

28. Offe, "The European Model of 'Social' Capitalism," 443.

29. Offe, "The European Model of 'Social' Capitalism," 444–46.

30. Carsten Strøby Jensen, "Trade Unionism: Differences and Similarities—A Comparative View on Europe, USA and Asia," *Industrial Relations Journal* 48, no. 1 (2006): 66–67, 74–75.

31. Jensen, "Trade Unionism," 77.

32. Mathias Reimann, "The Good, the Bad, and the Ugly: The Reform of the German Law of Obligations," *Tulane Law Review* 83 (2008): 890.

33. Benedikt Reinke and Peer C. Zumbansen, "Transnational Liability Regimes in Contract, Tort and Corporate Law: Comparative Observations on 'Global

Supply Chain Liability,'" King's College London Law School Research Paper No. 2019-18 (July 2019): 11–17.

34. Rachel Chambers and Gerlinde Berger-Walliser, "The Future of International Corporate Human Rights Litigation: A Transatlantic Comparison," *American Business Law Journal* 58, no. 3 (2021): 579–642.

35. *Sierra Club v. Morton, 405 U.S. 727, 736 (1972).*

36. *Milieudefensie et al. v. Royal Dutch Shell (2021), 77 m.nt. (Neth.).*

37. Chambers and Berger-Walliser, "The Future," 606.

38. Gerlinde Berger-Walliser and Inara Scott, "Redefining Corporate Social Responsibility in an Era of Globalization and Regulatory Hardening," *American Business Law Journal* 55, no. 1 (Spring 2018): 173–90.

39. Franklin A. Gevurtz, "Disney in a Comparative Light," *American Journal of Comparative Law* 55 (2007): 485.

40. R. Edward Freeman, *Strategic Management: A Stakeholder Approach* (Pitman, 1984), 52–83.

41. André O. Laplume, Karan Sonpar, and Reginald A. Litz, "Stakeholder Theory: Reviewing a Theory That Moves Us," *Journal of Management* 34, no. 6 (2008): 1156–64.

42. Berger-Walliser and Scott, "Redefining Corporate Social Responsibility," 173–82.

43. Martin Gelter, "Taming or Protecting the Modern Corporation? Shareholder-Stakeholder Debates in a Comparative Light," *New York University Journal of Law & Business* 7, no. 2 (2011): 38–72.

44. Gelter, "Taming or Protecting the Modern Corporation?," 72–81.

45. Mitbestimmungsgesetz [MitbestG] [Co-determination Act], May 4, 1976, BGBl. I at 1153, last amended by Artikel 17 des Gesetzes, Aug. 7, 2021, BGBl. I at 3311 (Ger.); see also Gelter, "Taming or Protecting the Modern Corporation?," 62–65.

46. Grundgesetz, Art. 20a (Ger.): "The state protects the natural foundations of life, also in its responsibility for future generations, within the framework of the constitutional order through legislation and in accordance with law and justice through the executive power and the judiciary."

47. Mark J. Roe, "The Shareholder Wealth Maximization Norm and Industrial Organization," *University of Pennsylvania Law Review* 149, no. 6 (2001): 2071–76; Kenichi Osugi, "What is Converging? Rules on Hostile Takeovers in Japan and the Convergence Debate," *Asian-Pacific Law & Policy Journal* 9, no. 1 (Winter 2007):156–59.

48. Edward B. Rock, Hideki Kanda, and Reinier Kraakman, "Significant Corporate Actions," in *The Anatomy of Corporate Law: A Comparative and Functional Approach*, ed. R. Kraakman, et al. (Oxford University Press, 2004), 131–56.

49. Ryoko Ueda, "How Is Corporate Governance in Japan Changing? Developments in Listed Companies and Roles of Institutional Investors" (OECD Corporate Governance Working Papers No. 17, 2015), 9–15.

50. Ueda, "How Is Corporate Governance in Japan Changing?," 8–18.

51. Amable, *The Diversity of Modern Capitalism*, 171–225.

52. Clift and McDaniel, "Capitalist Convergence," 12–14.

6

The American Model for Global Growth

David Bernell

The globalized market that has engaged countries in an increasingly mul-
tifaceted trading and financial system was accelerated at a rapid pace by
the economic program advanced by the United States after World War II.
This global economic system has been considered responsible for significant economic advances in terms of global growth and moving hundreds
of millions of people out of poverty. It has also been seen as responsible for
a succession of global economic crises over the decades, as well as worldwide environmental degradation in the form of overuse of resources and
pollution.[1] While it may be unfair to place the weight of responsibility for
this model solely on the United States, it can be acknowledged that the
United States has been the primary proponent and cheerleader for a globalization movement that has brought significant economic growth, but
also sizable social and environmental costs.

The American Way of Commerce and Growth

The American focus on a maritime-based, global trading and financial system has been part of the country since its inception, and even before. U.S.
foreign policy has been significantly and continually influenced by the process that today we call globalization. The Declaration of Independence itself
stated that one of King George's "injuries and usurpations" was "cutting off

our Trade with all parts of the world." Alexander Hamilton was one of the early proponents of the idea that American security and prosperity were tied to the global economy and America's role in it. What has been called a "Hamiltonian" foreign policy in U.S. history has viewed open sea lanes, access to foreign markets (also called the "Open Door" policy), and a stable global financial system that allows for currencies and investments to easily move across borders as vital national interests.[2] Trade and maritime relations with Great Britain and France were some of the first challenges a young United States faced in the early 1800s, and these conflicts ultimately led to war. After the Napoleonic wars (in the United States we refer to our part as "The War of 1812"), the United States eventually settled into a role in which it served as something of a junior partner to Great Britain, whose rapid industrialization and imperial reach favored an open global trading system, and whose navy—which was the strongest in the world—kept the sea lanes open for trade.

The United States prospered economically in this period of the Pax Britannica, which fostered trade and industry, and allowed the United States to grow—both physically and economically—without much foreign interference. The extensive territorial and economic growth of the era included the annexation of new states and territories all the way to the Pacific coast, to Hawaii and the Philippines, and into the Caribbean. It included the massive growth of productive farms through the Midwest and Great Plains, mining and resource extraction in the Mountain West, and the connection of east and west by a series of railroads. The period saw an astounding pace of industrialization that was characterized by growth and innovation in manufacturing, transportation, energy, and many other industrial sectors, such that names like Thomas Edison, Henry Ford, the Wright brothers, and J. P. Morgan are well known long after these people lived. Many made their fortunes, some became wealthy beyond a level the world had ever seen before, and the country became richer and stronger.

This positive view of American economic progress and growth has been a consistent feature of U.S. history. It was expressed early in the country's history by John Adams, who wrote in 1756 that prior to colonization, "The whole continent was one dismal wilderness, the haunt of wolves and bears and more savage men. Now the forests are removed, the land covered with fields of corn, orchards bending with fruit, and the magnificent habitations of rational and civilized people."[3] Adams's own family was a significant part of this story of progress of clearing the land to make way for better things to come. He stated in a letter in 1815 that "The New England Adamses ... have contributed more to the population of North America, and cut down more trees, than any other."[4] One could draw an unbroken through line from the thinking of John Adams to today.

These successes, however, were not cost-free, and those costs were often externalized. Economic growth and progress, and the power that came with it, were built on the backs of millions who were less fortunate and marginalized. The American project, left to its own devices, expanded across the continent by killing and relocating Native Americans, brutally enforcing slavery, exploiting immigrant labor while simultaneously selectively restricting immigration, legalizing racist violence and Jim Crow discrimination, subjugating women to second-class status, and creating a country where vast inequality, injustice, and racial and ethnic violence were not only widespread, but quite often openly practiced and celebrated by government, businesses, organizations of various stripes, and those lucky enough to have the opportunity to be on the right side of American growth and prosperity by virtue of their birth and race.

This inequality and injustice, which were also a part of this American project, prompted a reformist, progressive movement in the early 1900s. The continental, nineteenth-century version of American capitalism and economic expansion created its own backlash, as it was increasingly deemed unacceptable by a growing number of Americans. However, even though this progressive movement sought to limit some of the human costs of the country's growth and expansion (though it never did for Black Americans), the effort was relatively minor in scope with respect to reining in the excesses of social and economic inequalities. Over the twentieth century, the goal of mitigating these adverse impacts had some important political and economic successes (e.g., civil rights, voting rights, Social Security, Medicare, unemployment insurance), but their application has also been uneven. The United States has never established a welfare state as robust as other rich, industrialized countries, and it has largely left most Black Americans and other minority populations outside the boundaries of prosperity and equality, while making progress for women a continual uphill struggle.

Moreover, not only have the costs of success often been paid by the less fortunate, they have also been offloaded onto the physical environment, other countries, and the future. While the aim of mitigating the environmental impacts of industry and growth became more prevalent with the emergence of a global environmental movement in the 1960s and 1970s, the logic and ethos of economic growth have consistently prevailed over other goals and values.[5] Witness the practice of clearcutting forests to extract maximum short-term economic gain out of private and national forest lands; the mountaintop removal coal mining in the Appalachian region of the United States that continues to this day; the "fracking" revolution characterized by a mad dash by energy companies beginning in the early 2000s to find and secure every available parcel of land in Pennsylvania's Marcellus Shale and the Texas Permian Basin to develop oil and gas resources in previously inaccessible shale rock formations; or the export of American garbage to Malaysia and other Southeast Asian countries—materials which have been in theory meant for recycling but in reality simply sit out in the open in massive trash heaps and decompose.[6]

United States' Establishment and Maintenance of a Global Economic System

The limited efforts in the United States to mitigate the inequality of economic growth and the adversity of environmental impacts have translated even less into the realm of foreign relations, economic or otherwise. The British-led global economic system of the late nineteenth and early twentieth centuries was seen as a net gain for the United States for decades. Carving out a sphere of American influence—as exemplified in the Monroe Doctrine and the Roosevelt Corollary in the Western Hemisphere, and by maritime expansion across the Pacific—within the British system was desirable, but overturning the British system was not, nor was it feasible until after World War I.

However, British power and influence ultimately foundered in the wake of World War I, and the global trading and financial system broke down in the wake of war, postwar instability, and a worldwide economic crisis that became the Great Depression. Americans were left with three choices to safeguard their prosperity and security, which were bound up in the global trading and financial system: 1) try to prop up the British system to help it survive; 2) ignore turmoil in Europe and hope to prosper without worrying about the instability and fragility of the global political and economic order; or 3) replace the British as the world's hegemonic power. Over a period of about thirty years the United States tried all three, settling after World War II on replacing the British in their global role, and becoming the senior partner in what became known as a "special relationship" between the two countries.[7]

The establishment of the U.S.-led postwar international economic order was motivated by the United States and Great Britain wanting to bring back the best elements of the Pax Britannica after World War II. One of the lessons the United States and its allies took away from the war—in the aftermath of Japan and Germany pursuing economic strength, self-sufficiency, and security through war and conquest—was that there would be great value in rebuilding and maintaining a more open, liberal trading order so countries could acquire the resources they wanted by trading, rather than being tempted to seize or conquer lands with the resources and wealth they coveted.

To do this, U.S. foreign policy became oriented toward extending its own growth model onto the rest of the world. The United States had long championed trade and an Open Door policy, but now there was even greater will and opportunity—as well as a receptive Europe—to extending the American project well beyond U.S. borders. This would be done by institutionalizing an economic order, establishing and codifying a set of organizations and rules that resulted in the creation of the General Agreement on Tariffs and Trade (GATT), the World Bank, the International Monetary Fund (IMF), and the gold standard in exchange rates (which was in practice a dollar standard). This system, which promoted and expanded global trade for several decades by continually liberalizing trading rules and attracting more countries to join the GATT, and which has brought a measure of order and stability to the global financial and monetary system, can claim to have worked to a great extent to increase wealth and standards of living for millions, even billions of people around the world. Moreover, it can be argued that this liberal international order has helped to prevent war among the world's great powers (though others attribute this avoidance of war to nuclear weapons).

One country after another has benefitted in many ways from the post-World War II international economic order. First there was Western Europe and Japan, which recovered and grew economically to become major economic powers. It has been considered a great success to see two of the former Axis powers become integrated into the global order and achieve remarkable economic growth and success, along with democratic governance. Then there were South Korea, Taiwan, Singapore, and Hong Kong—whose economic development model and rapid growth were based on export-led growth and participation in the global trading and financial system. In the 1980s and 1990s, in the wake of debt crises, the collapse of Communism, the establishment of the World Trade Organization (WTO), and the strength of the Washington Consensus, much of the rest of the world—from Mexico and Brazil in the Americas, to India and China in Asia, to former Communist countries in Eastern Europe, and countries the world over—became further integrated into the U.S.-led economic order that eschewed protectionism, capital controls, and planned economies, and instead encouraged (and even mandated) opening up to global trade and foreign investment.[8]

The accelerated expansion of globalization over the past seventy-five years can be attributed to economic policies and institutions that promote ever-lowering trade barriers and liberalized cross-border investment restrictions, along with a massive reduction in costs of transportation and communications technologies. This process has also been protected by the lack of a world war, the ebb and delegitimation of anti-liberal ideologies, the avoidance of major trade wars and protectionist measures, and the adoption by many countries of the Washington Consensus to immerse themselves into globalized markets (though some went kicking and screaming while others made the move willingly). Participants in this global economic system have seen the ability to maintain financial stability, or return to it after confronting various crises such as the United States moving off the gold standard, the Latin American debt crisis, the Asian financial crisis, and the 2008 financial crisis. However, environmental degradation, outsourcing from richer to poorer countries, growing inequality and massive consolidation of wealth by a limited number of multinational corporations and individuals have also been strong contributors to faster growth. All of these elements have been promoted and/or led by the United States, which has fashioned itself as globalization's greatest advocate and defender.[9]

The Latest Entrant: China

China is the most significant recent example of how the growth and development model encouraged by the United States and the West is having massive impacts. The country's approach to economic policy is being called a "Chinese Model": one that is characterized by a capitalist economy managed by the state and the Communist party. However, this model has grown out of China's immersion into the postwar, U.S.-led, global economic order. The country joined the WTO in 2001, seeking to reproduce the success of the export-led growth model adopted by other countries. It seeks foreign investment, with a total stock of almost $2 trillion of investment inflows from other countries while its own businesses and wealth funds went from investing a total of $27 billion overseas in 2000 to more than $2.3 trillion in 2020.[10] China did not do this by creating its own separate global economic order (it may one day do this, or change the existing institutional order to the extent it no longer resembles its old self), but by succeeding in taking advantage of the existing order. In the process, China has become an economic giant and a global force to be reckoned with. In 1980, China's GDP was less than $200 billion; by 2020 it was $14 trillion.[11] In that time, the country has moved hundreds of millions of people out of poverty and become one of the world's major powers. This is a major achievement that is unprecedented in world history. The debate is not whether China will become the world's strongest political, economic, and military power, only when it will do so.

The Chinese success story, however, also comes with significant costs. The country is realizing growth, wealth, and power by means of extending the model of unsustainable capitalism. It is heavily favoring growth over sustainability, and in the process of becoming a rich and powerful country, it is leaving behind significant harmful impacts in its wake. China's energy use has risen on a per capita basis by more than one thousand percent since 1970.[12] The demand for electricity has been met to a great extent by burning coal, the dirtiest of all fossil fuels. China uses more than half of all the coal used in the world, and it provides almost 60 percent of the country's total energy consumption.[13] The number of automobile sales in China has grown from 2 million per year in 2000 to 25 million per year in 2017 (the peak in the United States was 17 million cars sold in 2017), and it has been the largest car market in the world for a decade.[14] To power all these cars China's use of petroleum has risen to 14.5 million barrels of oil per day in 2019, second only to the United States.[15] The result of all this use of fossil fuels has made China the world's largest emitter of carbon dioxide emissions since 2008. As a result, localized air pollution levels and related health impacts have risen significantly. The level of air pollution is so high at times that in recent years the government has even ordered air quality apps to stop reporting the air quality index when it exceeds an officially mandated cutoff point.[16]

The speed and magnitude at which China's economic growth is occurring is so significant that it may represent not only a difference in degree, but a difference in kind. It has been said that "quantity has a quality all its own." China seems to be demonstrating this, as the following examples can attest. In every two-year period from 2008 to 2017, the increment of growth in China's GDP has been the equivalent of India's entire GDP. In 2015, China's economy produced every sixteen weeks the equivalent of Greece's annual economy.[17] By 2005, the country's construction was so massive that it was building the square foot equivalent of Rome every two weeks. It has now built the equivalent of Europe's entire housing stock in fifteen years.[18] In 2011, a Chinese firm built a thirty-story skyscraper in fifteen days.[19] At the outset of the COVID-19 pandemic, the Chinese put up a 1000-bed hospital in Wuhan in ten days.[20] And in what seems impossible, in one three-year period, from 2011 to 2013, China consumed more cement than the United States did in the entire twentieth century.[21] It should come as no surprise that China is now the world's largest producer of steel (almost 50 percent of the total), aluminum, computers, and rare earth materials and the world's largest market for everything from energy to cars to cell phones to e-commerce.[22] The country has, in effect, done the equivalent of combining the achievements of the industrial revolution and the information revolution simultaneously in a period of forty years.

While China's annual levels of economic growth rates have tapered off and fallen below double digits since 2011,[23] the economic boom still continues. What this means is that the sheer magnitude of China's growth, consumption, and environmental impact threatens to have a larger environmental impact than all the rest of the economic activity of the past century and a half combined.

Can This Continue?

Herb Stein, the chair of the U.S. Council of Economic Advisors who served under Presidents Nixon and Ford, coined a phrase that has since become known as "Stein's Law." He said that "If something can't go on forever, it won't." The experiences of the United States and China demonstrate, in particular, the costs of what has historically been called economic success. Such success has also left a wake of human, economic, and environmental damage in the process, with massive exploitation of labor, great levels of inequality, and environmental degradation, with the climate itself (and the human and economic flourishing it can provide) being threatened rapidly. These human, economic, and environmental impacts seem unsustainable in the long term (and maybe the short to medium term), and they have over time become increasingly unacceptable to a growing number of people, countries, and organizations around the world.

The problems only seem to be getting worse. If economic growth in the past could at least be achieved by selectively externalizing the costs, those costs seem to be more broadly felt, while the growth itself is more elusive. In his book *Hot, Flat, and Crowded,* journalist Thomas Friedman stated that there's a reason that "Citibank, Iceland's banks, and the ice banks of Antarctica are all melting down at the same time." It is because our economic models and our environmental models, which are closely linked in the global economy, have both been based on two things: 1) consumption now that would be paid for in the future; and 2) privatizing the gains while socializing the losses. Friedman argues that the future is here now, and that we are all feeling the pain together, while what seems to be only a relatively small number of people and companies continue to benefit in the midst of crisis. "We have been growing in a way that is not healthy for either our markets or our planet, for either our banks or our forests, for either our retailers or our rivers."[24]

It remains to be seen if China on its own may threaten to upend the global economic system the United States helped to build and accelerate, or if the trends of the past continue. The economic and financial crisis of 2008, the movement of large numbers of refugees fleeing wars and escaping bleak economic prospects, the climate crisis that reveals itself with ever larger and increasing droughts, floods, fires, storms, and disasters, and most recently the absolute global upheaval prompted by the COVID-19 pandemic have all provided a strong impetus to make significant changes.

Some trends suggest a move away from past practices. Politically, the rise of populist politics, localism, and anti-globalization have diminished the appetite for liberal trade policies, including an increasingly open international economic order and the easy movement of goods, capital, and labor across borders. There is also growing demand in some quarters for policies to take action on climate change and to support renewable energy. In business and markets, trends include the falling costs of solar and wind energy, as well as longer-term goals of 3D manufacturing (a factory in every home?) and "just-in-time" manufacturing and inventory being replaced by "just-be-sure" as the global economy experiences unprecedented and unforeseen shipping bottlenecks and shortages. One thing seems certain, however. These trends, whatever their benefits, most assuredly have their costs, not only the ugliness and destructiveness of xenophobia, racism, and populist politics and ideologies that are already manifesting themselves, but others we have yet to see, or perhaps even imagine.

Perhaps it is unfair to place so much responsibility on the United States for the state of unsustainable capitalism and the adversity that the world is experiencing. After all, others have practiced the same. This is true, but it is also important to acknowledge the role that the United States has had in its history, serving for a long time as the proponent and bodyguard of a turbocharged, globalized economic engine that has had a great impact on the world, for much good, but also for some degree of ill.

Notes

1. Christina Prell, "Wealth and Pollution Inequalities of Global Trade," *Social Science Journal* 53, issue 1 (March 2016); Seema Jayachandran, "How Economic Development Influences the Environment," *Annual Review of Economics* 14, issue 1 (2022).
2. Walter Russell Mead, *Special Providence* (Routledge, 2002). This Hamiltonian outlook did not necessarily translate into advocacy of free trade. The United States for a long time was a strong proponent of its own protectionist policies, and vigorously implemented tariffs and trade restrictions on foreign goods prior to the two world wars. However, it has consistently sought to gain access to the markets of other countries.
3. Liza Gross, "No Place for Predators?," *PLoS Biology* 6, no. 2 (February 2008).
4. Paul M. Zall, ed., "Becoming a Lawyer: 1735–1758," in *Adams on Adams* (Lexington: University Press of Kentucky, 2004), 1–14.
5. Milton Friedman, "A Friedman Doctrine—The Social Responsibility of Business Is to Increase Its Profits," *New York Times Magazine*, September 13, 1970. It can also be added that the corporation, particularly as it developed in nineteenth-century America, created a pathway for a supercharged form of capitalism that gave companies significant freedom of action while limiting its liabilities. In addition, the American theory of corporate fiduciary responsibility, popularized in the 1970s and 1980s by Milton Friedman, argues that shareholder value is what matters most, and should matter most, in guiding the actions of corporations. See Chapter 6, page 13. Both of these developments have contributed to a global capitalism that has put growth and shareholder value at the top of the priority list, with relatively less value for individual, societal, and environmental well-being.

6. Dominique Mosbergen, "Why Southeast Asia Is Flooded With Trash From America And Other Wealthy Nations," *HuffPost*, March 8, 2019.

7. Mead, *Special Providence*, 59–63.

8. The Washington Consensus involved a series of economic policies that the United States, many of its allies, the World Bank, the International Monetary fund, and major banks around the world agreed to adopt beginning in the 1980s to promote economic growth and macroeconomic stability while reducing indebtedness among debtor countries. In order for indebted countries to renegotiate existing loans or take out new loans under more favorable repayment terms, several strict policy conditions—known as "structural adjustment" reforms, such as cutting government spending, deregulating, privatizing certain government functions, and opening up to global trade and investment—were often attached as conditions to securing the loans.

9. For a notable example of this argument, see Thomas Barnett, *The Pentagon's New Map: War and Peace in the Twenty-First Century* (Berkley, 2005).

10. United Nations Conference on Trade and Development, *The World Investment Report* (United Nations, 2021), 249.

11. World Bank, "GDP (Current US$)—China," 2023, https://data.worldbank.org/country/CN.

12. Hannah Ritchie and Max Roser, "China: Energy Country Profile," *Our World in Data* (2020).

13. United States Energy Information Administration, Executive Summary: China (2022), 2.

14. Statista Metals & Electronics, "Passenger and Commercial Vehicles," 2023; Statista Transportation and Logistics, "Light Vehicle Retail Sales in the US," 2023; Statista Transportation and Logistics, "Vehicles and Road Traffic," 2023.

15. United States Energy Information Administration, Executive Summary: China, 4.

16. Wang Lianzhang, "Government Orders Chinese Air Quality App to Limit Readings," *Sixth Tone*, January 11, 2017.

17. Graham Allison, *Destined for War: Can America and China Escape Thucydides's Trap?* (Houghton Mifflin Harcourt, 2017), 6–7.

18. Allison, *Destined for War*, 13.

19. Allison, *Destined for War*, 13.

20. Yuliya Talmazan, "China's Coronavirus Hospital Built in 10 Days Opens Its Doors, State Media Says," *NBC News*, February 3, 2020.

21. Daniel Yergin, *The New Map: Energy, Climate, and the Clash of Nations* (Penguin Press, 2020), 132.

22. Yergin, *The New Map*, 132.

23. World Bank, "GDP Growth (Annual %)—China," 2023, https://data.worldbank.org/indicator/NY.GDP.MKTP.KD.ZG?locations=CN.

24. Thomas L. Friedman, *Hot, Flat and Crowded: Why We Need a Green Revolution—and How It Can Renew America* (Farrar, Straus and Giroux, 2008), 6.

7

Racism and Capitalism

Elizabeth J. Kennedy

"Climate apartheid" is a term the United Nations uses to refer to the unequal and racialized distribution of the climate crisis's material impacts across populations. It recognizes that enduring forms of social inequality threaten our ability to meet the challenges of the climate crisis and operate as a barrier to a sustainable economy. This phenomenon has roots in the same history of racial exploitation that shaped and supported the development of American capitalism. For example, Black Americans own one-tenth the wealth of white Americans; at the current rate, it would take Black households 228 years to accumulate the wealth held by white families today. This disparity is mirrored across every metric of lived experience, including health, housing, education, environment, and liberty.[1] The rate of Black infant mortality is twice as high as that for white babies, a wider disparity than in 1850.[2] Black children are food insecure at three times the rate of white children.[3] Black Americans are incarcerated at five times the rate of white Americans and for significantly longer sentences.[4] This caste system forces us to interrogate the relationship between racism and capitalism. As Malcolm X claimed, is it impossible to have capitalism without racism? Ibram X. Kendi describes racism and capitalism as "conjoined twins," each dependent on the other for survival. To answer whether sustainable capitalism is possible, we must examine the history of capitalism and reckon with its continued reliance on racialized oppression.

This chapter examines the history of slavery as a racialized institution that coexisted with capitalism and evolved alongside it. It also considers the laws, institutions, and policies that reinforced racial oppression long after emancipation, which help us to identify the historical roots of present inequity and climate apartheid. At every point in capitalism's development, Black, Indigenous, and other people of color have resisted the economic, social, and political systems that sought to exploit and extinguish their existence. While a comprehensive discussion of the relationship between race and capitalism must include all people of color along intersectional axes of oppression, this chapter focuses on the Black wealth gap. It proposes reparations and cooperative economics as viable steps toward a more sustainable and just economy.

Slavery and the Rise of Global Capitalism

We cannot understand the relationship between racism and capitalism without fully accounting for the role slavery played in the growth of the global economy. Capitalism emerged as Medieval European feudalism—an economic, social, and political system by which those who controlled arable land (lords) demanded rent and labor from those who made that land productive (peasants or serfs)—had begun to wane.[5] Military resources required to maintain feudal inequality were increasingly expensive, particularly following the Black Death. Before the African slave trade or colonial expansion to the Americas, displaced and enslaved European peoples, such as the Irish, Jews, Roma, or Slavs, were viewed as racialized. The Germans used the racial doctrine of "herrenvolk" to justify enslaving eastern European peoples; religion and regionalism rationalized the indentured servitude forced by the British upon the conquered Irish.[6] European conquest created classes of "unfree" populations whose displacement and precarity made them willing to work for meager wages. Toward the end of the fifteenth century, this economic system in which labor was treated as a commodity—capitalism—began to take shape. Yet, even before the start of the transatlantic slave trade, the use of race and racism to classify—and economically devalue—the labor of different ethnic groups of Europeans was firmly established.

Nearly one in five of the 12 million African men, women, and children forced on the harrowing voyage across the Atlantic known as the "Middle Passage" died before reaching shore.[7] Those who survived worked under brutal conditions in Caribbean sugarcane fields or Virginia tobacco plantations, generating profits for European investors. Wealth extracted from slavery fueled the growth of a global capitalist economy, stoking the industrial engines of finance, insurance, shipping, manufacturing, construction, and education. As Manning Marable observes, the labor power of enslaved workers powered modern capitalist world accumulation.[8] But fear of white rebellion led the British to terminate many indentured contracts and extend land grants to white laborers, creating a class of white settlers with economic and political fortunes aligned with the ruling regime.[9]

This nascent capitalism of 1619 evolved into a highly efficient system capable of powering an industrial revolution. By 1860, cotton—grown on Indigenous lands expropriated using militarized violence—comprised 59 percent of American exports. It was, as the saying went, "king." Land resources were plenty, but harvesting cotton was labor intensive, driving demand for enslaved workers. At that moment, most people in South Carolina and Mississippi, almost half of those in Georgia, and roughly one-third of all Southerners were enslaved. While forced agricultural labor may have been performed predominately in the South, the Northern Industrial Revolution depended on it. The number of cotton spindles in northern textile mills exploded from 87,000 in 1810 to about 5 million in 1860.[10] Other countries could not compete with a nation that codified a caste of workers as non-human and legalized violence as a management technique. As the sociologist and ethnographer Matthew Desmond observes, "Given the choice between modernity and barbarism, prosperity and poverty, lawfulness and cruelty, democracy and totalitarianism, America chose all of the above."[11] Human bondage was the "beating heart" of this new American economy, pumping wealth to Southern planters, raw materials to Northern mills and British industrialists, and capital to European bankers.[12]

Whether capitalism could exist without racism ignores, as historian Walter Johnson affirms, that "there was no such thing as capitalism without slavery." Institutions like J.P. Morgan appraised, sold, and resold Black bodies as collateral for loans, bonds, and capital investment. By 1860, enslaved people were the single largest asset in the American economy, with a combined value exceeding the nation's railroads and factories. The purchase and sale of enslaved people spurred the creation of new financial products, insurance policies, tax revenues, and notary fees. Children born to enslaved women were sold and separated from their families, which Ta-Nehisi Coates describes as "the for-profit destruction of the most important asset available to any people, the family."[13] American business history largely ignores what Marx described as the "undisguised looting, enslavement, and murder" that powered the global economy.[14]

The profits extracted from the bodies of enslaved people would be woven everywhere into the American capitalist economy.[15] Caitlin Rosenthal traces the origins of quantitative management practices, record-keeping, and accounting methods to the plantation. These included scientific production quotas, elegant data dashboards, mark-to-market accounting, depreciation algorithms, and credit instruments.[16] Commercial journals and accounting ledgers helped planters "accelerate the pace of daily labor through calculation and comparison, bonuses and incentives, and, of course, punishment," a sophisticated human resource management system developed long before Frederick Taylor.[17] Though slavery pre-dates capitalism, and capitalism persists without slavery, it is hard to imagine a system of capitalism growing at that scale and pace in its absence.

Wealth is accumulated under capitalism by extracting planetary resources, including labor. The labor of enslaved people was necessary to transform raw materials, such as cotton, into marketable commodities. So, too, did the American coal industry rely almost exclusively on enslaved labor. But extraction also refers to the wealth accumulated from treating enslaved people as commodities. The sale of those people—"in whose bodies that money congealed"—triggered the creation of new financial products, such as policies insuring the property value of enslaved people, taxes on their sale, and notary fees for the transactions.[18] Unlike chattel property like farm machinery or railroad cars, enslaved men and women could reproduce voluntarily or through systemic rape and forced childbearing.

Law's Role in Shaping Post-Civil War Capitalism

On December 6, 1865, Georgia ratified the 13th Amendment, outlawing slavery "except as a punishment for crime."[19] Abolishing slavery was an opportunity to acknowledge and repair America's "original sin." If capitalism did not depend on racial subjugation, we would expect to see the era of slavery regarded as a holocaust, never to be repeated. The federal government would create an equitable economy supported by a just legal system. Reparations would be made to those formerly enslaved and their descendants. Instead, what followed was an extension of slavery's economic, social, physical, and emotional damages. Through terror, disenfranchisement, and exclusion, American capitalism survived the emancipation of the enslaved people upon whose labor it depended.

While emancipation meant a financial loss to Southern enslavers of their chattel property, that amount was small compared with the economic risks if agricultural fields remained fallow or coal mines lay empty. Federal oversight of what was intended to be a "reconstruction" fell to Andrew Johnson, the former Tennessee enslaver elevated to the role after Lincoln's assassination. Contrary to field orders issued by Union General William Tecumseh Sherman on January 16, 1865, that provided for the seizure and redistribution of Southern coastal lands to the newly freedmen ("forty acres" though not, in those orders, any mention of mules),[20] President Johnson returned those lands to former enslavers, granted amnesty to Confederates and allowed Southern states to elect new governments.[21] Their first order of business was criminalizing the autonomy of newly freed people by enacting "Black Codes," which criminalized the refusal to work as "vagrancy." Conviction under these codes resulted in fines that few could pay, leading to imprisonment. African Americans incarcerated for violating the Black Codes or breaching shareholder contracts were "leased" to planters, railroads, and mining companies under agreements that ranged from ten to thirty years. When the number of convicts was insufficient to meet labor demands, criminal laws were expanded and sentences extended.

Many Black farmers, lacking capital, were forced into coercive "sharecropping" contracts that required them to pay for using land, tools, and seeds in exchange for a share of harvest proceeds. They had to work in debt peonage or risk arrest if they could not repay the debt. When Black people accumulated even a meager amount of capital—tools, animals, land—local governments engaged in tactics ranging from "legal chicanery to terrorism" that resulted in seizure or foreclosure. Convict leasing ensured cotton would still be picked, textile looms would hum, and returns on capital investment would flow. This "slavery by another name" fueled an explosion of Southern prison populations in a system described in 1949 by historian Fletcher Green as akin to "the persecutions of the Middle Ages" and "prison camps of Nazi Germany."[22]

Lynching and other racialized violence pushed Black men, women, and children out of the deep South to cities in the North. As under slavery, violence—actual and threatened—was omnipresent and sanctioned, enabled, and participated in by law enforcement. Considered "a fate worse than death," lynching took grotesque and brutal forms, including burning, castration, crude cesarean sections, and amputation. The Ku Klux Klan, whose members included government officials, gave lynching the imprimatur of state authority. When Black Americans managed to accumulate wealth, they were met with an organized and violent racial backlash. During the "Red Summer of 1919," racial pogroms destroyed dozens of cities and neighborhoods from Texas to Chicago to Washington DC and Florida.[23] Tulsa's Greenwood neighborhood, known as "Black Wall Street," experienced a massacre. Over 300 residents were murdered, and businesses, civil, and cultural institutions were leveled.[24] As millions of Black people migrated away from the South between 1919 and 1950, Northern cities enacted Jim Crow laws, which excluded them from parks, restrooms, schools, restaurants, hospitals, nursing homes, public pools, jobs, and transportation.

The policies of the New Deal, intended to combat poverty on a national level, further entrenched Jim Crow segregation. Black agricultural and domestic workers were excluded from landmark labor protections, preventing them from saving for retirement, collectively bargaining for raises, or receiving compensation for workplace injuries. While these programs were a critical safety net for white working-class Americans, the NAACP called them "a sieve with holes just big enough for the majority of Negroes to fall through."[25] Other exclusionary opportunities for building wealth included the G.I. Bill and the Federal Housing Administration's (FHA) home mortgage program. While race-neutral in theory, the G.I. Bill did not require universities to admit non-white students, so few African Americans could take advantage of subsidized higher education. Likewise, the FHA developed a system that Richard Rothstein describes as "state-sponsored segregation."[26] The FHA relied on color-coded risk maps created by the Home Owners' Loan Corporation (HOLC) to determine which loans it would guarantee and thus make affordable to working-class Americans. A red line encircled neighborhoods with high concentrations of African Americans, making them ineligible for federally subsidized mortgages. Segregation laws and discrimination had already shaped neighborhood demographics; "redlining" cemented them as structural barriers.

The use of HOLC maps spread beyond the FHA into a private market rife with racism. The National Association of Real Estate Boards required realtors to steer Black home buyers away from white neighborhoods. Banks created predatory financing schemes that targeted Black home buyers and coerced them into contracts on which they would often default. Fledgling

Black banks attempted to meet the demand for mortgages. Still, without more affirmative federal support, they could not survive while serving communities experiencing high rates of poverty and depressed housing values. Federal prohibitions against racial discrimination by lenders, builders, and realtors could have built a Black middle class. Instead, as a New York City Housing Authority leader observed in 1955, the FHA "adopted a racial policy that could have been culled from the Nuremberg Laws."[27] This partnership between public agencies and private industry depressed property values and fortified barriers to Black homeownership for decades.

Structural Legacies of Racial Capitalism

The United States was so adept at using racial codes and laws that differentiated—and racialized—human values that Nazi Germany looked to the U.S. legal system for inspiration.[28] Civil Rights Era legislation banned many legal forms of discrimination but did not affirmatively reverse their impacts. For example, while the 1968 Fair Housing Act officially ended redlining, the impact and legacy of this practice endure. Redlining prevented Black families from living in racially integrated neighborhoods, attending high-quality schools, accessing clean air and green space, and benefiting from public investments in infrastructure and the economic diversity that generates employment opportunities.[29] State-sponsored devaluation of homes in Black neighborhoods trapped residents for generations. Rather than using homeownership to build wealth and achieve social mobility, those residing in once-redlined areas continue to suffer from higher rates of cancer,[30] asthma,[31] COVID-19,[32] educational disparities,[33] and the effects of climate change.[34] Communities of color are more likely to be located near an urban coal plant—an industry historically reliant on enslaved and Black prison labor and responsible for significant global carbon emissions. Environmental pollution and climate hazards are often created and reinforced by racist laws and policies.[35] Social scientists have noted that the significance of the neighborhood-level disparities that persist today—regardless of household income—make it impossible to compare the economic outcomes of Black and white children statistically. Furthermore, algorithms used in artificial intelligence often perpetuate these disparities, a phenomenon Safiya Umoja Noble termed "technological redlining."[36]

Redlining's connection to climate change precarity is just as pervasive. After analyzing the "flood potential" of properties in its database, the real estate listing company Redfin recently shared its discovery that homes in formerly redlined neighborhoods were at a disproportionately high risk of future flooding. Given the enduring nature of structural racism, people of color are still more likely to live in those neighborhoods, which, in a double blow, are less equipped to prepare for the increasing number of storms that climate change will produce. In another example of how historic discrimination creates contemporary opportunities for exploitation, Wells Fargo engaged in the predatory marketing of subprime, high-risk mortgages to communities of color under a banner of "building generational wealth." As revealed in a 2012 class-action lawsuit, the program targeted Black religious leaders whose influence the bank hoped would convince their congregants to take out risky mortgages.[37] According to the *New York Times*, affidavits found that loan officers referred to their Black customers as "mud people" and their subprime products as "ghetto loans."[38] In addition to this damning evidence of explicit bias, we again see how seemingly "neutral" data-driven algorithms—in this case, pointing loan officers to communities historically cut off from the finance industry—reinforce and replicate racial discrimination.[39] Wells Fargo would ultimately pay $175 million, but the damage created by what Cathy O'Neil calls a "weapon of math destruction" was complete.[40] Half the properties whose owners had been granted loans by Wells Fargo were vacant; 71 percent were in predominately Black neighborhoods. Fifty years after Jim Crow, the incentives to extract profits by exploiting racial inequality remain. As Ta-Nehisi Coates exhorts, "When we think of white supremacy, we picture colored-only signs, but we should picture pirate flags."[41]

Defenders of capitalism argue that racism is inefficient in a genuinely free market and that slavery, segregation, and structural discrimination are political and social issues, not economically driven problems. In *The Wealth of Nations*, Adam Smith proposed that the balance of power and distribution of advantages between capital and labor could be maintained in a society where "there was perfect liberty, and where every man was perfectly free both to chuse [sic] what occupation he thought proper and to change it as often as he thought proper."[42] Such conditions of equality did not exist in 1776, nor do they now. Writing nearly a century after Emancipation, W.E.B. Du Bois argued that "the first and fundamental and inescapable problem of American democracy is Justice to the American

Negro." Contemporary critical race theory helpfully instructs that racism is not the only form of discrimination impacting marginalized individuals or communities: sexism, classism, heteronormativity, and nativism (among others) combine, overlap, or intersect to rationalize inequality. By the mid-twentieth century, Du Bois had concluded that one could not struggle decisively against racism in the United States and remain a proponent of capitalism.[43]

Collective Resistance and Cooperative Economics

People have engaged in collective resistance at every point in the history of capitalism. As Manning Marable explains, "In the proverbial bowels of the capitalist leviathan, the enslaved people forged a new world culture that was in its origin African, but in its creative form, something entirely new."[44] Understanding this resistance culture may be the key to sustainable capitalism. For some, resistance meant to escape, engage in self-defense, or foment rebellion. For others, it took the shape of forging "maroon" communities with Indigenous peoples,[45] tending kitchen gardens to nourish their families, pooling funds to purchase one another's freedom, or organizing an underground railroad. Black women were always at the forefront of these efforts to preserve the dignity and humanity of Black people. Over time, this resistance assumed new forms, integrating Black Christianity,[46] Creole language and culture,[47] the labor union and civil rights movements, and mutual aid societies.[48] As the legal supports for capitalism shape-shifted from enslavement to de jure segregation to de facto discrimination and capital markets exclusion, Black resistance established Black banks, worker-owned cooperatives, and credit unions. Activists organized Black Power breakfast and educational programs,[49] environmental justice protests,[50] Black labor caucuses, and a Black Lives Matter movement against police violence and intersectional oppression.[51] The contemporary cooperative movement, which includes worker-owned cooperatives, investor cooperatives, producer cooperatives, credit unions, and consumer cooperatives, has roots in this Black radical tradition of cooperative economics. A cooperative governance model could serve as a model for a more sustainable and anti-racist form of capitalism.

Critics of capitalism contend that capital accumulates only when it moves through relations of severe inequality.[52] They argue that wealth in a capitalist society can only be generated—or extracted—by creating and maintaining this inequality. We can understand this in the context of a factory owner who accumulates capital through the labor his workers sell him for wages. If those wages were commensurate with the actual economic value that labor produced, what profit would remain for the factory owner? In this sense, capitalism requires inequality. But does it require extreme inequality? Does it require racialized inequality? Wages are lowest when workers have no other means of subsistence, though arguably, if they are too low, consumer demand and worker retention will fall, reducing the profit margin. Proponents of capitalism argue that these are some of the invisible market forces that serve as a check against exploitation. Capital also flows through inequality in other dimensions of a capitalist economy, such as rent from tenants to landlords and debt payments from borrowers to creditors. Yet, as we've seen throughout this chapter, systemic racism has metered those flows in various and disparate ways.

What might an economic production system resemble in the absence of racism? As Jacqui Patterson, Senior Director of the NAACP's Environmental and Climate Justice Program, explains, it would involve "moving away from a society functioning on extraction to one deeply rooted in deep democracy and integrating regenerative processes, cooperation, and acknowledgment of interdependence." Moving toward a more sustainable and anti-racist economy will require acknowledging that American capitalism was built upon racial violence, enslavement, and exploitation. From that acknowledgment must follow federal and state reparations for those past and ongoing harms.[53] Reparations fall squarely within the legal norms of our democratic, capitalist system: when someone is harmed, the law seeks to make that person whole. Reparations—repairing what has been harmed—are a fundamental purpose of our domestic civil justice system and are used internationally to compensate victims of human rights violations.[54] Yet, in repairing historic and ongoing harms Black and Indigenous people suffer, they are treated as morally questionable or practically unfeasible.[55] Until we recognize and restore the victims of racial capitalism, a system of non-racial capitalism will not be possible. These reparations cannot be achieved simply through "acknowledgment or an apology" or by "investment in underprivileged communities" and instead require, at minimum, the following pre-conditions established by the United Nations: cessation, assurances, and guarantees of non-repetition; restitution and repatriation; compensation; satisfaction; and rehabilitation.[56]

Du Bois predicted that America would eventually have to choose, explains Manning Marable, moving toward "worker self-management, antiracism, and a new democratic state apparatus," or "lapse into authoritarianism, racial barbarism, and militarization of the workforce."[57] We have reached that choice point. Widespread racial and environmental injustice protests have amplified critiques of extractive capitalism and its relationship to inequality and climate change. Yet corporate and public policies that promote sustainability often fail to address—let alone redress—capitalism's history of slavery, racism, and structural inequality. Scholars of racial capitalism have made critical contributions to our understanding of the relationship between capitalism, racism, and law. Their work can serve as a roadmap toward a new economic and political system that is equitable, sustainable, and just. Just as the rise of the automobile was deeply entwined with the use of fossil fuels, the development of capitalism was inextricably linked to the institution of slavery. Transitioning from a carbon-based to a sustainable economy is not as simple as swapping a combustion engine with a rechargeable battery. We must also unwind a century of economic, residential, and workforce policies prioritizing roads over rails, speed over security, and consumption over conservation. Likewise, a sustainable society requires unraveling and repairing the racialized violence, inequality, and exploitation woven into the fabric of American capitalism.

Notes

1. Hiroko Tabuchi and Nadja Popovich, "People of Color Breathe More Hazardous Air. The Sources Are Everywhere," *New York Times*, April 28, 2021; Sarah Mervosh, "How Much Wealthier Are White School Districts than Nonwhite Ones? $23 Billion, Report Says," *New York Times*, February 27, 2019.
2. Linda Villarosa, "Why America's Black Mothers and Babies Are in a Life-or-Death Crisis," *New York Times*, April 11, 2018.
3. Christianna Silva, "Food Insecurity In the U.S. by the Numbers," *NPR*, September 27, 2020.
4. Ashley Nellis, *The Color of Justice: Racial and Ethnic Disparity in State Prisons* (Sentencing Project, 2021); Jodi Melamed, "Racial Capitalism," *Critical Ethnic Studies* 1, no. 1 (Spring 2015): 77. Jodi Melamed notes that while we use the term "racial cruelty" to describe "extreme or surplus violence" against people of color, we accept racialized state violence when it takes the form of criminal justice. Racial profiling tactics and sentencing disparities codified by a

succession of federal crime bills fueled a profitable and destructive "prison industrial complex." Those who benefit, and even profit from, the construction and operation of prisons rely on a national narrative of Black criminality to ensure public support, justify stark racial disparities, and deflect criticism.

5. Cedric Robinson, *Black Marxism: The Making of the Black Radical Tradition* (Zed Books, 1983) 10–25.

6. Robinson, *Black Marxism*, 25–28.

7. Edward E. Baptist, *The Half Has Never Been Told* (Basic Books, 2016), 57.

8. Manning Marable, *How Capitalism Underdeveloped Black America* (South End Press, 1983), 24.

9. Michelle Alexander, *The New Jim Crow: Mass Incarceration in the Age of Colorblindness* (The New Press, 2012), 24.

10. Matthew Desmond, "To Understand the Brutality," *New York Times*, August 14, 2019, 34.

11. Desmond, "To Understand the Brutality," 32.

12. Sven Beckert and Seth Rockman, *Slavery's Capitalism: A New History of American Economic Development* (Philadelphia: University of Pennsylvania Press, 2016), 33.

13. Ta-Nehisi Coates, "The Case for Reparations," *Atlantic*, June, 2014 (quoting Walter Johnson).

14. Karl Marx, *Capital*, 535.

15. Caitlin Rosenthal, *Accounting for Slavery* (Harvard University Press, 2018), 51, 127.

16. Caitlin Rosenthal, "Capitalism when Labor was Capital: Slavery, Power, and Price in Antebellum America," *Capitalism: A Journal of History and Economics* 1, no. 2 (2020): 296–337.

17. Rosenthal, *Accounting for Slavery*, 90–92, 6.

18. Coates, "The Case for Reparations."

19. "Neither slavery nor involuntary servitude, except as a punishment for crime whereof the party shall have been duly convicted, shall exist within the United States, or any place subject to their jurisdiction." U.S. Const. amend. XIII, § 1.

20. U.S. War Department, Special Field Orders, No. 15, Headquarters Military Division of the Mississippi, January 16, 1865, Orders & Circulars, series 44, Adjutant General's Office, Record Group 94, National Archives.

21. William P. Quigley, "The Continuing Significance of Race: Official Legislative Racial Discrimination in Louisiana 1861 to 1974," *Southern University Law Review* 47, no. 1 (April 14, 2020): 10–13.

22. Marable, *How Capitalism Underdeveloped Black America*, 109–15.

23. Jessica Glenza, "Rosewood Massacre: A Harrowing Tale of Racism and the Road toward Reparations," *Guardian*, January 3, 2016.

24. Yuliya Parshina-Kottis, et al., "What the Tulsa Race Massacre Destroyed," *New York Times*, May 24, 2021.

25. Mehrsa Baradaran, *The Color of Money: Black Banks and the Racial Wealth Gap* (Harvard University Press, 2017), 102.

26. Richard Rothstein, *The Color of Law: A Forgotten History of How Our Government Segregated America* (Liveright, 2017), 21.

27. Andrew Wiese, *Places of Their Own: African American Suburbanization in the Twentieth Century* (University of Chicago Press, 2005), 101.
28. Isabel Wilkerson, *Caste: The Origins of Our Discontents* (Random House, 2023), 79.
29. Naa Oyo A. Kwate and Ji Meng Loh, "Separate and Unequal: The Influence of Neighborhood and School Characteristics on Spatial Proximity Between Fast Food and Schools," *Preventive Medicine* 51 (2010).
30. See, e.g., Lindsay J. Collins et al., "Neighborhood-Level Redlining and Lending Bias Are Associated with Breast Cancer Mortality in a Large and Diverse Metropolitan Area," *Cancer Epidemiology, Biomarkers, & Prevention* 30, no. 1 (2021)
31. See, e.g., Anthony Nardone et al., "Associations between historical residential redlining and current age-adjusted rates of emergency department visits due to asthma across eight cities in California: an ecological study," *Lancet Planetary Health*, 4, no. 1 (January 2020).
32. Maria Godoy, "COVID-19 May Have A More Serious Impact On Formerly Redlined Communities," *NPR*, September 18, 2020.
33. Dylan Lukes and Christopher Cleveland, "The Lingering Legacy of Redlining on School Funding, Diversity, and Performance" (working paper, EdWorkingPapers 21-363), 1–12.
34. Meg Anderson, "Racist Housing Practices from the 1930s Linked to Hotter Neighborhoods Today," *NPR*, January 14, 2020.
35. Laura Pulido. "Flint, Environmental Racism, and Racial Capitalism." *Capitalism, Nature, Socialism* 27, no. 3 (2016): 1–16. https:// doi .org/ 10 .1080/ 10455752.2016 .1213013.
36. Safiya Umoja Noble, *Algorithms of Oppression: How Search Engines Reinforce Racism* (NYU Press, 2018), 1, 167.
37. See Office of Public Affairs U.S. Department of Justice, "Justice Department Reaches Settlement in Suit to Block ASSA ABLOY's Proposed Acquisition of Spectrum Brands' Hardware and Home Improvement Division," May 5, 2023, https://www.justice.gov/opa/pr/justice-department-reaches-settlement -suit-block-assa-abloy-s-proposed-acquisition-spectrum.
38. Michael Powell, "Bank Accused of Pushing Mortgage Deals on Blacks," *New York Times*, June 6, 2009.
39. Cathy O'Neil, *Weapons of Math Destruction: How Big Data Increases Inequality and Threatens Democracy* (Crown, 2016), 40.
40. O'Neil, *Weapons of Math Destruction*, 3–11.
41. Coates, "The Case for Reparations."
42. Adam Smith, *The Wealth of Nations* (London: W. Strahan and T. Cadell, 1776).
43. Du Bois observed that "The United States, with its existing social structure, cannot today abolish the color line despite its promises. It cannot stop injustice in the courts based on color and race. Above all, it cannot stop the exploitation of black workers by white capital, especially in the newest South. White North America beyond the urge of sound economics is persistently driving black folk toward socialism." W.E.B. Du Bois. "Negroes and the Crisis of Capitalism," *Monthly Review* 4, no. 12 (April 1953): 91.

44. Marable, *How Capitalism Underdeveloped Black America*, 24.
45. "Marronage" can refer to very specific settlements formed by those who escaped slavery, either immediately after arriving in the Americas or at some later point. Examples of such communities, often forged with Indigenous people, can be found throughout the Caribbean, Central America, South America, and North America, including Black Seminole communities in Florida and Creole communities in New Orleans. It can also refer to various ways in which "less permanent, more flexible forms of marronage [that] enabled enslaved women to carve out semiautonomous space within slavery" and engage in systems of mutual aid with other enslaved people. Shauna J. Sweeney, "Gendering Racial Capitalism and the Black Heretical Tradition," in *Histories of Racial Capitalism*, ed. Destin Jenkins and Justin Leroy (Columbia University Press, 2021), 66–68.
46. Forrest Moore, *A History of the Black Church in Tuscaloosa* (Authorhouse, 2008).
47. Robinson, *Black Marxism*, 311.
48. See, e.g., Dominique Thomas and Tabbye Chavous, "The Black Radical Tradition of Resistance: A Series on Black Social Movements," *Medium*, February 6, 2019, https://medium.com/national-center-for-institutional-diversity/the-black-radical-tradition-of-resistance-7277f09ef396. See also Mohammed Elnaiem, "Black Conquistadors and Black Maroons," *JSTOR Daily*, April 1, 2021; Laura Flanders, "Solidarity Economics, a Forgotten Practice of the Black Radical Tradition: An Interview With Jessica Gordon Nembhard," *Truthout*, April 9, 2014.
49. Darryl Robertson, "The Black Panther Party and the Free Breakfast for Children Program," *Black Perspectives*, February 26, 2016.
50. Laura Pulido and Juan De Lara, "Reimagining 'justice' in environmental justice: Radical ecologies, decolonial thought, and the Black Radical Tradition," *Environment and Planning E: Nature and Space* 1, no. 1–2 (April 2018): 2.
51. Earle J. Fisher, "Black Liberation Theology and the Movement for Black Lives: A Match Made in Heaven," Georgetown University: Berkley Center for Religion, Peace & World Affairs, January 6. 2022.
52. Melamed, "Racial Capitalism," 77.
53. National Coalition of Blacks for Reparations in America (N'COBRA) defines reparations as "A process of repairing, healing and restoring a people injured because of their group identity and in violation of their fundamental human rights by governments, corporations, institutions, and families. Those groups that have been injured have the right to obtain from the government, corporation, institution, or family responsible for the injuries that they need to repair and heal themselves. In addition to being a demand for justice, it is a principle of international human rights law." Movement for Black Lives (M4BL), Reparations Now Toolkit (2020), 25.
54. Richard M. Buxbaum, "A Legal History of International Reparations," *Berkeley Journal of International Law* 23, no. 2 (2005): 314–17.
55. Joe Feagin, "Documenting the Costs of Slavery, Segregation, and Contemporary Discrimination: Are Reparations in Order for African Americans?" (CSD

working paper No. 00-10, St. Louis, MO: Washington University, Center for
Social Development), 9–11.

56. To elaborate, "cessation . . ." refers to the requirement that under "international law, a state responsible for wrongfully injuring a people" is under
an obligation to a) "cease the act if it is continuing, and b) offer appropriate assurances and guarantees of non-repetition. . . ." Restitution means
"re-establish the situation which existed before the wrongful act was committed." Changes traced to the wrongful act are reversed through the restoration of freedom, recognition of humanity, identity, culture, repatriation,
livelihood, citizenship, legal standing, and wealth to the extent they can
be, and if they cannot, restitution is completed by compensation. Concern-
ing compensation, "The injuring state, institution or individual is obligated
to compensate for the damage if the damage is not made good by restitution. Compensation is required for "any financially accessible damage
suffered . . ." to the extent "appropriate and proportional to the gravity of
the violation and circumstances." "Satisfaction" is "part of full reparations
under international law for moral damage, such as 'emotional injury, mental suffering, and injury to reputation.' In some instances where cessation,
restitution, and compensation do not bring full repair, satisfaction is also
needed. Apology falls under the reparative category of satisfaction." Lastly,
"[r]ehabilitation shall be provided to include legal, medical, psychological,
and other care and services." Movement for Black Lives (M4BL), Reparations Now Toolkit, 26.

57. Marable, *How Capitalism Underdeveloped Black America*, 18.

Part III
Capitalism and Corporations

8

Corporations
The Heart of American Capitalism

Ruth Jebe

Capitalism is the only economic system the U.S. has known. While it has undoubtedly produced benefits in the form of increased wealth, some argue that capitalism as practiced in America also acts as a barrier to a sustainable economy by increasing the wealth gap and degrading environmental quality. Capitalism may be defined as a system in which private actors own property and control it in accordance with their individual interests; as such, it has the opportunity to be a vehicle for extreme self-interest. Because of the extensive government intervention required to create, maintain, and protect these property interests, capitalism also provides an opportunity to recognize the interdependence between privately owned business, in particular privately owned corporations, and society.

This chapter explores the history and evolution of American capitalism through the development of the corporation as a business form and the creation of corporate governance tools. First, it examines the origin and evolution of the corporation as a form of business organization. Using this background, it then considers the changing and diverging ideas on the purpose of business and the role of corporations in society, including the relationship between corporations and their external environment, and more specifically, the philosophical question of the purpose of business: what is the purpose of business and what responsibilities does a corporation owe the stakeholders in the societies in which it operates?

Next, this chapter examines the corporation's internal relationships, specifically the relationship between the corporation and its shareholders.

The formal aspects of corporations' legal structures raise fundamental issues about what is commonly called corporate governance—that is, the collection of mechanisms, processes, and relations used by various parties to control and to operate a corporation. Some corporate governance mechanisms guide and control the relationship between corporate directors and corporate shareholders. Increasingly, corporate governance is also seen as creating the guardrails that shape the relationship between corporations and society.

At its heart, the story of American capitalism reveals the tension between notions of capitalism for shareholders and capitalism for stakeholders, as well as the fundamental question of the appropriate role of business in society.

The Corporation: Origins and Development

Before the nineteenth century, business enterprises operated on a small scale. Early businesses were embedded in and largely served only their local communities. Most business was specialized, often handling a single production function and a single product, and therefore, did not need sophisticated management structures.[1] Manufacturing concerns, for example, were usually operated by an artisan, assisted by apprentices or family members.[2] Until the mid-1800s, businesses were generally owned and managed by a sole owner or a small number of partners.[3]

While these smaller entities carried out the majority of commercial activities, forms of business organization with some of the characteristics of corporations have also existed for hundreds of years, from ancient Rome to fifteenth century Italy to seventeenth century England and the Netherlands.[4] These business organizations sought to address an important financial problem: how to attract large amounts of capital. Traditional business forms made raising large amounts of money difficult because contributing capital to a partnership, for example, would likely make one liable for the partnership's debts. Thus, there was a limit to how much capital a partnership could raise. The unique feature these corporate forms had in common is that all had mechanisms to shield shareholders—those who contributed capital to the corporation by purchasing "shares" in the corporation—from the corporation's debts.

Protection from liability for corporate debt made corporations useful for activities that required significant financial resources, such as public works projects. For example, some scholars argue that the Romans used the equivalent of corporations to build aqueducts and other large public projects. Early corporate forms were also used to finance high-risk ventures. The Dutch and British used a form of corporation for their East India trading companies, which allowed investors to pool their funds to reduce the risk of losing their entire fortune on a single voyage. Perhaps most notably for Americans, the British set up corporations to finance the founding of its colonies in America; the Virginia Company, which established the first colony in Jamestown, Virginia, was a British corporation.[5]

However, these early corporate forms were quite different entities from today's corporations. First, governments recognized the potential issues with large capital accumulations and wanted to exercise control over these large businesses. To this end, corporations could generally only be created by a special charter issued and overseen by the government. Charters were granted for the execution of specific projects (for example, the construction of a canal); once the project was completed, the corporation's charter would expire and the corporation would cease to exist. In addition, these early corporations were chartered primarily for public purposes, not for private profit. The Romans, for example, used corporations to deliver public services and the British East India Company was charged with support and development of communities where it established trading connections. Early U.S. corporations were chartered to build bridges and railroads and to dig canals.[6] While these companies wanted to make a profit, they had an equal or greater charge to serve the societies within which they operated.

The late nineteenth and early twentieth centuries saw a sea change in business. New communication and transportation technologies shortened distances and made it possible for entities to do business on an expanded geographic scale: business began to go global. Changes in U.S. law made it easier to form corporations, and corporations could be created for any lawful purpose, not solely for public purposes. For example, in 1896 the state of New Jersey passed a statute allowing corporations to define the scope of their corporate charters for themselves.[7] These developments combined to make possible the types of large corporations we know today.

Managerial Capitalism: Business as a Member of Society

As business grew in size, the need for management structure and expertise grew. The early 1900s saw the rise of corporations with thousands of
investors who expected a financial benefit from their investment but who
had no interest in managing the business. Managerial hierarchies developed, in which salaried managers made the day-to-day decisions about the
production and distribution of goods. Importantly, these salaried managers owned little or no stock in the enterprise they managed. This form of
capitalism came to be known as managerial capitalism.

Managerial capitalism dominated the narrative of American capitalism from around 1930 to the mid-1970s. Although corporations were no
longer chartered specifically for public purposes, the dominant view still
saw business as rooted in community. Many companies had strong ties to
the communities where they originated or had key operations and saw
their relationship with those communities as mutually supportive. Business only did well if the community around it did well. Managers viewed
their job as considering and balancing the interests of multiple parties to
fulfill the corporation's purpose of serving all of society. Harvard law professor Merrick Dodd summed up this view, arguing that the corporation
"is an economic institution which has a social service as well as a profit-
making function."[8]

Others disagreed with Dodd. They were particularly concerned about
a potential problem created by separating ownership (shareholders) from
decision-making (managers). According to this view, if managers did not
own shares in the corporation, they would have little incentive to do what
the corporation's owners want. At best, they might shirk their managerial
duties, and, at worst, their interests might diverge from the shareholders'
interests leading to management stealing from shareholders.

This tension between the interests of managers and shareholders—which
would later be incorporated into a theory called the "agency cost problem"—
raised red flags to some, who called for an accountability mechanism to
keep managers honest in the execution of their duties. For Columbia law
professor Adolf Berle, that mechanism was an exclusive focus on shareholders' interests. Berle argued that making the purpose of the corporation, and the sole focus of managerial decision-making, the creation of
profit for shareholders would rein in managers' discretion and keep them
accountable for their decisions.[9] Shareholder governance would be used

to control management power. Berle viewed corporate powers as held in trust for shareholders, while Dodd saw them as held in trust for the entire community.

Dodd's argument won the day, perhaps because it reflected the way business actually thought about itself. For the next few decades, business leaders generally believed that the corporations they operated should help address societal ills by, for example, providing employment to the long-term unemployed, avoiding pollution, or fighting discrimination. Generally, business was seen as owing something in return to the communities that granted them legal protections and provided an economy within which they could grow.

Shareholder Capitalism: Narrowing the Focus of Business Purpose

The managerial capitalist perspective saw its first significant challenge in 1970 when *New York Times Magazine* published an opinion essay titled "The Social Responsibility of Business is to Increase its Profits."[10] The essay, written by economist Milton Friedman, ushered in the age of shareholder capitalism. Friedman argued that the only objective of a business should be to increase profits for shareholders and that using corporate resources to address stakeholder concerns such as discrimination or pollution was essentially stealing from the shareholders. The ultimate measure of corporate success for Friedman was how much the corporation maximized wealth for shareholders, regardless of the impact of corporate actions on other stakeholders. Friedman did recognize that corporations must abide by the law and society's ethical norms, but argued that outside of that, corporations owed no responsibilities to anyone other than shareholders.

The concept of shareholder capitalism received a further boost when an economics article written several years later spelled out the so-called "agency cost problem."[11] Harkening back to Adolf Berle's contention that managers' and shareholders' interests diverged, the agency cost argument used agency law to go a step further. Shareholders, the theory contends, are the principals of a corporation who hire managers to act as their agents. Under agency law, the agent must act only for the principal and, in this context, that means the corporation's managers' sole focus is maximizing wealth for the shareholders. Any other use of corporate resources violates the principal-agent relationship, creating agency costs for the shareholders.

Despite the popularity of the arguments behind Friedman's article and the agency cost theory in academic circles, shareholder capitalism and what is generally known as shareholder primacy remained the minority position into the 1980s, with most business leaders retaining the traditional view that business bore responsibilities to all stakeholders, not simply shareholders. A statement issued by The Business Roundtable (TBR) in 1981 illuminates how corporate leaders viewed the relationship between business and society. That organization's "Statement of Corporate Responsibility" noted that corporations operate within a web of relationships with a variety of stakeholders; business recognizes its symbiotic relationship with society since the corporation's viability depends upon discharging the responsibilities it has to the society of which it is a part.[12]

By the mid-1980s, however, the situation had changed, and corporations rethought the notion of corporate purpose. Globalization loosened business's ties with local communities, weakening its stakeholder focus. Further, globalization altered the competitive landscape for American companies, exposing them to competition from foreign companies that decreased profits and returns to shareholders. The stock market decline of the 1970s was the result of this dynamic and created disappointment for shareholders. In the 1980s, companies with lagging stock prices became targets of hostile takeovers (i.e., attempts by rival companies or corporate raiders to buy the company's stock to gain control of the corporation). Shareholders dissatisfied with corporate stock performance were only too happy to sell out to the raiders. To counter the rash of hostile takeover bids, corporate executives adopted a single-minded focus on profits and share prices to keep shareholders happy and the executives in control of the corporation. The era of corporate concern for stakeholder interests as embodied in managerial capitalism gave way to shareholder capitalism and business's narrow focus on the interests of shareholders alone.

While TBR in 1981 espoused the view that a company's purpose was to serve society, by 1997 it had changed direction, declaring that the "principal objective of a business enterprise is to generate economic returns to its owners" and that the purpose of corporate governance is to ensure that focus on shareholder wealth maximization.[13] Before long, shareholder capitalism had become more than the dominant philosophy; it had become dogma that few questioned.

An elaborate corporate governance infrastructure in law and finance developed to support Friedman's vision of shareholder capitalism. For example, corporations in the United States were required to disclose information for investors, but the law presumed that the only information investors wanted was that on the financial condition of the company—not information related to other impacts the corporations might have on other stakeholders. Corporate lawyers contributed to the move toward shareholder capitalism by distorting a fundamental question of corporate governance: who does the board of directors owe duties to? Advocates of shareholder primacy began to argue that boards had duties only to shareholders, while corporate law had previously been clear that directors owe fiduciary duties to the corporation itself, rather than to shareholders.

The shareholder primacy position was strengthened by a 1986 case examining corporate directors' duties to shareholders when a company has put itself up for sale.[14] Under those narrow circumstances, the court held that the board was required to prioritize the financial gain to shareholders; as a result many corporate lawyers began to routinely advise their business clients against any actions that would lower the company's stock price.

Finally, while even Milton Friedman acknowledged that business must follow the rules of the game in pursuing profit, the laws and norms under which business operates are not set by impartial referees. Under the 2010 *Citizens United* case, business was granted the right to spend unlimited amounts on political campaigns.[15] In the years since this opinion, companies have routinely spent millions of dollars to support political candidates and lobby legislatures to gain regulation that is favorable to business and its shareholders, often at the expense of other stakeholders.[16]

The financial community, as personified by Wall Street, contributed to this infrastructure with its short-term mindset and fixation on quarterly earnings. Companies that miss earnings projections often see their stock prices drop and their chief executive's job in jeopardy. Corporate executives have another reason to cater to Wall Street's short-termism: executive compensation is routinely tied to the short-term performance of the company's stock.[17] The idea of connecting executives' pay to stock performance relates back to the agency cost problem. One way to keep the agent (here, corporate executives) acting for the interest of the principal (the shareholders) is to create a situation where they have the same thing at stake. Shareholders were presumed to care only about stock price and linking executive pay to stock price meant that the principal and agent now cared about the same thing—stock price. Presumably, then, executives would act to increase stock price because it served their interests as well as the shareholders' interests.

While shareholder capitalism may have produced positive impacts for a small cadre of corporate shareholders, it produced significant negative impacts for other stakeholder groups. Three trends—short-termism, deepening inequality, and the erosion of social capital—highlight this negative impact.

1. Short-termism: Shareholder primacy is the foundation for the current corporate focus on short-term profit making. As corporate executives concentrated their attention on satisfying shareholder and Wall Street demands for increased profits, they inevitably sacrificed long-term value creation for short-term profit increases. The short-term mindset eroded protections for workers, the environment, and even the long-term viability of the corporation as corporate leaders underinvested in innovation, research and development, workforce improvement, and capital expenditures. Profit that once was reinvested into the corporation to improve its performance was now paid out as dividends to placate shareholders. Short-termism devalues employee commitment to the firm and makes it impossible to plan for environmental issues such as climate change and resource scarcity that play out over the long term, in years or decades rather than quarters.

2. Deepening inequality: Shareholder capitalism with its short-term focus on creating value for shareholders deepened economic inequality and bred a populism that some say may threaten capitalism itself. In a 2014 article, billionaire entrepreneur Nick Hanauer worried that inequality was increasing at such a fast rate that the United States was becoming "less a capitalist society and more a feudal society"[18] characterized by an elite that controlled nearly all the wealth, with many poor people, and no middle class. For example, in 2020, the wealthiest one percent of Americans owned over thirty percent of the nation's wealth, while the bottom fifty percent of the population owned under two percent of the wealth.[19] Hanauer predicted that at some point extreme inequality would become destabilizing as the have-nots with little to lose start pushing back against the system that created the inequality.

Shareholder capitalism played a role in this concentration of wealth generally, as well as in the growing gap between executive compensation and worker pay. Corporations tied executive pay to company stock price to avoid the agency cost problem. Today, stock options comprise an average of 85 percent of CEO compensation, and this has created the huge gap between executive and employee pay. Since 1978, CEO compensation has grown 1,322 percent, while typical worker compensation has increased just 18 percent; in 2020, top CEOs earned 351 times more than the typical worker.[20] Executives worked to build profit for shareholders, often by minimizing expenditures for employee wages and benefits, but also benefitting themselves through the stock-related portion of their compensation. Ironically, even as corporate executives ostensibly championed shareholder capitalism, they worked to minimize shareholder involvement in corporate governance by lobbying against initiatives that would have given shareholders more voice in corporate decisions.

3. Erosion of social capital: Shareholder primacy ushered in a new phase of American economic life and weakened norms of behavior. The singular focus on profit gave rise to a situation where greed and the single-minded pursuit of self-interest became the norm rather than the exception, something to be proud of rather than frowned upon. "Greed is good" became the rallying cry for shareholder capitalism and normalized selfishness.[21] But this focus on corporations' and shareholders' self-interest ignored the fact that business was often complicit in creating social ills. Many people believed business had some responsibility to contribute to correcting those ills, especially because business benefitted so greatly.

Disillusionment with America's shareholder capitalism grew following the 2008 financial crisis in the United States. The Tea Party movement railed against what it called crony capitalism, the collaboration of government and business elites at the expense of workers and small business.[22] Meanwhile, the Occupy Wall Street movement, whose slogan was "We are the 99%," embodied objections to the economic inequalities and income disparities it viewed as created by the power of corporations.[23] For many, the crisis revealed the perils of short-termism and how shareholder primacy fueled systemic imbalance. It revitalized examination of the role of the corporation in society and Friedman's shareholder capitalism.

Stakeholder Capitalism: Business's Web of Relationships

The social movements of the 1960s and 1970s raised questions about the role of business in society. These concerns were eclipsed by the stock market decline in the 1970s and it was not until the early 1980s that the question resurfaced. Even as Friedman's doctrine of shareholder primacy was gaining traction among corporate executives, others were developing theories of more inclusive forms of capitalism, often called stakeholder capitalism. Management professor R. Edward Freeman's 1984 book *Strategic Management: A Stakeholder Approach* provided a platform to discuss stakeholder capitalism.[24] Freeman took issue with those who argued that corporations could maximize their value by focusing solely on profits for shareholders. He saw capitalism as a system where the interests of no one group dominated all others, where all stakeholders worked together to create long-term value. This view of capitalism jettisoned short-termism in favor of achieving sustainable value, value that existed over the long term. Serving stakeholders was essential to creating this sustainable value.

The tenets of stakeholder capitalism appeared to run afoul of existing corporate governance structures that focused on maximizing shareholder wealth, leading to creation of different mechanisms for pursuing stakeholder capitalism. For example, the corporate social responsibility movement can be seen as a corporate governance method where companies consider their responsibilities to stakeholders, not just shareholders. The latest iteration of this phenomenon is the 2019 Statement on the Purpose of Business released by TBR. In a position reminiscent of its 1981 statement, the organization recognized that all stakeholders are essential to business and proclaimed a commitment to deliver value to all stakeholders.[25] The rise of sustainability reporting by corporations is another tool of stakeholder capitalism. Environmental and social nonprofit organizations pressured companies to release information on their impact on the environment, workers, and communities where they operated. Organizations such as the Global Reporting Initiative created reporting frameworks for corporations to use to disclose their impacts on a broad array of stakeholder groups.[26]

Some U.S. states passed what are called corporate constituency statutes, statutes that allow corporate directors to consider the interests of stakeholders in addition to shareholders when making their decisions. These statutes are similar to the more recent innovation, the benefit corporation.

The benefit corporation is a form of corporation that includes in its initial charter a public purpose. As the corporation is created, the company's responsibility to society is explicitly stated in its founding document and becomes part of its legal responsibility. Under Delaware's law, for example, a public benefit corporation is intended to produce a public benefit or public benefits and to operate in a responsible and sustainable manner. A public benefit is some positive effect on people, entities, communities, or interests other than shareholders.[27] To date, thirty-eight U.S. states have passed benefit corporation legislation, demonstrating the growing movement to broaden corporate purpose.

As useful as these new corporate governance mechanisms may be, they are working largely at the fringes of corporate control without moving capitalism's focus away from shareholder power. However, a federal law proposed in 2018 seeks to fundamentally alter corporate governance infrastructure and has the potential to establish a form of stakeholder capitalism through stakeholder governance of corporations. The Accountable Capitalism Act (ACA),[28] introduced by Senator Elizabeth Warren, proposes sweeping structural changes in how large corporations are governed in the United States, changes that redefine corporate purpose while federalizing corporate governance. Under the ACA, corporations with more than one billion dollars in revenue must be chartered by the federal government as most corporations were until the late nineteenth century. The statute broadens corporate purpose and the obligations of corporate directors by requiring directors to consider the interests of all stakeholders. To promote accountability, the ACA would alter corporate control structures by having employees elect 40 percent of corporate board members. The idea behind Senator Warren's proposal is to close the gap between corporate law and social welfare by aligning corporate governance and business purpose with the interests of society, rather than just shareholders.

Conclusion

The story of American capitalism is the story of development and use of the corporation in an evolving American economy and society. Business and corporations started as relatively simple organizations, located in and with strong ties to communities. Business saw itself as a member of the communities whose success depended on the health of the community.

As business grew in size and complexity, shareholders' interests came to dominate a form of capitalism that no longer attempted to balance the competing interests of stakeholders. Shareholders' interests have reigned supreme since the 1980s when shareholder capitalism became the definition of American capitalism.

We might question, given the established tradition of business seeing itself as a member of the community, why so much of the American economic and business establishment ultimately flocked to Milton Friedman's view of capitalism. One possible answer is that Friedman's view of capitalism provides a simple answer to a complex question. Deciding the purpose of business and its appropriate role in society touches on the fundamental values and norms that undergird society, where deep disagreements may lie. Defining business as making profit for shareholders simplifies this question. It may also be thought to provide a bulwark against corporate executives having to engage in balancing a complex array of competing interests among stakeholders.

This simplified perspective, however, cannot eliminate the reality that business operates in an increasingly complex environment, with growing calls for improved environmental performance, better treatment of workers throughout global supply chains, and a longer-term view that considers the impact of today's actions on tomorrow's children. Managerial capitalism and stakeholder capitalism embrace complexity, while shareholder capitalism rejected it. Refusing to deal with complexity does not mean complexity disappears. Events such as the 2008 financial crisis highlight some of the fault lines in shareholder capitalism and threaten to rupture the social contract between the American people and American capitalism. To the extent that capitalism depends on public trust for its legitimacy and survival, it is clearly time to move toward a more sustainable form of capitalism.

Notes

1.   Alfred D. Chandler Jr., "The Beginnings of the Modern Industrial Corporation," *Proceedings of the American Philosophical Society* 130, no. 4 (December 1986): 382–89.
2.   Charles W. Carey Jr., "Corporations and Big Business," *Nineteenth Century U.S. Newspapers*, Cengage Learning, 2008, https://www.gale.com/intl/essays/charles-w-carey-jr-corporations-big-business.

3. Carey, "Corporations and Big Business."

4. For a detailed discussion of the evolution of the corporate form, see Colin Mayer, *Prosperity: Better Business Makes the Greater Good* (Oxford University Press, 2018), 63–80.

5. Duncan McCann and Christine Berry, *Shareholder Capitalism—A System in Crisis* (New Economics Foundation, 2017); Tyler Halloran, "A Brief History of the Corporate Form and Why it Matters," *Fordham Journal of Corporate & Financial Law*, November 18, 2018.

6. Halloran, "A Brief History of the Corporate Form"; Ciara Torres-Spelliscy, "Does 'We the People' Include Corporations?," *Human Rights Magazine* 42, no. 2 (American Bar Association 2018).

7. Harwell Wells, "The Modernization of Corporation Law 1920–1940." *University of Pennsylvania Journal of Business Law* 11, no. 573 (2009):584

8. E. Merrick Dodd Jr., "For Whom Are Corporate Managers Trustees?," *Harvard Law Review* 45, no. 7 (May 1932).

9. A. A. Berle Jr., "Corporate Powers as Powers in Trust," *Harvard Law Review* 44, no. 7 (May 1931).

10. Milton Friedman, "A Friedman Doctrine—The Social Responsibility of Business Is to Increase Its Profits," *New York Times Magazine*, September 13, 1970, https://nyti.ms/1LSi5ZD.

11. Michael C. Jensen and William H. Meckling, "Theory of the Firm: Managerial Behavior, Agency Costs and Ownership Structure," *Journal of Financial Economics* 3, no. 4, (October 1976).

12. The Business Roundtable (TBR) is a nonprofit lobbying organization whose members are chief executive officers of major U.S. corporations. Business Roundtable, Statement on the Purpose of a Corporation (2019).

13. Business Roundtable, Statement on the Purpose of a Corporation, 1.

14. The case was *Revlon, Inc. v. MacAndrews & Forbes Holdings, Inc.* and involved a situation where Revlon Inc. had decided to "go private," i.e., buy back all of its outstanding shares of stock. The Delaware Court of Chancery held that, in this circumstance, the directors must put the interests of shareholders first and accept the highest price offered for the company's stock. *Revlon, Inc. v. MacAndrews & Forbes Holdings, Inc., 506 A.2d 173, 175 (Delaware 1986).*

15. *Citizens United v. F.E.C., 558 U.S. 310, 318 (2010).*

16. See Chapter 3, this volume.

17. Steven Pearlstein, "Social Capital, Corporate Purpose and the Revival of American Capitalism" (Center for Effective Public Management at Brookings, 2014), 7, 9–10.

18. Nick Hanauer, "The Pitchforks are Coming . . . for Us Plutocrats," *Politico*, August 2014.

19. Tommy Beer, "Top 1% Of U.S. Households Hold 15 Times More Wealth Than Bottom 50% Combined," *Forbes*, October 8, 2020.

20. Abigail Johnson Hess, "In 2020, top CEOs earned 351 times more than the typical worker," *CNBC*, September 15, 2021.

21. This phrase was coined by the character Gordon Gekko in the 1987 film *Wall Street*. *Wall Street*, directed by Oliver Stone (1987; Twentieth Century Fox).

22. Michael Lind, "Why Big Business Fears the Tea Party," *Politico*, June 15, 2014. For an overview of the Tea Party Movement, see Michael Ray, "Tea Party movement," *Britannica*, May 5, 2023.

23. Brian Greene, "How 'Occupy Wall Street' Started and Spread," *U.S. News*, October 17, 2011; Michael Levitin, "The Triumph of Occupy Wall Street," *Atlantic*, June 10, 2015.

24. Edward R. Freeman, *Strategic Management: A Stakeholder Approach* (Boston: Pitman, 1984).

25. Business Roundtable, Statement on the Purpose of a Corporation.

26. Global Reporting Initiative, "About GRI," https://www.globalreporting.org/about-gri/.

27. Del. Code Ann., tit. 8, §§361-62 (2020).

28. Accountable Capitalism Act, S. 3348, 115th Congress (2017–2018).

9

Capitalism and Respecting Human Rights

David Hess

In the 1990s, the U.S. model of capitalism "reigned supreme" in the world.[1] The U.S. economy saw exceptional growth and corporations searched the globe for opportunities for greater returns. During this time, corporations established the complex supply chains that we know today, with networks of contractual relationships spread over multiple countries. By the early 2000s, for example, Nike's supplier network included over nine hundred factories in fifty different countries.[2] Due to globalization, corporations entered markets in countries with "challenging sociopolitical contexts"[3] and were often unprepared to face the ethical issues of operating in countries that had different standards on human rights issues than those corporations' home country.[4]

Likewise, national governments were not prepared to regulate the global economy; home-country governments were limited in regulating the operations of their corporations overseas and host-country governments were ineffective in regulating domestic operations. As a result, multinational corporations gained tremendous political power. Commentators described a "race to the bottom," where developing nations relaxed regulations on worker protections in the hopes of attracting international investment.[5] Activists complained that multinational corporations' quest to increase profits by reducing production costs led to "sweatshop" conditions in the factories that made their products. Corporations deflected responsibility by focusing on the fact that their suppliers were separate legal entities. This was reflected in Nike's initial response to allegations of sweatshop conditions in their suppliers, which was simply that "we don't make shoes."[6]

The attitude of the public was changing, however, and there was a demand that corporations respect human rights in their operations throughout the world, regardless of the local government's lack of action or whether the company committing the human rights abuse only had a contractual relationship with the corporation. Some of the key incidents that helped precipitate this change included the previously mentioned allegations of sweatshops in Nike's supply chain, Yahoo's disclosure of a journalist's identity to the Chinese government that led to the journalist's imprisonment, and Shell's refusal to intervene in the Nigerian government's execution of Ken Saro-Wiwa, an activist who protested the harm caused by Shell's oil operations in the country.[7] In response to such incidents, global actors' attention shifted from an exclusive focus on the human rights abuses of governments and towards the responsibilities of corporations such as Nike, Yahoo, and Shell.

This chapter explores the human rights impacts of capitalism and the ability of governments and other stakeholders to exercise social control over corporations through market and nonmarket pressures. In particular, this chapter focuses on a significant criticism of global capitalism: that corporations' pursuit of profits by continually seeking to lower input costs leads to the exploitation of labor (and other negative human rights impacts), especially in nations with ineffective regulatory systems. In other words, global capitalism is not always a story of the pursuit of profits bringing employment opportunities and beneficial economic growth to low-income countries but is also a story of increased labor exploitation due to the spread of global supply chains.

This chapter begins by discussing the human rights problem of modern slavery in global supply chains. This is a problem that has gained the attention of regulators in the past decade and illustrates the challenges of regulating a corporation's human rights responsibilities. It is an example that will be returned to throughout this chapter. The next section considers how business models contribute to the persistence of modern slavery. This is followed by a discussion of the limits of the law to hold corporations accountable for their negative human right impacts. The final sections concern recent soft-law and hard-law developments that seek to improve corporate behavior and increase accountability.

The Problem of Modern Slavery and Global Supply Chains

Modern slavery is an umbrella term that covers such practices as forced labor, debt bondage, forced child labor, and human trafficking.[8] In brief, the term "refers to situations of exploitation that a person cannot refuse or leave because of threats, violence, coercion, deception, and/or abuse of power."[9] Freedom from all forms of modern slavery is an established human right, such as under Article 4 of the Universal Declaration of Human Rights (UDHR),[10] and is prohibited by International Labour Organization (ILO) conventions[11] and United Nations Conventions.[12] The United Nations Sustainable Development Goals' Target 8.7 establishes the goal to "eradicate forced labour, end modern slavery and human trafficking and secure the prohibition and elimination of the worst forms of child labour."[13]

Despite the universal condemnation of the practice, modern slavery still thrives. In 2016, the ILO conservatively estimated that there were over forty million people in modern slavery.[14] This number included twenty-five million people in forced labor. Of that number, sixteen million people are victims of forced labor in the private sector and the ILO estimates that they generate profits for business of over $40 billion annually.[15]

Products known or presumed to have been produced at least in part by forced labor regularly reach consumers in developed country markets. For example, in 2020, the media reported that products from companies such as Apple, Dell, and Nike were linked to the forced labor of Muslim minority groups in the Xinjiang region of China.[16] In 2015, consumers sued Costco under allegations that it failed to disclose that the farm-raised prawns sold in its grocery section were fed with fishmeal caught by forced labor.[17] In addition, the U.S. Department of Labor maintains a list of international goods made with forced labor. This list includes food items, such as bananas, coffee, and cocoa, as well as minerals used in batteries and electronics, and cotton used in clothing.[18]

These examples demonstrate the numerous ways that forced labor can enter a company's supply chain. For an apparel company, for example, forced labor may exist in a tier-one supplier, such as a company that sews together the final product. However, these exploitive practices are more likely to enter the supply chain due to that tier-one supplier subcontracting part of its work to a third party, which may be part of the informal economy.[19] Or, looking further upstream in the supply chain, the producers of the cotton used in the garment may have used forced labor.

Business Models and Modern Slavery

Modern slavery does not appear in supply chains despite multinational corporations' best efforts to avoid it; instead, corporate practices can be a root
cause of these adverse human rights impacts. In their efforts to increase
profits, corporations place severe economic pressures on suppliers that
impact those suppliers' practices, and have ripple effects further upstream
in the supply chain. The primary pressure is for suppliers to reduce costs,
but corporations may also create pressures due to short lead times to complete work, severe penalties for missed deadlines, late changes on orders
already in progress, delays in making payments to suppliers, and encouraging competition between suppliers by agreeing to only short-term contracts. Combined, these actions place significant pressure on suppliers to
cut corners on safety measures, utilize questionable subcontractors, and
take other actions that can connect the lead corporation's operations and
products to adverse human rights impacts.

Despite corporations being a significant factor in the resulting labor
exploitation, corporations avoid accountability for their actions. Tsing refers
to this as "supply chain capitalism."[20] In the drive to increase efficiencies
and reduce costs, corporations establish "commodity chains based on subcontracting, outsourcing, and allied arrangements in which the autonomy
of component enterprises is legally established even as the enterprises are
disciplined within the chain as a whole."[21] Through a system of contractual
relationships—which allows a corporation to avoid legal responsibility
for the actions of others in the network as described further below—the
power becomes concentrated in the lead corporation.[22] Corporations seek
this power because there are significant agency and transactions costs in
these supply chain networks and the ability to exercise significant control
helps ensure that the corporation's gains exceed those costs.[23] Due to the
dependence of the supply chain actors on this business model to gain access
to markets, the lead corporation can use its power to negotiate contracts
that are unfavorable to suppliers.

Market and nonmarket actors, such as consumers, social investors, and
civil society organizations, have placed pressure on corporations to take
responsibility for potential human rights impacts in their supply chains
and to self-regulate. These pressures have had limited effectiveness, however, as corporations have been able to place those social performance
obligations on suppliers without the corporations changing their business

models. In brief, lead firms created new obligations on suppliers to improve on a variety of indicators measuring human rights performance, but those suppliers were still required to meet the same contractual terms on price, quality, and time, as well as continuing pressure to reduce costs.[24] Thus, corporations sought to demonstrate responsibility to external stakeholders without changing their own business practices.

Starting in the 1990s, the primary mechanism used by corporations to demonstrate responsibility in supply chains, such as avoiding modern slavery, was the social audit. Social audits are inspections of suppliers' factories carried out on behalf of lead corporations to determine if suppliers are in compliance with the corporation's standards of conduct. By contracting only with suppliers that pass the audit, this mechanism allows a corporation to claim that their products are not tainted by human rights violations. Unfortunately, social audits are well-known by those in the human rights field to be ineffective.[25] Among their problems, social audits rely on a very limited inspection process, focus only on tier-one suppliers, are subject to fraud and corruption, and the auditors may have significant conflicts of interest but little accountability for the quality of their work. In fact, some go so far as to claim that social audits are an elaborate ruse; corporations and suppliers both want a clean social audit with as little operational or cost change as possible, and social auditors, which suffer from conflicts of interest, are happy to provide such audits in return for continued business.

Lack of Accountability Under the Law

In addition to the ineffectiveness of self-regulation, government regulation has also been limited in its ability to control corporate behavior. The governments where the suppliers, subcontractors, and raw materials producers are located should protect the workers in those countries and prevent human rights abuses. However, those governments are often unable to do so, for a variety of reasons.[26] First, domestic legislation may be insufficient. Using the modern slavery example, domestic law may not adequately define forced labor, which hampers government efforts to prosecute perpetrators. Second, even with sufficient legislation, the government may lack the resources to investigate potential cases. Without the inspection of workplaces, violators of the law may act with impunity while compliant businesses operate at a competitive disadvantage. In addition, as stated above, the informal economy is a common way for modern slavery to enter supply chains, and operations in the informal economy are even more difficult for under-resourced government agencies to police.

The victims of human rights abuses not only have a lack of access to remedies in the country of the violation, but they are also precluded from seeking to hold the lead corporation—that benefits from the lower production costs related to modern slavery, for example—accountable in that corporation's home country. Chambers identifies three different "veils" that protect the multinational corporation: the corporate veil, the contractual veil, and the jurisdictional veil.[27] The corporate veil protects a parent corporation from the liabilities caused by a subsidiary corporation because the law treats them as two separate legal entities. Similarly, the contractual veil protects a corporation from the misdeeds of its suppliers, because they are separate entities and their relationship is based solely on contracts. The jurisdictional veil "limits the home state's power to exercise its legal authority extraterritorially in order to prescribe rules and adjudicate disputes when harm occurs in the host state."[28] There are some exceptions to the above veils, such as if the parent corporation itself owed a duty to victims based on its own actions and not the actions of the subsidiary, but those are limited and still developing.

The United Nations Guiding Principles on Business and Human Rights

Many in the international-policy community found the growth in power of corporations described above combined with their lack of accountability highly problematic. This led to the response that has had the greatest impact to date: the United Nations Guiding Principles on Business and Human Rights (UNGPs).[29] The United Nations Human Rights Council endorsed the UNGPs in 2011, and they have become the authoritative framework on business and human rights for business, states, and civil society.

The UNGPs are the implementation of the 2008 Protect, Respect, and Remedy Framework. This framework established that the state has the responsibility to protect human rights, business has a responsibility to respect human rights, and both have a responsibility to provide a remedy to victims of human rights abuse. The UNGPs explain how states and businesses should implement this framework.

Corporations' responsibility to respect human rights "means that they should avoid infringing on the human rights of others and should address adverse human rights impacts with which they are involved."[30] To meet their responsibilities, the UNGPs require businesses to conduct human rights due diligence (HRDD). This process involves "assessing actual and potential human rights impacts, integrating and acting upon the findings, tracking responses, and communicating how impacts are addressed."[31] Thus, businesses must "have in place policies and processes through which they can both know and show that they respect human rights in practice."[32]

Under the UNGPs, businesses can be connected to human rights abuses in one of three ways, which then impacts their required response. First, the business could cause the adverse impact by its own, direct actions. Second, a business could contribute to another party's violations either directly or indirectly. For example, in the previously mentioned instance, Yahoo directly contributed to a violation by disclosing a journalist's identity to the Chinese government. An example of an indirect contribution would be a multinational garment company making last-minute changes to a supplier's order that pushes the supplier to use exploitive labor practices in order to meet the new requirement. Finally, a business may be directly linked to an adverse impact if that impact is caused by a party with whom the company has a business relationship, and the actions relate to the company's operations, products, or services. Thus, a corporation would be directly linked to modern slavery if its tier-one supplier subcontracted part of its contract to an entity in the informal economy that used forced labor.

If the company causes or contributes to a human rights violation, then it "should take the necessary steps to cease or prevent its contribution,"[33] and provide, or cooperate in the provision of, remediation.[34] If the company is only in directly linked to the harm, then the company's response will depend on such factors as its leverage over the entity causing the abuse and the severity of the abuse.[35] If the company lacks leverage to end the other entity's abuse, then it should consider ending the relationship (if it can do so in a manner that does not cause an adverse impact).[36]

It is important to note that the UNGPs are "soft law," which means that they have no binding legal impact on corporations. Instead, the UNGPs establish norms of expected behavior. The next section discusses how states have used legislation to attempt to overcome the previously mentioned limits of self-regulation and legal accountability and incentivize corporations to meaningfully implement the UNGPs.

Business and Human Rights Legislation

Legislative attempts to codify the UNGPs, especially as they relate to modern slavery, have focused primarily on transparency. The goal of this regulatory approach is to harness market and nonmarket pressures to improve corporate performance. The first example of such legislation was the California Transparency in Supply Chains Act of 2010, which was soon followed by the U.K. Modern Slavery Act of 2015 and the Australia Modern Slavery Act of 2018.[37] Under these laws, corporations are required to disclose what due diligence actions, if any, they have taken to ensure that modern slavery is not present in their supply chains. Although these laws have raised awareness of the modern slavery issue, they have not had a significant impact on corporate practices.

The limited impact of this legislative approach on corporate behavior is not surprising, as transparency initiatives on corporate social responsibility (CSR) issues in general have had limited effect on corporate behavior.[38] Instead of transparency requirements forcing corporations to rethink their practices and adopt appropriate due-diligence procedures based on the risks related to their operations, corporations treat disclosure as an end in itself. That is, rather than using the disclosure process to evaluate their performance and make appropriate changes, corporations simply seek to match their existing practices to the requirements of the disclosure framework.[39] Typically, the disclosures focus on process-oriented metrics (e.g., percent of employees receiving training on the company's code of conduct) rather than performance outcomes. In addition, because stakeholders, such as consumers, are unable to meaningfully evaluate corporate practices—especially since different companies face different risks based on their size, industry, supply chain practices, and geographic location of operations and suppliers—they are not able to use market pressure to drive change.[40]

Due to the ineffectiveness of disclosure laws and the inability of the market to improve corporate practices, several home countries of leading multinational corporations are exploring more direct regulation and are mandating that corporations undertake human rights due diligence. The first country to adopt such a law was France in 2017, with the French Duty of Vigilance Act.[41] This was followed with different variations of mandatory human rights due diligence laws in countries such as the Netherlands, Germany, and Norway.[42] There is also work at the United Nations on a business and human rights treaty that would include mandatory due diligence.[43] Depending on how the law is structured, mandatory human rights due diligence is a significant government intrusion into the internal affairs of the corporation; that is, the appropriate governance structures and practices are not being determined by the market but by regulators.

Under the French law, corporations of a certain size are required to conduct, and publicly disclose, their human rights due diligence policies and practices for their supply chain. The corporation should consult its stakeholders when developing this "vigilance plan."[44] The law also provides victims of a human rights abuse with a cause of action against the company. The plaintiff must show that the company failed to adopt an adequate vigilance plan and that failure resulted in the victim's harm. In other words, the plaintiff must show that an adequate plan would have prevented the harm caused by the company or some other party in the supply chain with whom the company has an established commercial relationship. In some countries, the law does not provide for a cause of action for victims but focuses only on mandating due diligence practices under threat of penalty. A recent draft of the business and human rights treaty included both a mandatory due diligence requirement and a liability provision, including liability for the actions of certain business partners (including suppliers), if the company should have foreseen the risk of harm and "fail[s] to take adequate measures to prevent the abuse."[45]

In addition to actions that mandate certain governance processes or attempt to influence behavior by expanding potential liability to victims, governments are starting to directly intervene in the market. In the United States, Customs and Border Protection (CBP) has started using its authority under Section 307 of the Tariff Act of 1930[46] to ban goods from entering the United States that were produced, at least in part, with forced labor. If the CBP issues a ban—which is done through a Withhold Release Order (WRO)—then the importer has the burden to refute the finding with sufficient evidence that forced labor was not connected to their products.[47]

Currently, the use of WROs is limited. Between 2016 and January 2021, the CBP issued twenty-nine WROs.[48] The CBP has limited resources to investigate claims, especially if the violation is further upstream in the supply chain (though, non-governmental organizations (NGOs) may alert the CBP to cases). Other countries are calling for the adoption of similar laws,[49] which would potentially allow for coordination between governments' enforcement efforts. In addition, in the United States, the government has shown a willingness to take further actions in this area for high-profile cases. In 2021, the United States passed the Uyghur Forced Labor Prevention Act, which targets the problems in Xinjiang described above.[50] The Act creates a rebuttable presumption that all goods made at least in part in the Xinjiang region are made with forced labor and are therefore banned from entering the United States. Rebutting the presumption includes showing that the company has conducted appropriate human rights due diligence.

Conclusions

Global capitalism has the potential to bring employment and economic development throughout the world, including in lower-income countries. A key factor driving this global spread is corporations' pursuit of increased profits through reduced production costs. This pursuit, however, often comes at the expense of respecting human rights, such as through labor exploitation. For example, the pressures that downstream corporations place on their suppliers are a significant cause for the use of forced labor. Local governments are often unable or unwilling to adequately protect their citizens from such abuses, and the three different "veils" described above have prevented effective regulation by home country governments.

In response, governments are adopting new approaches. At first, governments focused on harnessing the power of the market to control corporate behavior by mandating certain nonfinancial disclosures. This approach has had limited effectiveness. Thus, some governments have experimented with more direct interventions. Mandatory human rights due diligence laws impact the corporate governance practices of corporations. Import bans are direct interventions into the functioning of markets. The goal of both approaches is to change respecting human rights from a voluntary, corporate social responsibility activity to a legal obligation. However, it is too early to know whether these approaches can be effective. If corporations do not meaningfully implement HRDD practices and the legal system is unable to distinguish symbolic versus substantive HRDD, then the harms caused by global capitalism and the pursuit of lower costs and higher profits will continue.

Notes

1. Joseph Stiglitz, *Roaring Nineties: A New History of the World's Most Prosperous Decade* (W. W. Norton, 2004).
2. Anna Tsing, "What Is Emerging? Supply Chains and the Remaking of Asia," *Professional Geographer* 68, no. 2 (2015): 148.
3. John Gerard Ruggie, *Just Business: Multinational Corporations and Human Rights* (W. W. Norton, 2013), 33.
4. Thomas Donaldson, "Values in Tension: Ethics Away from Home," *Harvard Business Review*, October 1996, 48.
5. Surya Deva, "Sustainable Good Governance and Corporations: An Analysis of Asymmetries," *Georgetown International Environmental Law Review* 18 (April 2006): 714–27.
6. David Hess, "Combating Corruption through Corporate Transparency Using Enforcement Discretion to Improve Disclosure," *Minnesota Journal of International Law* 318 (2012): 693.
7. Ruggie, *Just Business*, 9–16.
8. U.S. Department of State, "What is Modern Slavery?," https://www.state.gov/what-is-modern-slavery/.
9. United Nations, "International Day for the Abolition of Slavery, 2 December," https://www.un.org/en/observances/slavery-abolition-day.
10. G.A. Res. 217 (III) A, Universal Declaration of Human Rights (December 10, 1948).
11. International Labour Organization, "C029—Forced Labour Convention, 1930 (No. 29)."
12. International Covenant on Civil and Political Rights, March 1976, 999 U.S.T. 171.
13. United Nations, "Sustainable Development Goals: Target 8.7," https://www.unodc.org/roseap/en/sustainable-development-goals.html.
14. International Labour Organization and Walk Free Foundation, *Global Estimates of Modern Slavery: Forced Labour and Forced Marriage* (International Labour Organization), 9–10.
15. International Labour Organization, *Profits and Poverty: The Economics of Forced Labour* (International Labour Organization), 9–10.
16. Ana Swanson, "Nike and Coca-Cola Lobby Against Xinjiang Forced Labor Bill," *New York Times*, November 29, 2020; Ana Fifield, "China Compels Uighurs to Work in Shoe Factory That Supplies Nike," *Washington Post*, February 29, 2020.
17. *Sud v. Costco Wholesale Corp.*, 229 F. Supp. 3d 1075 (N.D. Cal. 2017).
18. U.S. Department of Labor, "List of Goods Produced by Child Labor or Forced Labor," https://www.dol.gov/agencies/ilab/reports/child-labor/list-of-goods.
19. International Labour Organization, Ending Child Labour by 2025 (2018), 29.
20. Tsing, "Supply Chains," 148.
21. Tsing, "Supply Chains," 148.
22. Dan Danielson, "Trade, Distribution, and Development Under Supply Chain Capitalism," In *Globalization Reimagined: A Progressive Agenda for World*

Trade and Investment, edited by Alvaro Santos, Chantal Thomas, and David Trubek (Anthem Publishing, 2019), 122–23.

23. Danielson, "Trade, Distribution, and Development," 122–23.
24. Robert C. Bird and Vivek Soundararajan, "From Suspicion to Sustainability in Global Supply Chains," *Texas A&M Law Review* 7, no. 2 (2020): 392–93.
25. David Hess, "Modern Slavery in Global Supply Chains: Towards a Legislative Solution," *Cornell International Law Journal* 54, no. 2 (2021): 268.
26. International Labour Organization, Organization for Economic Co-operation and Development, International Organization for Migration, and United Nations Children's Fund, *Ending Child Labour, Forced Labour and Human Trafficking in Global Supply Chains*, Geneva: 2019, 17–28, https://www.ilo.org/ipec/Informationresources/WCMS716930/ lang-en/index.htm.
27. Rachel Chambers, "Parent Company Direct Liability for Overseas Human Rights Violations: Lessons from the U.K. Supreme Court," *University of Pennsylvania Journal of International Law* 42, no. 3 (2021): 529.
28. Chambers, "Parent Company Direct Liability," 530.
29. U.N. Special Representative of the Secretary General, Guiding Principles on Business and Human Rights: Implementing the United Nations "Protect, Respect and Remedy" Framework, U.N. Doc. HR/PUB/11/04 (United Nations, 2011).
30. U.N., Guiding Principles, 13.
31. U.N., Guiding Principles, 17–19.
32. U.N., Guiding Principles, 23–24.
33. U.N., Guiding Principles, 21.
34. U.N., Guiding Principles, 24–25.
35. U.N., Guiding Principles, 22.
36. U.N., Guiding Principles, 22.
37. Cal. Civ. Code § 1714.43 (2019); Modern Slavery Act 2015 c. 30 (UK), https://www.legislation.gov.uk/ukpga/2015/30/contents/enacted; Modern Slavery Act 2018 (Cth) (Austl.).
38. David Hess, "The Transparency Trap: Non-Financial Disclosure and the Responsibility of Business to Respect Human Rights," *American Business Law Journal* 56, no. 1 (Spring 2019): 31.
39. Michael Rogerson, Andrew Crane, Vivek Soundararajan, Johanne Ward-Grosvold, and Charles Cho, "Organisational Responses to Mandatory Modern Slavery Disclosure Legislation: A Failure of Experimentalist Governance?," *Accounting, Auditing & Accountability Journal* 33, no. 7 (2020): 1516–17.
40. Adam Chilton and Galit Sarfaty, "The Limitations of Supply Chain Disclosure Regimes," *Stanford Journal of International Law* 53, no. 1 (2017): 5–6.
41. Loi 2017-399 du 27 mars 2017 relative au devoir de vigilance des sociétés mères et des entreprises donneuses d'ordre (1) [Law 2017-399 of March 27, 2017 relating to the duty of vigilance of parent companies and ordering companies (1)] Journal Officiel de la République Française [J.O.] [Official Gazette of France], March 28, 2017.
42. Sam Eastwood, Susanne J. Harris, and Wei Na Sim, "Business and Human

Rights: New Universal Human Right To Access A Clean, Healthy And Sustainable Environment," Mayer Brown, August 5, 2022.

43. United Nations Human Rights Office of the High Commissioner, "Mandatory Human Rights Due Diligence," https://www.ohchr.org/en/special-procedures/wg-business/mandatory-human-rights-due-diligence-mhrdd/.

44. Légifrance Loi 2017-399 du 27 mars 2017, https://www.legifrance.gouv.fr/jorf/id/JORFTEXT000034290626/.

45. "Open-ended Intergovernmental Working Group on Transnational Corporations and Other Business Enterprises with Respect to Human Rights," https://www.ohchr.org/en/hr-bodies/hrc/wg-trans-corp/igwg-on-tnc//.

46. 19 U.S.C. § 1307.

47. Christopher A. Casey, Cathleen D. Cimino-Isaacs, and Katarina C. O'Regan, *Section 307 and U.S. Imports of Products of Forced Labor: Overview and Issues for Congress* (Congressional Research Service R46631, 2021), 1.

48. U.S. Government Accountability Office, "Forced Labor: Actions Needed to Better Prevent the Availability of At-Risk Goods in DOD's Commissaries and Exchanges" (February 3, 2022), 10.

49. Ursula von der Leyen, "State of the Union 2021," September 15, 2021, *European Commission.*

50. Uyghur Forced Labor Prevention Act, Pub. L. No. 117-78, 135 Stat. 1525-32 (codified as amended in scattered sections of 19 and 22 U.S.C).

10

Whose Capital?
Is Cooperative Ownership a More Sustainable Model for Capitalism?

Mark J. Kaswan

When we think of capitalism, particularly with regard to sustainability, we tend to think of large, investor-owned corporations: Walmart, GM, United Airlines, Chevron, and so on. This is reasonable, since these companies dominate not only the economy itself but also our thinking about the economy. However, "capitalism" can take different forms depending on who controls the capital. In this chapter I will discuss an alternative to the traditional investor-owned model,[1] one that, because it is inherently democratic and rooted in community, tends to be more sustainable: the cooperative.

Cooperatives are owned by their members and are democratic by design on the basis of one-member-one-vote. There are several different forms of cooperative—agricultural (producer) cooperatives, consumer cooperatives, worker cooperatives, and service cooperatives, as well as hybrid forms that combine parts of different forms. The members of the cooperative supply some of its capital through membership fees, and it may retain capital from its operations, but other capital needs are met without giving outside investors property rights—in other words, by renting it. The question is whether these member-controlled enterprises (which in some cases translates into their being community-controlled) are inherently more sustainable than the traditional form.

Although often dismissed as a fringe practice, cooperatives represent the largest alternative to traditional capitalism. With over a billion members worldwide, including an extensive presence in the United States and other advanced economies, they represent a kind of low-hanging fruit for reorienting the economy toward a more sustainable model. By rooting capital in communities through a structure that is inherently democratic, what we might call cooperative capitalism could lead to a more sustainable economic system.

What Is a Cooperative?

According to the International Cooperative Alliance (ICA), the apex organization for cooperative societies worldwide, "[a] cooperative is an autonomous association of persons united voluntarily to meet their common economic, social, and cultural needs and aspirations through a jointly owned and democratically controlled enterprise. Cooperatives are based on the values of self-help, self-responsibility, democracy, equality, equity, and solidarity. In the tradition of their founders, cooperative members believe in the ethical values of honesty, openness, social responsibility and caring for others."[2] This is notably different from the standard view of the typical for-profit corporation, which has a single purpose: increasing the value of the holdings of its stockholders, reflected in the current share price of its stock—so-called "shareholder primacy."[3]

A cooperative is a business, but with some significant differences from your typical company: it is owned and democratically controlled by the people who use it, who also are the ones who retain its net revenue, or profit. From humble beginnings in England in the first half of the nineteenth century, the global cooperative movement today is both extensive and diverse. The ICA bills itself as the world's largest non-governmental organization, with 233 member organizations representing over a billion people in over one hundred countries worldwide. In 1995 the United Nations (U.N.) estimated that nearly half the world's population is in some way affected by cooperatives. Indeed, the U.N. declared 2012 the International Year of the Cooperative in light of the movement's extensive global presence and substantive impact on people's lives.[4]

Cooperatives are well-integrated into all of the world's leading economies, including the U.S. As of 2009, there were nearly thirty thousand cooperatives in the United States operating seventy-three thousand places of business. Altogether, cooperatives in the U.S. own over $3 trillion in assets, generate over $500 billion in revenue and pay over $25 billion in wages. While the number of individuals who are co-op members is difficult to estimate (because one person or family can belong to more than one cooperative), cooperatives nationwide count over 350 million members, reflecting an estimated 120 million individuals.[5]

Any kind of business can be organized as a cooperative. A cooperative can be thought of as a kind of association, and the owners are the members of that association. In this way, they are no different from stockholders in a corporation. Also, like any other corporation, most cooperatives operate as for-profit entities,[6] and the profits are returned to the owners as a dividend (at least, what isn't used for debt service, held as retained earnings, or used in some other way the members may choose).

There are some important differences between a cooperative and a traditional corporation. One is that all of the members of the cooperative are equal as owners—that is, they all pay the same amount to join, and they are governed on the familiar democratic principle of one person-one vote.[7] This may take the form of direct participation in decision-making (common in small cooperatives), or there may be an elected board of directors. Another difference is that the profits are returned to members not on the basis of their level of investment (i.e., how many shares they own—since all members only own one share), but on the basis of how much they use the co-op.[8]

In terms of their operation, some small cooperatives are organized as collectives, in which all members participate in decision-making at a high level. However, many cooperatives operate like any other business, with a CEO and a hierarchical management structure. Yet even in these cases, rather than being answerable to investors, the management is answerable to the members of the cooperative.

Cooperatives can be categorized in different ways, depending on the way ownership is structured. These are the following:

- Consumer cooperatives, which are owned by those who purchase the goods or use the services of the cooperative. These include credit unions, as well as retail, service, and utilities such as electrical and telecommunications cooperatives. Credit unions generally operate as non-profit companies, generally offering higher interest on savings and lower interest rates on loans, with fewer and lower fees than most banks or other savings institutions.

- Producer cooperatives, which are owned by people or enterprises who are engaged in producing similar goods, and who use the cooperative for distribution and marketing. This includes agricultural cooperatives, as well as independent craftspeople and artisans. Agricultural cooperatives are common around the globe, including familiar brands (e.g., Sunkist and Yoplait) and in some cases dominate national markets (e.g., 90 percent market share for dairy cooperatives in the United States).
- Service or supply cooperatives, often called "purchasing cooperatives," are a cross between consumer and producer cooperatives. These are usually formed by independent businesses, like Best Western hotels or Ace Hardware, or public agencies that come together to utilize advantages of scale and to establish services collectively that none would be able to provide separately. Municipal agencies sometimes form cooperatives to provide such things as fire services, or to reduce costs through shared purchasing arrangements.
- Worker cooperatives are owned and governed by the people who carry out the functions of the enterprise—the workers. Worker cooperatives tend to be small, although they can be quite large—some of the cooperatives in the Spanish cooperative conglomerate Mondragon have thousands of workers. In order to adhere to the cooperative principles, workers must govern their business, but they may hire outsiders to manage the day-to-day operations.
- Multi-stakeholder cooperatives, a relatively new form, distribute ownership and governance rights among different stakeholder groups, including producers, consumers, workers, and even members of the broader community who don't fall into any of those three groups (for example, recipients of home care services paid for by the government). Depending on the situation (and the laws in effect), only some stakeholders may have ownership (and receive a distribution of the profits), but all stakeholders have some representation on the board of directors in order to have a share in governance.

Something common to all these forms is that the cooperative's capital is controlled by its members—people who are directly engaged with the activity of the cooperative. This connection can be quite intensive, as it is in worker cooperatives where the members may work side-by-side, or more remote, or as in consumer cooperatives where most members may have little or no interaction with other members. But even in a cooperative where the members don't have much interaction, the difference from traditional corporate capitalism is substantial—the members enjoy governance rights because they are part of a community of members, as opposed to the traditional model where governance rights flow from the investment of capital and nothing else.

Cooperatives and Sustainability

In a typical corporation, the principle of shareholder primacy means that all that really matters is the "bottom line," reflected in the level of the company's profits (the dividends it pays out) and its share price. Many companies may claim to be "values-based," and corporate social responsibility (CSR)—including a focus on sustainability—is increasingly popular. But in many enterprises CSR is only considered valuable if it contributes to profitability; moreover, CSR may not be part of the core of a company's identity.[9]

In theory, cooperatives should be more sustainable than traditional capitalism for a number of reasons. First, the absence of shareholder primacy means that co-op members can put other priorities before profits. This is most clear in consumer cooperatives. Although they receive the profits of the business in the form of dividends, those profits come out of the purchases the members themselves have made. In a way, it's like they get some of their money back at the end of the year (or quarter, or whatever period the co-op chooses). For them, there is no value in maximizing profits. This is less true in producer and worker co-ops, for which profit may still be a powerful motive, but even these will be more likely to advance sustainability goals. In the first place, in contrast to shareholder-owned companies, they are more strongly rooted in the communities of which they are a part—instead of extracting wealth, they help communities retain it and spread it more evenly. In fact, they reduce inequality and can help to alleviate poverty by enabling people in lower socioeconomic groups to obtain and retain wealth. As community-based enterprises, cooperatives are more likely to place greater priority on the health of the community and engage in long-term planning that emphasizes stability and modest growth.

Some arguments for the greater sustainability of cooperatives are less economic in nature and more social. Social capital—the kinds of social connections that exist within a community and link it to other communities—has been identified as an important contributor to sustainability.[10] At the same time, cooperatives contribute in important ways to both the development and strengthening of social capital, as Saz-Gil, Bretos, and Díaz-Foncea show in a recent review of the literature.[11] Sustainability is also often associated with democracy, albeit in complex ways.[12] Indeed, the difficulties major democratic republics have had in addressing pressing issues of climate change can easily lead to skepticism about whether the two ideas are even compatible. However, a good argument can be made that the problem here is not democracy itself, but the need for greater opportunities for public engagement, participation, and active deliberation.[13] Cooperatives, as democratic institutions, can help with this, because they are places where people can gain direct experience in democratic practices that they can then make use of in engaging with the political institutions of their community.[14]

In fact, these theoretical advantages are reflected in real life. Sustainability is an important part of the cooperative identity. At its 100th anniversary congress in 1995, the ICA adopted seven principles as central to cooperative identity. Many of these had been a part of the organization since its founding a hundred years earlier, but a new principle was adopted at that meeting. Principle Seven, Concern for Community, reads, "[c]ooperatives work for the sustainable development of their communities through policies approved by their members."[15] Thus, the connection between cooperatives and their community, and the commitment to sustainability, is at the core of the cooperative difference.

The ICA has taken a number of steps to advance sustainability. In 2012 it adopted the *Blueprint for a Cooperative Decade*, which included sustainability as one of its five key priorities.[16] The ICA has worked to push the recommendations included in the *Blueprint* through various means. As part of this initiative, the ICA performed a "sustainability scan" to identify markers or indicators of sustainability within the cooperative movement. The report found that "[t]he UN is correct to place its hope in the co-operative model as an engine of sustainability. There is a clear and direct relationship between sustainability and how co-operatives describe themselves. The linkages to social dimensions of sustainability are stronger than the linkages to environmental and economic dimensions, but all three are present. ... [C]o-operatives embed sustainability into their operating model and values." Still, they acknowledge that "further study is required to understand definitively the degree to which co-operatives are 'walking the talk.'"[17]

Are cooperatives "walking the talk"? Quantifying the sustainability impacts of such a large and dispersed object as the cooperative movement is quite difficult. Nonetheless, the Committee for the Promotion and Advancement of Cooperatives (COPAC) has produced a series of reports that attempt to accomplish this—one brief for each of the seventeen UN Sustainable Development Goals. These provide examples of the ways cooperatives all over the world are contributing to the sustainability of their communities. Most of these are small and local in scope, but in some ways, that's part of the point—sustainability is more often associated with small-scale projects than large ones, and the democratic character of a cooperative is usually stronger when it is smaller.[18] A few examples will suffice.

- Ending Poverty (SDG 1): Pipinas Viva in Pipinas, Argentina, is a worker-owned hotel that was started after a local cement factory closed, leaving the community of one thousand people with 65 percent unemployment. Pipinas Viva employs an approach it calls "community-based tourism," which places sustainability as a primary principle. According to COPAC, the cooperative has helped to bring tourists into the town and contributes to the "flourishment of other micro and small enterprises in the local economy."[19]
- Sustainable Water and Sanitation (SDG 6): Kuapa Kokoo is a cocoa-growing cooperative in West Ghana. In addition to supporting local cocoa farmers, Kuapa Kokoo has worked to improve sanitation and access to clean water in three communities.[20]
- Responsible Consumption and Production (SDG 12): The cooperative movement has long been at the forefront of the organic movement.[21] Both consumer and agricultural cooperatives have demonstrated a strong commitment to sustainability, as the COPAC report shows. Consumer cooperatives, in particular, engage in a number of different sustainability practices, and some of these co-ops are very large businesses.[22]

The advantages of cooperatives for sustainability should not be taken for granted. For one thing, sustainability is a complex constellation of different elements that, in some cases, may conflict with one another.[23] It's also true that the producers and workers in agricultural cooperatives and worker cooperatives may still be motivated by a desire for profit in a way that can undermine sustainability.[24] Consumers that run consumer cooperatives may be motivated by a desire to keep prices low and may be resistant to investing large amounts of money that would be required to change a fundamental component of the business to make it more sustainable (for example, for an electrical cooperative to change the way it generates its power).[25] If cooperatives are really democratic entities, then the way they operate should reflect the values of their members—so if their members are not concerned about sustainability, then it is unlikely that the cooperative will be.

Conclusions

The experience of the past two hundred-plus years seems to suggest that capitalism as we know it is not sustainable. However, perhaps the problem is not capital itself, but the way it is used. So, the question is, who controls the capital? If capital is controlled by capitalists, people whose primary goal is to accumulate more wealth, then achieving sustainability may be difficult. But if capital is controlled by a broader group rooted in local communities with a diverse set of interests, ends, and values, then a more sustainable approach is not only possible, but probable. It is not a magic wand—if the global economy were to become cooperativized in an instant the challenges of sustainability would not suddenly disappear. But it seems clear that a society in which more enterprises are cooperatives would be more sustainable than otherwise.

Notes

1. I refer to this as "traditional" because investor ownership is more common and more familiar to most people than cooperative ownership.
2. International Cooperative Alliance, "Cooperative Identity, Values & Principles," http://ica.coop/en/whats-co-op/co-operative-identity-values-principles.
3. This concept is considered by some to be a "foundational concept of corporate law and corporate governance." Robert J. Rhee, "A Legal Theory of Shareholder Primacy," *Minnesota Law Review* 122 (2018): 1951; however, there have been some recent challenges to it, with some scholars saying that "shareholder primacy is losing its grip on the corporate world." Grant M. Hayden and Matthew T. Bodie, "The Corporation Reborn: From Shareholder

Primacy to Shared Governance," *Boston College Law Review* 61 (2020): 2422. See also Ian B. Lee, "Efficiency and Ethics in the Debate About Shareholder Primacy," *Delaware Journal of Corporate Law* 31 (2006): 536.

4. United Nations, "2012—International Year of Cooperatives," https://www.un .org/en/events/coopsyear/.

5. Steven Deller et al., *Research on the Economic Impact of Cooperatives* (University of Wisconsin Center for Cooperatives, 2009), 2.

6. They can also be organized as non-profits. In fact, the two largest cooperative sectors, credit unions and electrical cooperatives, are required to be non-profits by statute.

7. In contrast, in most joint-stock corporations the shareholders receive one vote per share owned, meaning that the more shares one owns, the more votes one has.

8. What "use" means varies depending on the type of cooperative, as I discuss below. For example, in a consumer cooperative, it typically means the amount the member purchases; in a worker cooperative, it may mean the number of hours worked.

9. Adam Lindgreen and Valérie Swaen, "Corporate Social Responsibility," *International Journal of Management Reviews* 12, no. 1 (2010): 3.

10. Paul Selman, "Social Capital, Sustainability and Environmental Planning," *Planning Theory & Practice* 2, no. 1 (2001): 14.

11. Isabel Saz-Gil, Ignacio Bretos, and Millán Díaz-Foncea, "Cooperatives and Social Capital: A Narrative Literature Review and Directions for Future Research," *Sustainability* 13 (2021): 534.

12. This is evident from the diversity of essays in *Democracy and Sustainability*. Basil Bornemann, Henrike Knappe, and Patrizia Nanz, eds., *Routledge Handbook of Democracy and Sustainability* (Routledge, 2022).

13. Maija Setälä, "Inclusion, Participation, and Future Generations," in *Routledge Handbook of Democracy and Sustainability*, ed. Basil Bornemann, Henrike Knappe, and Patrizia Nanz (Routledge, 2022).

14. Mark J. Kaswan, "Developing Democracy: Cooperatives and Democratic Theory," *International Journal of Urban Sustainable Development* 6, no. 2 (2014): 190.

15. International Cooperative Alliance, "Cooperative Identity, Values & Principles," http://ica.coop/en/whats-co-op/co-operative-identity-values-principles.

16. Cliff Mills and Will Davies, *Blueprint for a Co-operative Decade*. International Co-operative Alliance (Jan. 2013), 4.

17. Ann Dale et al., *Co-operatives and Sustainability: An Investigation into the Relationship* (International Co-operative Alliance, 2013), 1.

18. Kaswan, "Developing Democracy," 197.

19. United Nations Department of Economic and Social Affairs, "Sustainable Development Goals," https://sdgs.un.org/goals.

20. United Nations, "Sustainable Development Goals."

21. M. Sligh and T. Cierpka, "Organic Values," in *Organic Farming: An International History*, ed. W. Lockeretz (Cabi, 2011), 33.

22. United Nations, "Sustainable Development Goals."

23. Joni Valkila, "Fair Trade Organic Coffee Production in Nicaragua—Sustainable Development or a Poverty Trap?," *Ecological Economics* 68, no. 12 (2009): 3023.

24. Julie A. Hogeland, "The Economic Culture of U.S. Agricultural Cooperatives," *Culture and Agriculture* 28, no. 2 (2006): 67–68.

25. In 2020, approximately 20 percent of total US electricity production was through renewable sources (2021). In 2019, electric cooperatives, which cover 56 percent of the U.S. land mass and serve 42 million people, produced 19 percent of power through renewables. While this is a negligible difference, the fact is that electric cooperatives are not more sustainable than the U.S. electric system as a whole. National Rural Electric Cooperative Association, "Electric Co-op Facts & Figures," April 13, 2023.

11

The Structural Barriers to Eco-Capitalism

Ryan Katz-Rosene

Is an ecologically sustainable variant of capitalism possible? In this chapter I attempt to answer this question, first by enumerating the core features of a capitalist economy, and second by identifying what parameters would allow that structure to be ecologically sustainable. I argue that eco-capitalism is possible in theory, but unlikely in practice. While there are several essential features of a capitalist economy—including private property rights, wage labor, commoditization, free markets, and a growth imperative derived from capital's insatiable desire for profit—I argue it is the latter which, in the long-run, makes contemporary capitalism unsustainable. To become ecologically sustainable, the process of growing capital must become entirely decoupled from material throughput. This type of "absolute decoupling" could be achieved in theory through the formation of a fully regenerative mode of production, wherein waste streams are fully cycled back into production; all energy is generated by renewable and/or self-sustaining reactions; ecosystems recovery is built in to resource extraction or ecological damage; and a significant share of capital accumulation becomes de-materialized (through processes such as financialization or the transition to information- and service-based economies). In practice, however, this would be very difficult to achieve in a capitalist system, not least because of the physical difficulties of meeting these conditions while simultaneously seeking to grow capital, but moreover because it would require near-monopolistic levels of control over systems of production and impose limitations on consumer choice—both of which are anathema to capitalism's espousal of market freedom.

Defining Capitalism

As the introductory chapter in this book notes, there is no consensus on the definition of capitalism. I begin by offering my own definition, which in turn shapes how I see it relating to ecological sustainability: Between the sixteenth and nineteenth centuries, the world political economy completed a transition from feudalism to capitalism. In contrast to the feudal system of inherited rights, privileges, and resource allocation based on a socially embedded aristocratic hierarchy, the world economy began to orient itself around freer market relations.[1] In the new capitalist system, any individual had the "freedom" to amass wealth and fortune, choose what professions they wished to pursue, own land, and benefit from the exploitation of resources to which they owned the rights.[2] Liberal political economists like Adam Smith and David Ricardo promoted this system of wage labor, private property rights, and commodity exchange within and between different nations, on the premise that it was the economic system most commensurate with the pursuit of individual liberty and prosperity.[3] Subsequent political economists like Karl Polanyi (2001) and John Ruggie (1982) pointed out that "free markets" were not truly free; their underlying frameworks and rules had to be delineated by states, and different variations of capitalism in different places would feature unique market structures (consider, for instance, the differences through which neoliberal capitalism has manifested in places like the United Kingdom, Chile, and China).[4]

Karl Marx famously pointed out how the capitalist system was also founded upon the principle of capital accumulation. In the simplest terms, the capitalist system enables wealth accrual by providing conditions through which the monetary value of a commodity (including not just material things, but labor and services as well) can be increased.[5] So, for instance, a manufacturer can purchase raw materials, transform or reprocess them, and then sell the resulting material for a greater value than originally paid for the raw materials and the labor that went into transforming them, thus extracting "surplus value." Or, as another example, a property owner can purchase real estate and rent it out, earning more back than what was originally paid. This dynamic of capital accumulation is integral to capitalism. The motive to obtain profit in this manner, underlying all forms of capitalist exchange, creates pressure to expand the capitalist system itself, as capitalists seek profits in new frontiers. This can manifest in things like imperialism (as capitalists seek profits in foreign lands);[6] innovation (as capitalists seek profits from owning the rights to new ideas, technologies, or highly coveted items); and financialization (as capitalists seek profits from new intangible spaces where value is unmoored to the costs of fixed capital and labor).[7] As we shall see, this definition of capitalism has important implications for the prospects of a hypothetical ecological variant of capitalism in the future, as it effectively means the process of capital accumulation would have to become sustainable itself.

Unsustainable Capitalism

With a definition in hand, we can now ask: What is it exactly about contemporary capitalism that currently makes it ecologically unsustainable? Is it private property rights? Is it the commoditization of natural resources and labor? The profit motive? While all of these can play a role in causing ecological damage, I would argue there is no reason why they inherently must. Critics of capitalism have argued that the commoditization of things like land and natural resources inevitably leads to a sort of exploitation of nature in the same way that the commoditization of labor leads to the exploitation of workers.[8] At the same time, proponents of free market capitalism have argued the exact opposite—that ultimately only by commoditizing things and subjecting them to the "invisible hand" of supply and demand, will the forces of scarcity and innovation kick in, allowing people to accurately value a clean environment.[9] This is in part the principle underlying carbon pricing—it turns the "right to pollute" into a commodity that then costs polluters and, in theory, discourages their polluting behavior.[10] Similar arguments both in favor and against enclosure (the integration of land into a regime of private property rights) have been made: It could result in ecological degradation if, for instance, a property owner has no regard for the ecological integrity of the land.[11] On the flip side, private property rights can also be beneficial if ecological degradation becomes internalized as a cost to the private landowner (a degraded landscape will often devalue the property and, so the theory goes, this incentivizes property owners to protect the property from ecological damage). So we might conclude that commoditization and private property relations can result in ecological damage, but they can also incentivize environmental protection if the costs of ecological damage are adequately internalized.

There are also debates about the effects of wage labor itself on the environment. Historically, the institution of wage labor has brought sub-sistence peasants and artisanal producers into cities where they could earn an income working at industrial factories in order to buy goods needed for survival.[12] Whether this urbanization process has been inherently "good" or "bad" for the environment is also a matter of debate. Viewed holistically, the process of industrialization is often initially tied in with disruptions to the earth's biogeochemical cycles (or in Marx's terms it cre-ated various types of "metabolic rifts").[13] At the same time, new systems of production and trade linked to the institution of a wage economy gave rise to innovations and efficiencies which, others argue, have helped lessen the toll on the environment, at least on a per capita or per unit of output basis (think, for instance, of the way that new energy technologies have produced more efficient and less ecologically damaging variants than their predecessors—from coal, to oil, to natural gas, to renewables, etc.).[14] In this sense, even though we know that the historical period of capitalism has coincided with major degradations of the global environment, there is debate about whether private property and commoditization (including of labor), and the freedom of individuals and firms to buy and sell property and commodities as they desire, have made this impact larger or smaller (with some arguing that it is both—at first making things worse and then eventually, once enough wealth has been accrued, becoming better).[15]

It is in conjunction with the process of capital accumulation, however, that capitalist features like commoditization and private property lean toward producing negative outcomes for the environment. In essence, this is a combined problem relating to scale in production in conjunction with the current way that energy and material commodities tend to be produced. The global energy system is highly reliant on fossil fuel sources that emit greenhouse gases; the global food system relies on agricultural lands that must be continually fertilized to remain productive; and all of the other material things and goods that we consume—even so-called "green" goods like electric vehicles and compostable packaging, etc.—all rely on the extraction of raw materials or energy-intensive production or disposal processes that work away at Earth's bio-capacity.[16] In different terms, Allan Schnaiberg and colleagues pointed out long ago that the capitalist system is founded upon a "treadmill of production" that causes "additions" and "withdrawals" to and from the environment that are ecologically harmful, such as the addition of pollutants to marine and terrestrial ecosystems and the atmosphere; and the withdrawal of non-renewable resources from the Earth System.[17] Here, the accumulation of capital becomes a compounding factor, by turning this vicious cycle of the treadmill of production into an ever-expanding system drawing upon even more energy, raw materials, and land, thus producing ever more additions and withdrawals. So long as the systems of production continue to be degenerative and extractive, capitalism's push for additional profits—the growth imperative, in short—only works at exacerbating the ecological crises we face. The current geological epoch of the "Anthropocene," wherein human disruptions to Earth's bio-geochemical cycles have grown in exponential terms, is thus best understood as a "Capitalocene," a result of the way capitalism has re-organized nature itself.[18]

A Model for Eco-Capitalism

The obvious response to this vicious cycle of ecological degradation is to find ways to green production. Eco-capitalism thus hinges on the idea of "decoupling"; that is, finding ways to continue to pursue capital accumulation in a way that does not drive additional environmental degradation. With successful decoupling, we can create all of the things we need for humans, even the things we want, and simultaneously pursue limitless surplus value without damaging the environment.[19] There are two main ways to do this: One is to pursue the dematerialization of the economy, such that most value can be derived from non-material goods. To a certain extent, we have seen some forms of dematerialization through the growth of service- and information-based economies, and through "financialization." By shifting an economy such that it is organized more around service provision, knowledge creation, and new non-material commodities like information and intellectual property, it could be possible to lessen the overall material burden associated with surplus value creation while continuing to enable profit. And by continuing to build a financial infrastructure in which capitalists can apparently create limitless profits through markets centered on financial products (via interest, stock value appreciation, monetary exchange, etc.), we could allow the capitalist economy to continue to grow in ways that have minimal relation to material throughput.

The second main way to support decoupling is to invent new technologies and innovative production methods that lessen (and eventually neutralize) the material footprint of production. Currently the world extracts about 100 billion tons of raw materials used in production, but only about 10 percent is reintegrated back into the production process.[20] In an eco-capitalist system, then, we might set up self-sustaining renewable energy production and new fusion-energy nuclear reactors to create abundant emissions-free electricity, and an associated recycling infrastructure to help reuse or derive value from the spent solar panels and wind turbines and other waste products associated with the energy system. We could also find ways to significantly reduce the size of annual waste stocks, in part by bringing about changes to packaging, incentivizing recycling, monetizing markets for reused products, etc., but also by re-integrating most waste streams back into production, thereby minimizing the amount of waste added to ecosystems and limiting the amount of raw materials withdrawn to produce new goods. Also, we could set up new markets (through, for instance, putting a price on pollution and enabling emissions trading credits—even create a price for biodiversity and ecosystem services as commodities), thereby incentivizing companies and individuals to reduce their ecological impact in order to avoid costs and maximize profits.

This is therefore the theoretical basis for a potential eco-capitalism: A profitable and circular economy wherein both value creation and even material consumption are largely decoupled from the ecological impacts of production. But how likely is this model in practice? There are good reasons to be skeptical of the various arguments undergirding decoupling: For one, a service- and information-based economy still has material needs, and historically, as rich nations have transitioned to these types of "advanced" economies, they have merely moved production elsewhere.[21] In such cases we see evidence of decoupling only on a territorial basis, not on an absolute basis, since the ecological impacts of domestically consumed goods are also offshore.[22] Similarly, capitalists who earn tremendous wealth through immaterial financial markets tend to have higher material footprints, as higher incomes usually translate into higher rates of material consumption (larger homes requiring more energy, more vehicles, more travel and possessions, etc.).[23]

Notwithstanding such limitations pertaining to the sheer scale of change required to achieve decoupling, there are also some structural limitations that make it difficult for capitalists to support the model portrayed above. That is, current market frameworks do not lend themselves nicely to regenerative forms of production, because the latter require states to intervene with the intention of creating a regulatory system mandating that waste be reintegrated into production, and to mandate changes in technologies and the very processes used in commodity production. In turn, this type of extensive state control over markets, particularly on the scale required to create the conditions for a circular economy, is anathema to the principle of market freedom that is central to capitalism. Alternatively, if the state could somehow create the regulatory framework for a circular economy without contravening market freedom, a secondary risk would be that in doing so it might limit the ability of capital to profit—which again, works against the core principles of capitalism.

There is perhaps one way around this: An oligopoly of corporate agglomerations focused on circularity, competing with one another for profits in a capitalist economy. Here, very large agglomerations of national- and global-scale corporations would partner up to gather waste at the pre-disposal stage and reintegrate materials back into their own supply chains. One commercial prototype of what this might look like is provided by Loop, a corporate partnership led by Walgreens and Kroger and dozens of food and household product brands: Individual consumers order groceries and other household goods from the online Loop store. The consortium then delivers the goods in reusable or recyclable packaging, and simultaneously picks up spent containers or packaging from goods consumed during the previous week, which then get reincorporated back into the company's packaging supply chain. Of course, for this type of circularity to work at the scale of an entire economy, it would require massive agglomerations of corporate entities across multiple economic sectors, to make sure everything from spent electronics to automotive parts to broken appliances and furniture and so on get fully re-integrated into supply chains. It takes high-level coordination between sectors to guide a circular economy because often spent materials are used as feedstocks for goods in other subsectors (as an example, when recycled, most plastic bottles get broken down into fibers that then go into carpets and pillows and futons, etc.).[24] Thus, for this model of eco-capitalism to work, the corporate agglomerations would have to be large-scale entities with global reach. At the same time, there ideally would be multiple corporate entities to choose from (remember, in a capitalist system consumers must have market freedom). We might then imagine a situation wherein a few mega-corporations compete for the patronage (and brand loyalty) of every household, offering to provision all required consumer goods while also taking care of waste disposal for those same clients, and further supplying packaging or raw materials back to participating brands to start the production cycle anew.

Conclusions

In this chapter I have made the case that an ecologically sustainable variant of capitalism is possible in theory, but unlikely in practice. The main element of contemporary capitalism that makes it unsustainable at present is its growth imperative, which in turn is a result of capital's insatiable quest for profit: The pursuit of profits drives economic activities that require evermore levels of raw materials extraction and additional forms of ecological degradation. To overcome that, eco-capitalism would have to find ways of decoupling growth from its material footprint. This itself is an enormously difficult task in a capitalist economy, since states would have to completely restructure domestic and global supply chains, in the process placing major limitations on consumer choice and market freedom (which raises the question of whether such a system would still be "capitalist"). One potential model for eco-capitalism, then, which still enables capital accumulation and market freedom, is for corporations to take on the organizing role of a regenerative economy themselves. A handful of very large agglomerations of corporations practicing circularity and vying for customers could play this role. Nevertheless, it is worth considering whether such a structure would be desirable in the first place: It is evident from the discussion above that structuring the conditions for a sustainable world requires powerful actors to coordinate markets and supply chains. Either states can oversee this process, or—given their growing power—private entities can. Which is more likely to be the most comprehensive and efficient overseer? Which is more likely to be most democratic? Which is most likely to account for winners and losers, and make special considerations to ensure no one gets left behind as the world seeks to transition to a sustainable economy? These are the questions we ought to be asking about the theoretically possible eco-capitalism.

Notes

1.   Richard Bellamy, "Liberalism: Political Doctrine and Impact on Social Science," in *International Encyclopedia of the Social & Behavioral Sciences*, edited by James D. Wright (2nd ed., Elsevier, 2015), 26–31. Marx, *Capital*: Everyman's Library, No. 848-849 (J. M. Dent & Sons, 1967), 915–16.
2.   Of course, as Bohrer explains, this was a highly theoretical "freedom," as legacies of inequality, imperialism, racism, and patriarchy made it extremely difficult, if not impossible, for just about anyone other than white and wealthy men to become wealthy in this new political economic system. Ashley J. Bohrer, *Marxism and Intersectionality: Race, Gender, Class and Sexuality under Contemporary Capitalism* (Columbia University Press, 2019), 15.
3.   David Ricardo, *On the Principles of Political Economy and Taxation* (John Murray, 1817); Adam Smith, *The Wealth of Nations* (London: J. M. Dent, 1958).
4.   See David Harvey, *A Brief History of Neoliberalism* (Oxford University Press, 2007); Jamie Peck and A. Tickell, "Conceptualizing Neoliberalism, Thinking Thatcherism," in *Contesting Neoliberalism: Urban Frontiers*, ed. Helga Leitner, Jamie Peck, and Eric S. Sheppard (New York: Guilford Press, 2007), 26–50.
5.   Marx, *Capital*, 60–65.
6.   Vladimir Lenin, *Imperialism, the Highest Stage of Capitalism* (Petrograd, 1917).
7.   David Harvey, *The Enigma of Capital: and the Crises of Capitalism* (Oxford University Press, 2000), 47; David Harvey, "The Geography of Capitalist Accumulation: A Reconstruction of the Marxian Theory," in *Spaces of Capital*, ed. David Harvey (New York: Routledge, 2001), 19–21.
8.   James O'Connor, "Capitalism, Nature, Socialism: A Theoretical Introduction," *Capitalism Nature Socialism* 1, no. 1 (1988).
9.   Tim Worstall, "Peak Stuff has Been and Gone," *Adam Smith Institute Blog*, November 6, 2011, https://www.adamsmith.org/blog/energy-environment/peak-stuff-has-been-and-gone.
10. William D. Nordhaus, "After Kyoto: Alternative Mechanisms to Control Global Warming," *American Economic Review* 96, no. 2 (May 2006): 31–34.
11. Fred Block, "Karl Polanyi and the Writing of 'The Great Transformation,'" *Theory and Society* 32, no. 3 (June, 2003): 275–306.
12. Linda Clarke, *Building Capitalism: Historical Change and the Labour Process in the Production of Built Environment* (Routledge, 1992), 35–48.
13. John Bellamy Foster, "Marx's Theory of Metabolic Rift: Classical Foundations for Environmental Sociology," *American Journal of Sociology* 105, no. 2 (September 1999): 366–405.
14. Vaclav Smil, *Energy and Civilization: A History* (The MIT Press, 2018).
15. See David I. Stern, "The Rise and Fall of the Environmental Kuznets Curve," *World Development* 32, no. 8 (August 2004): 1419–39.
16. William E. Rees, *Our Ecological Footprint: Reducing Human Impact on the Earth* (New Catalyst Books, 1996).
17. Kenneth A. Gould, David N. Pellow, and Allan Schnaiberg, *The Treadmill of*

Production: Injustice and Unsustainability in the Global Economy (Routledge, 2008), 25.

18. Elmar Altvater, et al., *Anthropocene or Capitalocene? Nature, History, and the Crisis of Capitalism* (PM Press, 2016).

19. Reed Smith LLP, "Reed Smith Guide to the Metaverse," May 2021.

20. Robert K. Kunzig, "Here's How a 'Circular Economy' Could Save the World," *National Geographic*, February 18, 2020.

21. William Milberg and Deborah Winkler, "Globalization, Offshoring, and Economic Insecurity in Industrialized Countries" (DESA Working Paper No. 87 ST/ESA/2009/DWP/87, November 2009).

22. James D. Ward, et al., "Is Decoupling GDP Growth from Environmental Impact Possible?," *PLoS One* 11, no. 10 (2016).

23. See Peter Newell, Freddie Daley, and Michelle Twena, "Changing Our Ways? Behaviour Change and the Climate Crisis" (Cambridge Sustainability Commissions, 2021), 1–13.

24. Emily Chung, "What Really Happens to Plastic Drink Bottles You Toss in Your Recycling Bin?," *CBC*, January 7, 2001.

Part IV

Institutional Structures to Support Sustainable Capitalism

12

Sustainability and Labor

Liz Brown

Sustainable capitalism depends in large part on a sustainable labor force. Capitalist economies and many businesses have been able to avoid confronting the problem of making labor more sustainable in the past. In the United States, this is due in part to their ability to outsource employment and manufacturing to less developed nations, and the political power of wealthy businesses and their owners. Now, many of the institutional protections against sustainable labor practices are eroding, and this erosion is likely to continue. Factors such as the legal expansion of worker rights, the technological automation of basic functions once assigned to less-skilled workers, and the increased global competition for talent are increasingly making it imperative for businesses to develop a more sustainable approach to the labor market. In addition, global reporting on and disclosure of labor practices and sustainability impacts have created greater transparency and demand for sustainable labor practices.

As the Introduction to this book notes, sustainability can be defined in many ways. Sustainability is a concept that extends beyond its most common physical and environmental applications. The United Nations' SDGs recognize this, encompassing the goals of promoting "full, productive and decent employment for all," reaching "gender equality and empower[ing] all women and girls," and "foster[ing] innovation."[1] In order to have truly sustainable development, we must attend to the wellbeing of people in addition to our physical environment.

This broad understanding of sustainability applies to capitalism as well. In order for capitalism to support all forms of sustainability, therefore, it needs to have a sustainable source of labor itself. Challenges to the sustainability of the labor market, however, are increasing every year. These challenges include disincentives to the full participation of parents in the workforce, decreasing numbers of workers who can innovate and take on other higher-order roles, and the risks lower-income workers face both during and at the end of their working years. Ensuring that the human engines of capitalism can not only survive but thrive is essential to maintaining the ability for businesses to support every other kind of change this book explores. There can be no sustainable capitalism without the sustainability of the people on whom that system depends.

This chapter examines five basic concepts regarding labor that will help support the development of a more sustainable form of capitalism. These are the expansion of worker voice; the empowerment of women in the workforce; increased investment in education; federal regulation of a livable wage; and increased investments in sustainable resources to support people at the end of their working lives. Public and private commitments to certain key initiatives relating to each of these concepts could help create jobs and make sure that those jobs are sustainable in the long run.

In the past several decades, many corporations have externalized responsibility for large-scale environmental and social damages their business practices may create. Corporations have been encouraged to make decisions based on maximizing returns to shareholders in the short term, and pass along costs for business decisions to workers, governments, and communities. In fact, the regulation of the financial sector is largely designed to support shareholder primacy.[2]

This focus on shareholder primacy and on short-term thinking has encouraged the private sector to avoid making the kinds of long-term investments that would make the workforce more sustainable overall. At the same time, market forces and laissez-faire approaches to parental leave, childcare, and education have exacerbated inequality. Deregulation and cutbacks in the terms and enforcement of environmental laws have let employers get away with the kinds of pollution that have led to climate change. A sustainable workforce requires the reversal of many of these regulatory trends as well as new regulations to compel private action and support the protection of marginalized workers.

Expanding Codetermination

One specific threat to sustainable capitalism is the potential disenfranchise-ment and disempowerment of the workforce. Although historically there has been little regard for the needs and wants of lower-skilled workers in the United States, government and corporate leaders are beginning to realize that in order to make capitalism sustainable, the workforce must be more engaged and involved in decision-making in the future.

This can be accomplished in part through the expansion of worker voice. In recent years, the labor market has developed unprecedented power not just to express their concerns directly but also to use the leverage of social media to expose problems that used to be considered private mat-ters. Workers are using their voices to demand change more often. What might once have been the province of labor unions is no longer restricted to collective bargaining, and both shareholders and corporate boards are taking notice. As can be seen at Google and Amazon, among other leading employers, workers are accomplishing at least some of their goals. Work-ers are also increasingly concerned with global sustainability and using their collective power to demand responses from their employers to the climate crisis.[3]

Corporations have a strong incentive to hear more often and more directly from the workers who were once considered largely fungible. The employees who want to convey information to their leadership are generally among those who are the most committed to the company's success. When employees feel disengaged, their morale, performance, and retention rates are likely to be lower, having a negative impact on productivity.[4]

In order to improve sustainability, corporate leaders need to find new and improved ways of listening to and talking with, not at, their workforce. Workers need better ways to convey their concerns to corporate boards. Without direct engagement, corporate leaders will not know whether they are taking the right concerns into consideration. It will also be hard for them to determine whether they are developing the most efficient and effective means of addressing those concerns. Employers therefore need to learn how to listen to and accommodate worker voice.

The practice of sharing corporate governance between shareholders and workers is called codetermination. The codetermination systems used in Germany, Norway, and Sweden may provide a useful model of how this might be done in the United States. Codetermination is most often associated with Germany, where it has been legally mandated for many decades. The extent to which German codetermination laws require employee representation on corporate boards varies depending on the type of industry, the number of employees, and other factors.[5] Codetermination, in general, is an important element of the German and European economic systems. Codetermination gives more voice to the workers than the alternative governance model of shareholder primacy, which assumes that the shareholder owners should be the primary decision-makers for corporations, usually through the directors they elect. Compared with shareholder primacy, codetermination has not been especially popular in the United States, although it is much more common in northern Europe. Recent research shows, however, that codetermination offers significant advantages over traditional U.S. shareholder primacy governance systems.

The benefits of increasing worker voice in the boardroom through codetermination are tangible. According to one study conducted by Simon Jäger at MIT and others, companies who have worker representatives on their boards have lower outsourcing costs, a 16–21 percent increase in labor productivity, and between 40–50 percent more capital stock invested in fixed assets like factories and equipment, all resulting in greater productivity per employee.[6] Another report, issued by the office of Senator Tammy Baldwin, found that companies with worker representation on their boards created 9 percent more wealth per shareholder and paid wages 18–25 percent higher than comparable companies without worker representation.[7] Senator Baldwin has proposed a bill that would require a third of the board-to-worker representation for all publicly listed companies, reflecting a growing demand for increased employee involvement in corporate decision-making.[8]

Increasing worker voice in corporate governance would also support other global goals. In several studies, codetermination was associated with higher levels of corporate social responsibility, better climate policy, broader community support, and increased job security during industry downturns.[9] Overall, according to a comprehensive analysis of codetermination literature, "the emerging consensus of the studies of the effects of codetermination on firm performance is quite positive. A number of studies have shown that employee representation is accompanied by higher productivity, profitability, and capital investment."[10] This broader view of the benefits of codetermination is consistent with the

United Nations' SDG framework that promotes fuller and better employment alongside environmental goals. It also supports the conclusion that
greater investment in people tends to accompany more sustainable business growth overall.

If codetermination is so beneficial, why don't more companies adopt
it? One reason is that they are not legally required to do so. The laws governing who sits on a board of directors are usually state laws, not federal
laws. No corporation in the United States has to include worker representation on its board as a matter of law because no state mandates such
representation.[11] Another reason is that the shareholder primacy model
of corporate governance has been championed for decades in the United
States with little resistance. Corporate law scholars and thought leaders
have argued that it is now time to reconsider the longstanding assumption that codetermination should be required by law, in part because of
the many benefits associated with it.[12]

Codetermination is not the only way to amplify worker voice. Limiting
the use of mandatory arbitration clauses in employment agreements would
also have a powerful impact on worker equity. Arbitration clauses are often
used to ensure that employees who have a dispute with their employers
do not go to court to enforce their legal rights in the workplace.[13] Instead,
employees who sign employment agreements containing mandatory arbitration clauses are forced to bring their disputes before an arbitrator, typically one the employer chooses, pays, and uses frequently.[14] Employers have
justified this practice in the past by pointing out that workers do not have
to sign these employment agreements. Instead, according to this argument,
the employees could choose to work elsewhere. Employees, however, usually do not have the broad freedom of choice that this argument assumes.
These agreements are also not visible to job applicants before they go
through the application process and are commonly introduced at the last
stages of hiring. It is therefore hard for applicants to assess whether they
will be required to sign an agreement containing a mandatory arbitration
clause before they apply. Even if applicants could make that assessment
early in the application process, it might not help them. When mandatory
arbitration provisions are ubiquitous, employees cannot avoid them by
going to a different employer.

Limiting mandatory arbitration clauses in employment contracts
would help to provide workers with more leverage in their dealings with
management. Over time, this increased power to recognize and reform

unjust practices will compel employers to accord workers more respect, resulting in higher retention rates and a more satisfied and productive workforce. In the United States, there would be challenges to limiting these clauses through regulation. The United States has a strong tradition of freedom of contract, which supports the right of people to enter into contracts under any terms they choose, so long as the contract is voluntary and for a legal purpose, and the people signing it have the legal capacity to do so. In the context of sexual harassment claims, however, there has been strong pushback in recent years against the use of mandatory arbitration clauses.[15]

Amplifying the voices of workers will be more productive and meaningful when the population of workers itself is as broad and diverse as possible. In order to maximize the potential of the labor market, employers and policy makers also need to confront the institutional problems that limit the participation of some sectors of workers. Workers who are not native Caucasian cisgender heterosexual males tend to face greater barriers to participation in the workforce, including racism, sexism, violence, and more limited opportunities to access jobs.

An important element of a sustainable work force is the removal of these barriers to entry and success for people who have been marginalized by various social and economic pressures including racism, sexism, and other pernicious forms of bias. Capital spending on programs that alleviate these pressures is an important investment in the sustainability of labor in the U.S. economy.

Structural Change to Support Women and Families

A second structural change would focus on making capitalism more sustainable for women workers in particular. Women have been adversely affected by recent shifts in the labor market, and current societal structures limit the long-term viability of women's full participation in the workforce. During the COVID-19 pandemic, women left the workforce in much higher numbers than men, creating an unsustainable imbalance.[16] In order to restore that balance, businesses should consider several structural changes. These might include changes in hiring and retention practices as well as eliminating mandatory arbitration clauses in employment contracts that harm the interests of victims of sexual harassment and other forms of gender discrimination. When half of the potential labor market faces structural barriers to their full participation in the workforce, there are serious consequences for the sustainability of that market.

In 2021, there were nearly four million fewer women in the United States workforce than in 2020, primarily because of the coronavirus pandemic.[17] Many more women reduced their participation in the workforce. Women were forced to cut back on their hours because of increased caretaking responsibilities and uncertain working conditions. The sharp downturn in women's economic success during the pandemic revealed how fragile and unstable the labor system is for women, especially those with caretaking responsibilities.

In order to have a truly sustainable workforce, the capitalist system must dismantle the longstanding barriers to women's full participation in the labor market. Business leaders and legislators should reconsider the ways in which gender and racial bias are addressed. These changes also include the structural renovation of the childcare system, public education, and the provision of elder care. At a fundamental level, they require the reconceptualization of care, and family, as gender-neutral things.

One critical challenge to women's full economic participation is discrimination and bias in the workplace. Women face the challenges of gender bias when they apply for jobs and when they are considered for promotion. They face sexual harassment at work as well as outside of work. The legal protections that we have in place are deeply flawed, in part because they require the victims of discrimination and harassment to take an adversarial position toward the source of their income. The process of bringing these claims usually requires the intervention of a federal or state agency, which the victim must notify within a short period of time after experiencing some incident of bias. Women who experience bias are challenged to pinpoint and document damaging behavior in ways that tend to predetermine their failure. Bringing a claim forward can be exhausting, humiliating, and demanding. The fact that the victim must then confront the source of the discrimination against her creates what can be an overwhelming burden for someone who is already disadvantaged simply because of how she was born.

It is not just sexual harassment and gender discrimination that must be addressed more fundamentally in order for women to have more economic security. The impact of racism and ethnic discrimination also serves to limit women of color's participation in the workforce. Women of color earn less in average annual wages and experience sexual harassment at higher rates than white women.[18] The intersectionality of racism and sexism has no truly effective legal remedy in the United States.

Companies that fail to prevent discrimination and perpetuate patterns of bias face few repercussions, especially when they win or settle claims brought on behalf of victims of discrimination. Few federal or state laws mandate companies to take proactive steps to protect women in the workplace. But this could change. If employers were obligated to ensure that their workplaces were fair and unbiased, rather than placing the initial burden on employees to complain, there might be a more consistent corporate culture of fairness and a lower incidence of bias. If there were, for example, requirements that the officers, directors, and senior management of companies over a certain size represented a more diverse range of races, ethnicities, and genders, employers might have a stronger incentive to tamp down bias before it harms women in the first place. Similarly, if employers were required to provide dedicated training and support to groups underrepresented in upper-level management, including but not limited to women, women might find themselves on a more equal footing when it comes to participation in the workforce.

Additionally, sustainable capitalism requires more support for working families. While women still bear primary responsibility for the care and education of children, they cannot participate fully in the workforce. The United States is the only first-world country that does not provide for paid maternal leave, forcing hundreds of millions of women to sacrifice income and professional opportunities as soon as they give birth. Without reliable and affordable childcare, women are still presumed to have primary responsibility for taking care of children before kindergarten. When childcare is unavailable, unsafe, or unreliable, women leave work more often than men to take care of young children. When those children are old enough to go to school, mothers are presumptively charged with arranging for after-school care because the public school system does not account for the gap between the end of the school day and the end of the workday. The burden on women to arrange for, monitor, supplement, and replace after-school care represents an enormous drain on the sustainability of their role in the workplace overall.

Women face an even more complex additional burden as caretaking daughters. As people live longer, women are more likely than men to take on the additional burden of caring for elderly parents.[19] There is no structural support for this kind of responsibility in most workplaces. The illnesses of the elderly do not follow the kind of episodic, occasional scheduling that the Family and Medical Leave Act (FMLA) allows for. Under the FMLA, some employees are entitled to take up to twelve weeks of unpaid leave if they have worked for a large enough employer for a long enough period of time. But the FMLA is only available to 56 percent of workers in the United States. And relatively few workers can afford the reduction in salary that unpaid leave represents, let alone the reduction in professional growth opportunities that go along with such absences from work. The burden of caring for elderly parents, and the uncertainty and ambiguous grief that women often feel in balancing that care with their other obligations, is a burden that few public or private support systems tend to ease.

There is an important role for government to play here. In April 2021, President Biden introduced the American Jobs Plan, which aimed to support working women by upgrading childcare facilities and investing in schools.[20] Within schools, the plan earmarked funds to strengthen educational outreach to underrepresented students in STEM and other subjects that tend to lead to higher-paying jobs. The plan also called for investing $400 billion in expanding access to better quality care providers for the elderly and people with disabilities. Noting that the caregivers in these facilities are disproportionately women of color, the plan encompassed the expansion of home and community-based services that would support increased compensation for caregivers and improved infrastructures for care facilities.

The private sector can and should do more to improve the quality of women's working lives. Employers can create more opportunities for women returning to full-time employment after caretaking leaves and provide flexible career pathways for working parents.

Increasing Investment in Education
Will Make Innovative Leadership More Sustainable

A third complementary approach to making labor more sustainable is increasing private and public investment in education. Providing "inclusive and equitable quality education and promot[ing] lifelong learning opportunities for all" is one of the United Nations' SDGs.[21] Investing in education will lead to a more sustainable workforce in several different ways.

First, education increases the ability of workers to earn higher wages. People who attain the highest levels of education earn the most and enjoy the lowest rates of unemployment. According to the Bureau of Labor Statistics, workers who had not earned a high school diploma had median weekly earnings of $619 and an unemployment rate of 11.7 percent.[22] Workers who had earned a professional degree had median weekly earnings of $1,893, three times as much as those without a high school degree. Those more educated workers had an unemployment rate of 3.1 percent, almost 75 percent less than those without a high school degree. Especially as automation replaces workers with the lowest skill levels, and as low-skill jobs continue to be outsourced to other countries, education becomes an increasingly critical aspect of preparation for a sustainable career.

Schools also play an important role in providing a strong foundation for a healthy workforce. Improving education should encompass increasing the availability and quality of both early childhood development and nutrition. These, in turn, will further support the mental and physical health of workers. If every child in the United States received adequate nutrition in school, as well as screening for vision, hearing, and mental-health problems, that would increase the overall health and wellbeing of workers at every skill level.

Expanding educational opportunities is also important in reducing socioeconomic disparities. Because local taxes are used to fund local schools, lower-income areas tend to face the greatest challenges in providing high-quality schools and educational programming for their children. This tends to perpetuate geographical centers of poverty, exacerbating the gaps between the poorest and the wealthiest communities.

Without a sufficiently well-educated workforce, companies will face increasing competition for responsible leadership and competitive innovation. The lack of public-school funding creates not only an opportunity but an imperative for private investment in education. This might take the form of providing longer and better supplemental care in schools to fill the gaps between the end of the school day and the end of the workday. This would reduce the burden on the primary caretakers, more often women, simultaneously improving the educational system and supporting women workers.

Improving public education will support sustainability in other, less direct ways as well. A more educated workforce is likely to make better and more informed voting choices. They are more likely to elect political leaders based on objective information and be better equipped to analyze information for themselves, instead of depending on received influence. Improving education, including critical-thinking skills, will improve the abilities of workers to make better decisions both in the workplace and in their communities.

Providing All Workers with a Livable Wage Will Make the Labor Force More Sustainable

There are other ways in which federal investments in infrastructure could help to close the gaps in the racial, economic, and social inequities in the labor market.[23] A fourth requirement for a more sustainable labor force requires legislative action: raising the federal minimum hourly wage. This refers to the minimum amount a worker who is paid on an hourly basis can be paid per hour according to federal law, which sets the floor for such income across the country. States are free to set higher minimum wages, and some cities within states may set even higher minimum wages to attract talent and help offset the higher cost of living. Because states and cities take such widely varying approaches to this issue, it is more impactful to focus on the federal "floor." The federal minimum hourly wage of $7.25 has not been increased since 2009.

Increasing the federal minimum wage to at least the amount needed for the head of a household to work forty hours a week and stay above the poverty line will help ensure that workers can maintain a sufficient standard of living. If the minimum wage were increased to $15 by 2025, an estimated 59 percent of workers whose total family income is below the poverty line would see a rise in their pay.[24] There is also a significant racial justice component to the argument for raising the federal minimum wage. People of color make up a disproportionate number of the workers who are affected by minimum wage laws. According to one study, raising the federal minimum wage would provide a raise for nearly one-third (31 percent) of African Americans and one quarter (26 percent) of Latinos.[25] Nearly one-quarter of those who would benefit are African American or Latina women.[26]

Raising the minimum wage is not the only way in which federal regulation could improve the economic position of workers, especially those who have been marginalized. Ensuring that more workers can afford to cover their essential costs during retirement is another important labor-related policy that will support sustainable capitalism. A complementary policy would encourage employers to invest in environmental, social, and governance (ESG) funds as part of the retirement plans they offer. A federal mandate that incentivized certain employers to invest their 401(K) plans in ESG funds would help sustain not only the labor force but also the planet as well. In 2020, during the final months of the Trump administration, the Department of Labor proposed a rule that would have done just the opposite.[27] The proposed rule would have prevented 401(K) and other qualified retirement plans from including funds that were managed to include ESG factors in their due diligence analysis.

There are encouraging signs of increased commitment to a more sustainable approach to labor. In 2020, a coalition of business associations representing over 70,000 businesses formed with the mandate of developing a more inclusive approach to economic success.[28] This alliance, called Imperative 21, argues for an economic reset that is based on designing for interdependence, investing for justice, and accounting for stakeholders. Focusing on stakeholders, rather than shareholders, underscores the importance of labor and the need to consider workers in measuring success. In fact, one of the economic goals of Imperative 21 explicitly recognizes the need to focus on many of the elements described in this chapter as prerequisites for a more sustainable workforce. Imperative 21 seeks an economic system that "removes structural inequality; ensures leadership and ownership are more representative and investment more accessible; uses technology to advance democratic ideals and human rights; and promotes greater voice, power and opportunity for those currently marginalized." Its commitment to a more inclusive approach to capitalism may take time, but it is an idea whose time has certainly come.

Notes

1. Jeffrey Sachs, "6 Ways America Can Get Back on Track with the UN Sustainable Development Goals," Columbia Climate School, September 21, 2018; United Nations Sustainable Development Goals, "Leave No One Behind," https://unsdg.un.org/2030-agenda/universal-values/leave-no-one-behind.
2. See Chapter 13, this volume.
3. Labor Network for Sustainability, "Labor, Sustainability and Justice," https://www.labor4sustainability.org/post/labor-sustainability-and-justice/.

4. Gallup, *State of the American Workplace Report* (2013), 17–19, https://www.gallup.com/workplace/238085/state-american-workplace-report-2017.aspx .
5. Grant M. Hayden and Matthew Bodie, *Reconstructing the Corporation: From Shareholder Primacy to Shared Governance* (Cambridge University Press, 2021), 24–78.
6. See Simon Jäger, Benjamin Schoefer, and Jörg Heining, "Labor in the Boardroom" (working paper, National Bureau of Economic Research, November 1019), 22.
7. See Office of Senator Tammy Baldwin, *Reward Work Not Wealth* (March 2019), 4.
8. Reward Work Act, S. 915, 116th Congress (2019); see Tammy Baldwin, "Baldwin Reintroduces Legislation to Lower Health Care Costs & Expand Access to Insurance for Millions More Americans," Office of Senator Tammy Baldwin, January 24, 2023.
9. David J. Berger, "Expanding Diversity in the Boardroom by Adding Worker Voice," in *Worker Voice and the New Corporate Boardroom* (Aspen Institute, 2021) 2–5.
10. Grant M. Hayden and Matthew T. Bodie, "Codetermination in Theory and Practice," *Florida Law Review* 73, no. 2 (November 2021): 354.
11. Hayden and Bodie, "Codetermination in Theory and Practice," 325.
12. Aspen Institute, "Idea Lab on Worker Voice in Corporate Governance," 2023, 19.
13. Katherine V. W. Stone and Alexander J. S. Colvin, *The Arbitration Epidemic: Mandatory Arbitration Deprives Workers and Consumers of Their Rights,* (Economic Policy Institute, 2015).
14. Stone and Colvin, *The Arbitration Epidemic,* 17.
15. Stone and Colvin, *The Arbitration Epidemic,* 25; Jean R. Sternlight, "Mandatory Arbitration Stymies Progress Towards Justice in Employment Law: Where To, #MeToo?," *Harvard Civil Rights-Civil Liberties Law Review* 54 (2019): 201–5.
16. Naomi Cahn and Linda M. McClain, "Gendered Complications of COVID-19: Towards a Feminist Recovery Plan," *Georgetown Journal of Gender and the Law* 22, no. 1 (2020): 1.
17. U.S. Bureau of Labor Statistics, "Women in the Labor Force: A Databook," April 2023, 1.
18. National Partnership for Women & Families, "Sexual Harassment and the Gender Wage Gap Fact Sheet," 2.
19. Andre J. Mutschler-Supplee, "The Caregiving Burden on the Caregivers of Aged Loved Ones: Qualitative Interviews of Female Caregivers With Male Siblings," Professional Psychology Dissertations (2019).
20. White House, "Fact Sheet: The American Jobs Plan," March 31, 2021, https://www.whitehouse.gov/briefing-room/statements-releases/2021/03/31/fact-sheet-the-american-jobs-plan/.
21. United Nations, Sustainable Development Goals.
22. U.S. Bureau of Labor Statistics, "Education Pays," 2021, https://www.bls.gov/emp/chart-unemployment-earnings-education.htm.

23. Marcela Escobari, Dhruv Gandhi, and Sebastian Strauss, *How Federal Infrastructure Investment Can Put America to Work* (Brookings, March 2021), 3.

24. Economic Policy Institute, "Why the U.S. Needs a $15 Minimum Wage," (Fact Sheet), January 26, 2021, https://www.epi.org/publication/why-america-needs-a-15-minimum-wage/.

25. Economic Policy Institute, "Why the U.S. Needs a $15 Minimum Wage," 2.

26. Economic Policy Institute, "Why the U.S. Needs a $15 Minimum Wage," 2.

27. Lisa Woll and Judy Mares, "The Department of Labor Is Attacking Sustainable Investments—And Harming Plan Participants," *Institutional Investor*, August 25, 2020.

28. Maureen Kline, "How to Build a Sustainable Capitalism," *Inc.*, September 14, 2020.

13

From Neoliberal to Hybrid Corporate Social Responsibility

Rajat Panwar, Natalia Vidal,
and Ellen Alexandra Holtmaat

Corporations are core to the existence of capitalism. They drive economic progress and they also offer enormous promise to provide social goods that individuals and governments cannot. Yet, corporations are often thought to epitomize the evils of capitalism. Increased social inequalities, environmental degradation, forced labor, and corruption have all been linked to corporations working to maximize profits and expand economic prowess. Increasingly, proponents of sustainable capitalism have recognized the adverse societal impacts of corporate pursuits and argued that corporations owe a duty to society beyond simply maximizing profits. Instead, they suggest, corporations should prioritize social responsibilities alongside profit making. In this chapter, we argue that corporations can and should espouse corporate social responsibility (CSR) but also that CSR cannot effectively generate desired societal outcomes if it is always tied to a neoliberal lens of profitability and wealth maximization. Therefore, our core contention is that CSR should be guided by a hybrid mix of government and self-regulatory structures that are not explicitly organized around shareholder wealth maximization. If this is achieved, corporations indeed have much good to offer the world, and capitalism has a chance to operate sustainably.

The Danger of Neoliberal CSR

Business involvement in addressing social and environmental problems is not a new concept. Rajat Panwar, Tomi Rinne, Eric Hansen, and Heikki Juslin explain that businesses have always had some type of social responsibilities that have been evolving through time and across geographies.[1] In many Eastern civilizations, giving back to society by those who had enough was believed to be a moral imperative and an essential approach to keep the social fabric intact. Mahatma Gandhi's trusteeship doctrine, through which he stipulated that all people having money or property must hold it in trust for society, is a more recent yet vivid reflection of that ancient belief system.[2] In other parts of the world too, corporations have been giving back to society through philanthropic contributions. For example, a rich and almost unparalleled history of philanthropic contributions in the United States has helped build many institutions including some of the leading universities.[3] Whether in the East or West, corporate contributions have helped fill institutional voids by building hospitals, parks, public libraries, schools, and universities. Corporations, it seems, provided what governments in many cases could not!

Considered through this historical lens, we can see that the origins and roots of what is now called CSR are predominantly altruistic. It is rooted in a moral principle that corporations have an obligation to advance societal interests, going beyond wealth creation as their sole objective. This moral underpinning of CSR is explicit in Howard Bowen's seminal book *Social Responsibilities of the Businessman*, which is often regarded as the first comprehensive scholarly work on the topic.[4] It was following this publication that CSR began to receive attention from a growing group of business scholars who approached it primarily from a normative perspective.

Over time, however, others began to suggest that corporate social responsibility should be examined through an economic lens. In 1970, Milton Friedman offered a vehement critique of CSR, making his (in)famous proclamation that the social responsibility of business was to increase its profits.[5] This perspective sowed the seeds for what would later turn out to be a thick and hard coating of neoliberalism on CSR. Neoliberal CSR refers to corporations pursuing CSR initiatives with the aim of increasing profits either directly or indirectly through "a deeper opening up of social life to the dictates of the marketplace."[6] The core spirit of neoliberal CSR is to view social problems as investment opportunities.

By bringing CSR into the domain of economics, Friedman, even if inadvertently, put morals and markets on essentially the same pedestal.[7] As a result, the questions whether it was morally desirable for corporations to give back to society or how best they can do so were no longer the supreme inquiries for CSR scholars. The Friedman doctrine—putting shareholders' interests first—pushed CSR scholars to establish what became known as the "win-win" or the "business case" paradigm of CSR, the essence of which is that shareholders and societal interests are not at odds and that the corporation can materially benefit by being socially responsible. The question of whether giving back to society had a payoff for the corporation became more salient than questions of moral significance. Over time, the business case of CSR has emerged to be one of the most researched topics in CSR literature. A direct result of this is the institutionalization of CSR as a means to advance the corporation's financial ends. CSR became a mere tool of neoliberal economics.

We do not suggest here that there is no business case for a neoliberal CSR. In fact, there is plenty of empirical evidence—of course, with occasional exceptions—for a business case underlying CSR.[8] Neither are we suggesting that it is inherently wrong if corporations can profit from acting responsibly. Far from that; we recognize that the job of the executive will only become easier if the corporation can advance its financial interests in the course of addressing societal problems. They will not be accused of subjugating their fiduciary obligations to societal concerns or, in Friedman's words, of misappropriating shareholders' funds. What we are suggesting is the need to raise the question whether there is a societal case underlying CSR. In other words, whilst we know that CSR helps businesses, we also ought to know whether CSR actually helps society. Can CSR, as Barnett and colleagues ask, help avert social and ecological collapse?[9]

Our answer to this question is a categorical no. CSR, as normally practiced, is truly a risk-management strategy aiming to legitimize the actions of the corporation and corporate elites, and advance the interests of shareholders. Resultantly, CSR actions are typically symbolic in nature and rarely substantive enough to trigger transformative changes even if individual CSR projects might make a small difference in a contained context. The real problem of CSR, however, is not its impotency. Numerous programs that are carried out by governments can be equally or even more ineffective. The real danger of CSR is that it serves as a strategy to help the corporation prevent future regulations that would enhance cost of compliance for the corporation but otherwise safeguard societal interests. Reviewing the expansive literature at the intersection of business and polity, Neil Malhotra, Benoît Monin, and Michael Tomz find that corporations adopt CSR type self-regulatory measures so that they can dissuade government officials, interest groups, and the public at large from demanding more stringent regulations.[10] The authors follow up with a robust experimental study and conclude that voluntary corporate actions reduce public demand for environmental regulations.[11] In fact, some business scholars have included "the ability to prevent future regulations" as a key business benefit of CSR.[12] Whether one takes an anecdotal or an empirical approach, both arrive at the conclusion that CSR is a tool for further deepening the roots of neoliberalism and weakening the state's power to govern, all the while giving hopes of a better governance and brighter future. Joel Bakan criticizes CSR through a scathing remark:

> [T]he priority of the corporation is always going to be to create profit for its shareholders. To the extent that we embrace CSR, we're allowing the psychopath to be charming. The corporation is constituted to be profoundly self-interested, unconcerned with others, incapable of feeling guilt or remorse, criminal if it can get away with it, disdainful of social conventions—the very definition of the psychopath. Another characteristic of human psychopaths is their ability to portray themselves as benevolent and charming. That makes them all the more dangerous, because you don't see what they truly are. To some extent, corporate social responsibility plays that role.[13]

Bakan's jabs are not unfounded. The list of companies that were once lauded as CSR pioneers but later found to be engaged in criminal activities is not short. Think Enron, Volkswagen, Wells Fargo, or even Tesla, which recently put its workers in harm's way by defying lockdown orders during the COVID-19 pandemic. The expanding literature on greenwashing and corporate hypocrisy reflects growing concerns about the sincerity behind CSR. Uchechukwu Nwoke argues that CSR promotes corporate-centric capitalism, and Sarah Kaplan cautions that CSR breeds false hopes that contemporary corporate capitalism will solve the problems that it in fact creates.[14] Similarly, Gerlinde Berger-Walliser and Inara Scott argue that CSR promotes shareholder primacy while absolving firms from "any form of universal moral responsibility other than obeying the law."[15] In a similar vein, Roy Suddaby and Rajat Panwar argue that CSR communication hides more than it reveals and that CSR initiatives typically engender perverse outcomes undermining societal interests while giving an impression of protecting them.[16] At a time when we are running out of time to reverse the course on such problems as climate change and biodiversity loss, the neoliberal form of CSR appears to be a distracting and dangerous experiment.

Hybrid CSR as a Promising Way Forward

Should we then write off CSR and instead turn to state regulations to control corporate behavior and safeguard society and the planet? Should we take away corporate discretion and hand over the responsibilities of tackling societal challenges to the state? In light of the foregoing discussion, an intuitive answer would be yes. However, we also need to be mindful of the immense unique capabilities and efficiencies of the private sector that can play a critical role in addressing complex societal problems. Solutions to these problems require not only the mandate of the state but also the creativity, innovativeness, entrepreneurialism, agility, resources, and reach that the state often lacks but the corporation often possesses. So, the solutions to societal problems can be achieved when the corporation and the state work in tandem with rather than in isolation from each other. What we then need is an innovative and creative amalgamation of regulations and corporate discretion. We need a hybrid form of CSR.

Fortunately, such innovative governance arrangements are emerging in many parts of the world.[17] The governments of Indonesia, India, and the Philippines have enacted CSR regulations mandating private firms to contribute resources to societal well-being while providing concrete guidance about how this should be done. In 2007, the Indonesian government passed legislation requiring firms to invest in CSR activities and to consider these investments as part of the cost of doing business in the country. Failure to comply would result in sanctions.[18] In June 2017, the Economy Ministry of the United Arab Emirates (UAE) announced that large companies would be required to report their CSR initiatives. Already, countries including Australia, Brazil, China, South Africa, and several in the European Union have published regulatory guidelines for CSR reporting.[19] India has enacted by far the most elaborate and stringent CSR regulation. In 2014, India passed what is known as the "CSR law of India"—which many view as an oxymoron. This law stipulated that large Indian firms with a certain level of profitability must spend two percent of their average net profit from the previous three years on CSR activities and also make public their total expenditures along with allocations to different CSR practices.

The increasing number of CSR regulations worldwide demonstrates that governments can routinely and directly influence CSR practices.[20] Tom Fox, Halina Ward, and Bruce Howard developed a four-part typology of government influence in CSR.[21] The first category, endorsement policies, refers to government support for CSR through development of public procurement policies and symbolic actions, such as awards, acknowledging responsible behavior. The second category encompasses public policies that facilitate the adoption of CSR practices by encouraging firms to be more responsible through tax incentives, penalties, and subsidies. For example, governments can lower reporting requirements when firms adopt environmental management programs.[22] The third form of government influence in CSR includes policies that encourage cross-sector collaborations among the private sector, government, and non-profit organizations. These types of policies are intended to diffuse CSR best practices. The fourth form of government influence manifests as CSR mandates.

CSR policies can have different regulatory strengths. Jette Steen Knudsen, Jeremy Moon, and Rieneke Slager classified the regulatory strength of CSR policy in different European countries based on the above described four-part typology.[23] They found that policies that mandate CSR adoption have the highest regulatory strength; facilitative and partnership policies have moderate strength, and endorsement policies have the lowest strength. In addition, these scholars found that all—or most—European governments adopted a combination of the four policy types, with the UK, Northern Europe, and Scandinavia adopting all of them.[24] In contrast, Mediterranean countries tended to focus mostly on endorsement policies.

Although all forms of CSR policies have proven to be effective to some extent, mandatory policies can be particularly effective in promoting CSR practices and have been the preferred mechanism in some countries. Laura Albareda, Josep M. Lozano, and Tamyko Ysa found that, amongst the fifteen countries included in their study, soft regulations were the most common form of government intervention to encourage responsible business behavior.[25] Similarly, Jean-Pascal Gond and Nahee Kang found that soft regulation is the prevailing mode of CSR public policy in Japan, South

Korea, and China.[26] Unfortunately, although unsurprisingly, the United States is lagging behind the world in catching on to the notion of hybrid CSR, although the recent proposal by the U.S. Securities and Exchange Commission to enhance and standardize disclosures related to environmental, social, and governance (ESG) is an important step in that direction.

What do government CSR policies emphasize and who is responsible for implementing these policies? To answer the former questions, Fox, Ward, and Howard examined CSR policies established by developing and developed countries and found that CSR public policies comprised such themes as setting and ensuring compliance with minimum standards, responsible investment, community development, and pro-CSR production and consumption.[27] Knudsen, Moon, and Slager answer the latter question by explaining that most European countries were distributing CSR responsibilities across multiple ministries, including Social and Employment, Environment, Economy (including Trade and Industry) and Foreign Affairs and International Development.[28]

With a wide range of initiatives and formal structures in place to implement public CSR policies, we are entering an emerging era of CSR regulations wherein the relevance of the long-held dichotomy between regulation and self-regulation as distinct governance choices is diminishing. In its place, a hybrid CSR model, which blends the two, is gaining support from governments, civil societies, and surprisingly, also from corporate investors. For example, Panwar and colleagues empirically demonstrated that the passage of the Indian CSR law gained widespread support from Indian investors.[29] They argue that amidst increasing societal distrust of neoliberal CSR, corporations and investors prefer regulatory oversight even of self-regulating actions.[30] These empirical findings concur with recent initiatives by large technology companies calling for regulatory interventions. For example, rocked by privacy scandals, Google, Microsoft, and others have urged governments to enact regulation simply because the discretionary measures that they have long fought for are proving to be utterly ineffective and the public distrust of these measures is rising. Similarly, food-sector companies such as McDonald's and chocolate manufacturers such as Mars Wrigley, Mondelez, and Barry Callebaut have publicly asked for tighter regulation as they can no longer afford to defend what is an apparent failure of self-regulation in protecting tropical forests.

In this new CSR era, corporations will have to go beyond symbolic actions and seek to enhance the societal impact of their actions. This pursuit will inevitably blur the boundaries between regulation and self-regulation and thus further propel the growing trend of hybrid CSR. This impact-oriented CSR will also bleed into what is known as corporate political responsibility (CPR) and corporate political activity (CPA), both of which refer to corporate engagement in policy formulation. Often, corporations have lobbied for less regulation, but as corporations face more intense pressure from stakeholders, we expect to see more and more instances of progressive lobbying. More than three decades ago, Donna J. Wood emphasized the importance of impact-oriented CSR and called upon CSR scholars to focus on corporate social performance (CSP).[31] CSP refers to how businesses operationalize their definitions of CSR, including their "processes of social responsiveness, and policies, programs, and observable outcomes as they relate to the firm's societal relationships."[32] However, with the complete usurpation of CSR by the neoliberal ideology, research on CSP has been appallingly sparse. Resultantly, our understanding of such fundamental issues—such as how to assess CSP—is at a rudimentary level. This is one core area of research where significant progress must soon be made. Unless we can reliably measure what societal impacts CSR initiatives are making, the promising field of hybrid CSR will have the same fate as the neoliberal CSR, that is, corporations will use hybrid CSR as an instrument to advance their financial interests. They will identify initiatives that give them the greatest bang for their bucks rather than those that could make a societal impact. Therefore, holding corporations accountable to generate CSP and demonstrate it through reliable impact assessment measures is critical.

In closing, our core contention is that the role of the private sector in helping address societal and environmental problems is preeminent. We need CSR; in fact, there is a need for greater investments in CSR. However, the neoliberal form of CSR that is premised upon a sharp division between markets and governments is not going to help resolve social and environmental crises. We call for an end to this laissez-faire CSR that leaves the fate of the planet and society to market forces. The role of the government in guiding CSR is critically important to bring discipline to CSR practices, prevent it from being a tool of profiteering, and establish it as a force of societal good. The emerging hybrid form of CSR holds considerable promise to leverage the capabilities of the private sector and the power of regulations to avert societal and climate crises.

Notes

1. Rajat Panwar, et al., "Corporate Responsibility: Balancing Economic, Environmental and Social Issues in the Forest Products Industry," *Forest Products Journal* 56, no. 2 (February 2006).
2. Bidyut Chakrabarty, "Universal Benefit: Gandhi's Doctrine of Trusteeship: A Review Article," *Modern Asian Studies* 49, no. 2 (March 2015); Kazuya Ishii, "The Socioeconomic Thoughts of Mahatma Gandhi: As an Origin of Alternative Development," *Review of Social Economy* 59, no. 3 (September 2001).
3. João R. Faria and Franklin G. Mixon Jr., "Entrepreneurial Philanthropy and University Creation: An Economic Model," *Journal of the Knowledge Economy* 9, no. 3 (September 2018); Fiona Murray, "Evaluating the Role of Science Philanthropy in American Research Universities," *Innovation Policy and the Economy* 13 (2013).
4. Howard Bowen, *Social Responsibilities of the Businessman* (Harper, 1953).
5. Milton Friedman, "A Friedman Doctrine—The Social Responsibility of Business Is to Increase Its Profits," *New York Times Magazine*, September 13, 1970, https://nyti.ms/1LSi5ZD.
6. Gerard Hanlon, "Rethinking Corporate Social Responsibility and the Role of the Firm—On the Denial of Politics," in *Oxford Handbook of Corporate Social Responsibility*, ed. Andrew Crane (Oxford University Press, 2008), 157.
7. Friedman, "A Friedman Doctrine."
8. See Qian Wang, Junsheng Dou, and Shenghua Jia, "A Meta-analytic Review of Corporate Social Responsibility and Corporate Financial Performance: The Moderating Effect of Contextual Factors," *Business & Society* 55, no. 8 (November 2016) for a comprehensive review.
9. Michael Barnett et al., "Reorient the Business Case for Corporate Sustainability," *Stanford Social Innovation Review* (May 2021).
10. Neil Malhotra, Benoît Monin, and Michael Tomz, "Does Private Regulation Preempt Public Regulation?," *American Political Science Review* 113, no. 1 (February 2019).
11. Malhotra et al., "Does Private Regulation Preempt Public Regulation?"
12. Geoffrey B. Sprinkle and Laureen A. Maines, "The Benefits and Costs of Corporate Social Responsibility," *Business Horizons* 53, no. 5 (2010).
13. Joel Bakan, *The Corporation: The Pathological Pursuit of Profit and Power* (Free Press, 2005).
14. Uchechukwu Nwoke, "Corporations and Development: The Barriers to Effective Corporate Social Responsibility (CSR) in a Neoliberal Age," *International Journal of Law and Management* 59, no. 1 (February 2017); Sarah Kaplan, "Beyond the Business Case for Social Responsibility," *Academy of Management Discoveries* 6, no. 1 (April 2020).
15. Gerlinde Berger-Walliser and Inara Scott, "Redefining Corporate Social Responsibility in an Era of Globalization and Regulatory Hardening," *American Business Law Journal* 5, no. 1 (Spring 2018): 190.

16. Roy Suddaby and Rajat Panwar, "On the Complexity of Managing Transparency," *California Management Review* 65, no. 1 (2022).

17. Berger-Walliser and Scott, "Redefining Corporate Social Responsibility"; Rajat Panwar, Shweta Nawani, and Vivek Pandey, "Legislated CSR: A Brief Introduction," *Corporate Social Responsibility* (May 2018).

18. Patricia Rinwigati Waagstein, "The Mandatory Corporate Social Responsibility in Indonesia: Problems and Implications," *Journal of Business Ethics* 98, no. 3 (February 2011).

19. Ioannis Ioannou and George Serafeim, "The Consequences of Mandatory Corporate Sustainability Reporting," Harvard Business School Research Working Paper No. 11-100, May 2017.

20. Jette Steen Knudsen, "Government Regulation of International Corporate Social Responsibility in the US and UK: How Domestic Institutions Shape Mandatory and Supportive Initiatives," *British Journal of Industrial Relations* 56, no. 1 (2018).

21. Tom Fox, Halina Ward, and Bruce Howard, *Public Sector Roles in Strengthening Corporate Social Responsibility: A Baseline Study* (International Institute for Environment and Development, 2002).

22. Matthieu Glachant, et al., "Companies, Participation in EMAS: The Influence of the Public Regulator," *Business Strategy and the Environment* 11, no. 4 (July 2002).

23. Jette Steen Knudsen, Jeremy Moon, and Rieneke Slager, "Government Policies for Corporate Social Responsibility in Europe: A Comparative Analysis of Institutionalization," *Policy & Politics* 43, no. 1 (January 2015); Fox, et al., *Public Sector*.

24. Knudsen, et al. "Government Policies for Corporate Social Responsibility."

25. Laura Albareda, Josep M. Lozano, and Tamyko Ysa, "Public Policies on Corporate Social Responsibility: The Role of Governments in Europe," *Journal of Business Ethics* 74 (2007).

26. Jean-Pascal Gond, Nahee Kang, and Jeremy Moon, "The Government of Self-regulation: On the Comparative Dynamics of Corporate Social Responsibility," *Economy and Society* 40, no. 4 (November 2011).

27. Fox, et al., *Public Sector*.

28. Knudsen, et al., "Government Policies for Corporate Social Responsibility."

29. Rajat Panwar, et al., "Did India's CSR Mandate Enhance or Diminish Firm Value?," *Business & Society* 62, no. 2 (February 2023).

30. Panwar, et al., "India's CSR Mandate."

31. Donna J. Wood, "Corporate Social Performance Revisited," *Academy of Management Review* 16, no. 4 (October 1991).

32. Wood, "Corporate Social Performance Revisited," 693.

14

Smart Regulation
to Enhance Wealth Creation
and Sustainable Capitalism

Victor B. Flatt and Inara Scott

One of the myths surrounding capitalism is that it is in tension with government regulation—that regulation interferes with "pure capitalism" and minimizing regulation always benefits wealth creation.[1] This argument has found its home in the left-right political debates over the role of government in the private marketplace. But far from being interferences with capitalism, government regulation and law are in fact central to its operation and success. Well-designed, smart regulation supports the creation of wealth even as it discourages undesirable behavior, including cheating, lying, and illicitly preying upon vulnerable members of society. In this chapter, we trace the early development of capitalism and the legal foundations that it required. We then discuss the myth that deregulation will always lead to greater economic development and offer specific instances where a lack of regulation undermined economic growth and progress. We conclude by arguing that capitalism—and particularly sustainable capitalism—will only thrive when paired with smart regulation.

Capitalism and Markets Require Legal Foundations to Operate

An old adage suggests that fish don't know what water is because they swim in it. Similarly, it can be hard to see the legal foundations of capitalism because they are essential to how we operate our society. However, in order to understand the importance of regulation to capitalism, it is essential to start seeing these foundation elements.

Perhaps most importantly, law and government regulation are essential to defining and enforcing rights to ownership of property and creating markets for its disposition. At the most basic level, a system of law is necessary to create the expectation that private ownership can be defended, whether against other citizens or against the government itself. From this jumping off point, law must be engaged to answer a deluge of future questions that deeply impact the economic structure of markets within a capitalist economy. Can intangible items, such as dance, art, or music, be property? What about interest on loans, or the expectation of profits from a future transaction? Even if these things do constitute property, law must determine what the boundaries of such ownership are. Is it time limited or endless? Can it be passed along to future generations? Before there can be a market in intellectual property—including patents for technological development, or copyrights for literary works—or other intangible elements of capital, the legal structure of that property right must be determined and the law must recognize it.

Second, law and regulation govern the ways transactions—including contracts—occur in the marketplace. You know when you go to buy a bag of potato chips for a certain price that you can make the exchange for that price in a quick and easy manner and that your right to the potato chips at the agreed upon price will be respected. This certainty that the elements of an exchange transaction will be enforced by courts and legal structures is essential to the development of markets. Consider that in the United States today, a court will uphold a contract made for future services like the creation of a website or the promise to drive a passenger to a new location. These are promises to perform an intangible act of service, yet they may be adjudicated in a court of law. If these contracts were not judiciable, businesses could not predict whether they could market their services or get from one place to another. The certainty of these contracts fuels the ability of markets to develop.

Importantly, the boundaries of these rights are in a constant state of evolution that reflects changing political interests, economic development, and technological evolution. In the United States, for example, the Supreme Court recently considered what type of intellectual property rights can be claimed in genes and in the development of animal species.[2] Those who work in the "gig" economy are subject to a constantly changing slate of laws that determine if they are employees (and therefore entitled to benefits), or independent contractors. In 2018, unions were turned upside down by a Supreme Court decision prohibiting mandatory collection of dues in public employee workplaces.[3] All of these changes to the "rules of the game" impact the ability of particular markets to grow and thrive and also define the success of individual capitalists within those markets, reflecting an ongoing relationship between the evolution of capitalism and a society's political environment. "Both capitalism and its legal foundations are outcomes of an ongoing interaction between interest groups competing and cooperating in a world of scarcity, and there are no transcendent, metaphysical, or natural laws toward which socially generated human law will or should tend."[4]

Economies thrive where the rules of the game are known and predictable. Think of what we might consider "lawless places"—areas where the rule of law is limited.[5] In a globalized economic system, businesses have little incentive to locate themselves in these markets, where their ability to return a profit may be contingent on the whims of a ruling party or individual. Indeed, research indicates economic growth correlates directly with the strength of the rule of law.[6] Here, the concept of the rule of law is broader than simply infrastructure for property and contract rights—it also includes an independent judiciary, physical security, and effective limits on corruption. In fact, a variety of government regulations are necessary for economic efficiency. You buy potato chips without expending your own time and money worrying about whether or not they are poisonous because you know the government sets and enforces standards for such goods. You make long-term investments in home ownership or save money in a retirement fund because you trust that the government will be stable over time and will have the ability to protect these economic interests. Pharmaceutical companies invest billions into the development of a vaccine for COVID-19 because they believe they will be allowed to sell the resultant vaccines without government corruption interfering with their ability to profit.

In short, the so-called invisible hand of the market[7] can only operate when rules are clear and trusted and government can provide economic certainty and market information at a lower cost to society than private infrastructure. Alternatively, a lack of regulation can increase the possibility of major economic disasters, which we discuss in the next part.

Enron: When Insufficient Regulation Leads to Disastrous Results

Without effective government regulation, we see repeated examples of tremendous losses to individuals and society. Consider Enron. After years of building complex accounting devices to conceal losses, artificially prop up its stock price, and manipulate energy markets, Enron collapsed in 2001, destroying $67 billion in assets held by financial institutions, retirees, and stock investors.[8] However, the seeds of the Enron debacle were sown decades earlier—when a regulatory system (and partial dismantling of that system) created inherent incentives to cheat an efficient information ecosystem.

The Securities and Exchange Commission (SEC) was created in the 1930s to regulate accounting principles. It quickly decided that accounting did not need significant federal oversight and could instead rely on self-regulation, either in applying its own standards or those standards adopted by an independent standard setting body (the Financial Accounting Standards Board (FASB)).[9] This worked reasonably well, primarily because there was little incentive for the private sector accounting industry to misreport. Industry deregulation in the 1990s, however, allowed the accounting industry to begin offering other financial services. This created a conflict of interest that the SEC failed to address. Companies that both audited and provided financial services now had an incentive to "enforce" accounting standards in a manner that benefited their new financial services businesses.[10]

During 2000, for example, Enron paid a total of $52 million to Arthur Andersen: $25 million for auditing services and $27 million for non-auditing (consulting) services. The consulting services provided Enron with advice for structuring its business deals; in fact, over half of Andersen's annual revenues came from its consulting services, creating a massive incentive for Anderson not to find problems with the system.[11] The $27 million that Andersen received from Enron in 2000 could easily have compromised Andersen's independence and its judgment in determining the nature, timing, and extent of audit procedures. Further, these economic interests likely deterred Andersen from asking Enron to make revisions to its financial statements. The disastrous fall of Enron and related scandal at Arthur Andersen were not isolated incidents, and in short order, a series of massive corporate scandals, fraud, and financial collapse caused a stock market crash in 2002 on the scale that had previously only been seen in the Great Depression.[12]

In its heyday, Enron was admired for its disruption of the current market norms and its exploration of wealth creation through more use of hedging and financial instruments, ostensibly increasing efficiency by segmenting market risk and allocating it based on comparative appetite for risk. The problem was not the idea of a company pursuing innovation or testing disruptive ways of doing things; the problem was that essential government regulation had been eliminated (due to deregulation) or hamstrung (though a tradition of self-regulation), preventing it from effectively channeling the positive forces of innovation and disruption toward sustainable wealth creation.

Enron's failure was not simply due to economic miscalculation, but was also a clear ethical failure. Indeed, when the law does not punish cheating, falsification, or exploitation, such conduct is likely to result—one might even argue that such behavior is embedded in a capitalist system that offers a potential reward for cheating or unethical behavior. Business may calculate the cost of compliance and choose to engage in harmful conduct if the potential profit margin is high enough. In the illustrative case of the Ford Pinto, for example, the Ford Motor Company chose not to redesign the Pinto despite a known safety risk related to the placement of the gas tank. "The safer gas tank design imposed an additional cost of $137.5 million, which greatly exceeded what Ford considered to be the safety benefit from moving the tank, which it estimated to be approximately $50 million. Ford used a $200,000 value to monetize each fatality that would be reduced by changing the risky gas tank placement, which was in line with wrongful death awards at that time."[13] In short, Ford determined that the cost of killing people was less than the cost of a redesign.

Though the facts of the Enron and Pinto cases are particularly glaring, they are by no means the only examples. A deeply troubling pattern of safety violations by BP[14] led straight to the Deepwater Horizon disaster that took eleven lives and created an environmental disaster of epic proportions.[15] Or consider the 2022 Inflation Reduction Act (IRA),[16] which included additional funding for the Internal Revenue Service, in part to hire more auditors and increase enforcement. Based on this increased enforcement and collection, the Congressional Budget Office estimates the IRS will raise an additional $203 billion over ten years.[17] Clearly, regulation and enforcement matter—one without the other may ultimately prove unable to meaningfully change corporate behavior. As Professor Partnoy suggests, "market crashes . . . are due to various market failures, including investor cognitive error, moral hazard, and information asymmetry. [L]aw can do something about crashes, in addition to minimizing agency and information costs."[18] Or as Professor Lynn Stout argues, "The law plays an important role in promoting [prosocial behavior], not only by creating incentives but also by signaling what conduct is appropriate and expected; by encouraging prosocial behavior in others; and by educating us about how our own choices help or harm those around us."[19]

Economic Growth Through Smart Regulation

If capitalism (and society) so clearly benefits from law and regulation—indeed, requires it in order to operate—why do many persist in claiming that businesses grow best when they are "deregulated"? Perhaps the key to understanding this argument is that "deregulation" or "free markets" in this context does not mean the absence of all regulation—it means eliminating regulation that is believed to impede economic growth. Thus "deregulating" the airline industry did not mean erasing all regulations related to airlines—passengers would be unlikely to travel thirty thousand feet in the air in a metal tube subject to no safety regulations, let alone eliminating legal protection of private property, contracts, and credit for the business owners—it simply meant reforming entry and pricing regulations that significantly limited the operation of the airline industry.[20] When politicians advocate for less environmental regulation, what they generally want are less regulations related to the protection of endangered species, pollution controls, or limits on the use of public lands.[21] In the field of antitrust, confusingly, calls for "free markets" and deregulation can mean either enforcement of limits on consolidation (as was the case when the courts broke up the oil and telecommunications industries)[22] or the elimination of restrictions on consolidation (as in current calls for "deregulation" of the radio industry).[23]

Given that "deregulation" does not actually mean the absence of regulation, and that, as discussed in Part II, economic growth and individuals can be significantly harmed by an absence of regulation, we suggest that what is needed for capitalism to thrive is smart regulation—regulation designed to increase beneficial economic activity and long-term economic sustainability, while minimizing harmful externalities. In many cases, truly supporting the private sector, innovation, and wealth creation requires more government regulation, not less.

What types of regulations may be considered "smart" in a capitalist society? First, regulations that internalize externalities, such as the cost of pollution. In the absence of such regulation (i.e., requiring companies to pay for pollution control devices or limiting the amount of discharge into public waterways) a corporation will not factor the "cost" of the externality into its operations. Markets cannot efficiently address this problem—an individual market will not price in an invisible cost borne by society. Second, regulation must consider the potential harm to individuals in society of a cost-benefit analysis that puts the economic value of social harm at a lower cost than compliance with regulations. Whether it is the loss of a pension (Enron), a life (Ford), or an ecosystem (BP), regulation and enforcement must be sufficient to incentivize the kind of behavior that we want from corporations.

Regulation must also be aware of creating perverse incentives where the system can be gamed. Or failing that, must ensure sufficient enforcement and penalties to discourage such behavior. Again Enron's actions in the deregulated California electricity markets provide a good example. Because shortages in supply drove up the spot price for energy, the California restructuring actually encouraged producers to withhold electricity from the market because they would make more money doing so.[24]

Finally, regulation must be able to identify and address the kind of "irrational exuberance" and risky behavior that creates the risk of catastrophic losses and market collapse.[25] While economists might argue that markets will account for irrational behavior in the long run, as John Maynard Keynes aptly noted, "In the long run, we're all dead."[26] The time it takes for markets to calibrate can result in inefficient societal losses that cannot be fully remedied or corrected by the market later receiving or processing better information. One of the authors of this chapter has called this market failure adjustment costs, and in some cases, these can be quite exorbitant, and may fall unequally.[27]

Market forces might increase the price of the tusks of an endangered African elephant, but the market won't stop people from driving the animals into extinction. Rising sea levels and increasingly intense rain events may destroy property values in flood-prone areas, but this economic reaction won't stop the production of fossil fuels or the profound economic losses and even death that individuals and society suffer from climate change.[28] Conscience might suggest that corporations should not produce cars that are likely to kill people, but law is necessary to reinforce the type of pro-social behavior that makes people likely to comply with legal obligations. Markets will not prevent market crashes or the loss of individual liveli-hoods and futures that may result, but sound regulation can mitigate the ability of individuals to drive billions of dollars (theirs and others') off the cliff with them.

Proponents of "deregulation" fail to recognize the significant legal infrastructure that is required to build wealth through capital markets, and the regulatory apparatus that is needed for innovation, creativity, and disruption to lead to positive social change. Capitalism—and particularly sustainable capitalism—requires smart regulation to allow individuals to build wealth and societies to flourish. If we focus on smart regulation, we can avoid the next Enron, and other things we can't yet imagine.

Notes

1. Mark A. Martinez, *The Myth of the Free Market: The Role of the State in a Capitalist Society* (Kumarian Press, 2009), 3–6, 26–29.
2. *Diamond v. Chakrabarty, 447 U.S. 303 (1980)* (reaffirming that a live, human-made microorganism is patentable subject matter); *Association for Molecular Pathology v. Myriad Genetics, Inc., 569 U.S. 576 (2013)* (holding that a naturally occurring DNA segment is not patent eligible, but a lab-synthesized strand of complementary DNA is patent eligible because it is not naturally occurring).
3. California Legislative Analyst's Office, "Proposition 22: Exempts App-Based Transportation and Delivery Companies from Providing Employee Benefits to Certain Drivers," November 2020 (a ballot initiative that passed but later was overturned classifying drivers for app-based transportation and deliv-ery companies as independent contractors); *Janus v. American Federation of State, County, and Municipal Employees, Council 31, 141 S.Ct. 1282 (2021)* (certiorari denied); *Janus v. American Federation of State, County, and Munic-ipal Employees, Council 31, 942 F.3d 352 (7th Cir. 2019)* (prohibiting manda-tory collection of dues in public employee workplaces).
4. John R. Commons, Jeff E. Biddle, and Warren J. Samuels, *Legal Foundations of Capitalism* (Transaction Publishers, 1995), xxxi.
5. World Justice Report, Rule of Law Index 2020 (World Justice Project, 2020).
6. Stephan Haggard and Lydia Tiede, "The Rule of Law and Economic Growth: Where Are We?," *World Development* 39, no. 5 (2011): 673–85.

7. Adrian Vermeule, "The Invisible Hand in Legal and Political Theory," *Virginia Law Review* 96, no. 6 (October 2010): 1418.
8. See generally Marianne M. Jennings, "A Primer on Enron: Lessons From A Perfect Storm of Financial Reporting, Corporate Governance and Ethical Culture Failures," *California Western Law Review* 39, no. 2 (2003).
9. Donna M. Nagy, "Playing Peekaboo with Constitutional Law: The PCAOB and Its Public/Private Status," *Notre Dame Law Review* 80 (2005): 984–86.
10. Jennings, "A Primer on Enron," 213–29.
11. Jonathan D. Glater, "Enron's Many Strands: Accounting; 4 Audit Firms Are Set to Alter Some Practices," *New York Times*, February 1, 2002.
12. André Douglas Pond Cummings, "'Ain't No Glory in Pain': How the 1994 Republican Revolution and the Private Securities Litigation Reform Act Contributed to the Collapse of the United States Capital Markets," *Nebraska Law Review* 83 (2004): 990–91, 998–1003.
13. W. Kip Viscusi, "The Fatal Failure of the Regulatory State," *William & Mary Law Review* 60 (2018): 642.
14. Abrahm Lustgarten and Ryan Knutson, "Years of Internal BP Probes Warned That Neglect Could Lead to Accidents," *ProPublica*, June 7, 2010.
15. Richard C. Bishop, et al., "Putting a Value on Injuries to Natural Assets: The BP Oil Spill," *Science* 356, no. 6335 (April 2017).
16. Inflation Reduction Act, Pub. L. 117-169, 136 Stat. 1818 (2022).
17. Katie Lobosco, "The IRS Is Set to Get Billions for Audit Enforcement. Here's What It Means for Taxpayers," *CNN*, August 11, 2022.
18. Frank Partnoy, "Why Markets Crash and What Law Can Do about It," *University of Pittsburgh Law Review* 61 (2000): 817.
19. Lynn A. Stout, *Cultivating Conscience: How Good Laws Make Good People* (Princeton University Press, 2010), 237.
20. Gary McDonnell, "What Caused Airline Deregulation: Economists or Economics?," *Independent Review* 19, no. 3 (Winter 2015).
21. Hannah Perls, "Deconstructing Environmental Deregulation Under the Trump Administration," *Vermont Law Review* 45, no. 591 (2021).
22. Maham Usman, "Breaking Up Big Tech: Lessons from AT&T," *University of Pennsylvania Law Review* 170 (2021): 531–33.
23. Adam Jacobson, "Deregulation Meltdown: Is More the Answer For Radio?," *Radio + Television Business Report*, September 3, 2021; Gene Ely, "Can Deregulation Fix What's Broken About Radio? That's The Hope," *Forbes*, May 14, 2018.
24. Adrian Moore, "California: How Not to Deregulate Electricity," *reason Foundation*, January 7, 2001.
25. Sharon Reier, "5 Years Later, Greenspan's 'Irrational Exuberance' Alert Rings True," *New York Times*, December 1, 2001.
26. John Maynard Keynes, *A Tract on Monetary Reform* (London: Macmillan, 1923), 80.
27. Michael Pappas and Victor Flatt, "Climate Changes Property: Disasters, Decommodification, and Retreat," *Ohio State Law Journal* 82 (2021).
28. Kevin Rennert, et al., "Comprehensive Evidence Implies a Higher Social Cost of CO_2," *Nature* 610 (2022).

15

Environmental Law
The Paradox of Property Rights for Environmental Protection

Christy Anderson Brekken

Although the term "environmental law" was not coined until 1970, human societies have always governed individual use of collective resources.[1] Today, U.S. law directly governs many environmental resources, including clean air and water, while the capitalist economic system also serves as an "indirect system of governance" that impacts these collective goods.[2]

Despite arguments in favor of "free markets" and distaste for government interference, capitalism can only exist and thrive within legally defined and enforced property rights, firms, markets, infrastructure, and provision of public goods. If capitalism is here to stay, the essential question is not whether capitalism can be sustainable, but whether public policy can and will meaningfully "redefin[e] economic settings and circumstances" to constrain economic decisions that degrade our common environment.[3] Moreover, if property rights, markets, and profit-driven firms got us into a climate crisis, can we get out with these structures intact?

While property rights are essential to a capitalist economy, individual rights are essential to democratic governance. Surprisingly, given the current national interest in "rights talk,"[4] many individual environmental rights remain undefined. For example, should there be a "right" to a stable climate and healthy environment? Should environmental law give polluters a "right" to pollute? If these legal rights were adopted, could they work to ensure the sustainability of the capitalist economic structure?

To navigate these questions, we will take a brief tour through the history of U.S. environmental law. Then we can ask: Which policy tools are best suited to constrain economic actors within our current legal, economic, social, technological, and bio-physical circumstances to preserve collective resources? Can property rights and markets be effectively regulated in a manner that limits damage to the environment? Are environmental rights compatible with or even necessary for a sustainable capitalist economic system?

Ultimately, public policy adopted through the democratic process is the only direct control a society has over economic actors.[5] In this chapter, I argue that redefining rights can bring about a new landscape for cultural and market interactions, creating a decentralized, flexible, and adaptable policy landscape that adjusts as circumstances change. Democratic and economic equity and participation are essential legal foundations for sustainable capitalism, and environmental justice is a foundation for democratic and economic equity. Environmental, social, and economic equity and sustainability are inextricably linked.

A Brief History of U.S. Environmental Law: Deploying the Environmental Policy Toolkit

As human communities experience environmental harm, new policy is designed to reshape the institutional landscape. Environmental conditions improve, change, or persist in response to environmental law, and in turn, society's expectations and demands change in response, motivating new environmental law, continuing as long as the democratic process endures.

Environmental policy is designed to correct the capitalist market failures that cause environmental harm—such as negative externalities, under-provision of public goods, and asymmetric information. Policy tools that have developed over time include public management, liability, command and control, procedural requirements, pricing (taxes or subsidies), market-based property rights, and information.[6] As a result, today's U.S. environmental law is much more than the Clean Air Act, Clean Water Act, or Endangered Species Act. Environmental law permeates U.S. institutions and the economy, accumulating over the Western legal tradition and progressing through a set of environmental policy tools designed to address a type, source, and extent of environmental harm, enacted through legitimate government authority.

To chart a course to the future, it is helpful to first understand how our past choice of policy tools and use of legal authority have shaped our current economic and environmental landscape. The U.S. colonists threw off the British monarchy while maintaining colonial legal frameworks and capitalist economic assumptions. Property law justified the seizure of Indigenous land and continued ownership of human beings under chattel slavery.[7] The public trust doctrine embodies both public management and procedural policy tools, requiring states to hold defined public resources in trust for the benefit of the public while demanding public process when allocating public trust resources.[8] State tort law claims of trespass, private or public nuisance, or strict liability act as liability-based environmental policy, empowering courts to stop private activities that cause harm or requiring compensation for environmental damages.[9]

The legal authority of government actors also shaped U.S. environmental policy. Much of U.S. legal authority is implicit, such as the federalist structure in which states are sovereigns possessing the "police powers" to regulate for the health, safety, and welfare of the people and conferring that power to local governments. The federal government possesses explicit but limited powers enumerated in the Constitution; most relevant to environmental policies are the Property Clause (Art. IV Sec. 3 Cl. 2), Commerce Clause (Art. I Sec. 8 Cl. 3), Tax and Spend Clause (Art. I Sec. 8 Cl. 1), and the Treaty Power (Art. II Sec. 2). The U.S. economic system of private property rights and a market economy is implied in the Due Process Clause (Amend. 5) and Contracts Clause (Art. I Sec. 10).

These federal powers have been used to protect natural resources long before the 1970s. Under the Property Clause, the federal government may own and manage natural resources on public lands for multiple uses. The Treaty Power enables the Migratory Bird Treaty Act (1918), among others.[10] The Rivers and Harbors Act (1899) protects navigable waters using both public management and command-and-control policy tools to prohibit waste disposal into waters without a permit—which became both a motivation and model for the modern Clean Water Act permit system.[11]

Public management of infrastructure and natural resources facilitated industrialization, which increased the scale and toxicity of pollution. Industrialization and urbanization brought people closer to pollution and each other, while poor labor standards and poverty exposed them to environmental hazards.[12] Tort law principles became a barrier to remedying private environmental harm, as people without property lacked resources and legal claims to hold polluters accountable while proof of causation became more complex. Courts favored money damages over court orders to control pollution as the economic value of industrial facilities rose and their operation created jobs and a tax base for local jurisdictions.

Cities and states sued polluters using cross-border public tort claims as they dealt with the broadening scope and impact of pollution, but had limited success or very slow remedies.[13] By the early 1900s, social justice movements pressured state and local governments to pass command-and-control laws covering waste disposal, air quality, noise, zoning, and others.[14] Some communities suffered extreme pollution impacts, such as the 1948 "killer fog" in Donora, Pennsylvania, and the infamous 1969 Cuyahoga River fire—a "routine" river fire that caught the attention of the nation. By the 1950s, many large cities and some states had air quality laws and forty-seven state laws regulated water pollution; by 1967, states had passed 112 pollution control laws.[15]

During and after the Great Depression and World War II (WWII), local and state governments used command-and-control laws to limit pollution, while the federal government used public management and pricing policy tools to fund massive government projects and provide public goods. The hydroelectric dams of the West, extension of electricity distribution; intensification of agriculture; interstate highways; and other initiatives changed the natural and economic landscape. Federal government bureaucrats made decisions with little input from local or state residents or governments. National markets led to increased consumption for consumer goods and energy. The post-WWII baby boom and suburbanization emerged alongside demand for outdoor recreation. Conservation groups pushed for new procedural policy tools such as the Administrative Procedures Act of 1946 (APA), giving the public a right to participate in administrative agency decision making, still a cornerstone of citizen participation and the basis for the right to litigate many environmental issues today.[16]

Citizens also pushed for federal command-and-control policies that are the forebearers of today's pollution control laws, regulating products under the Commerce Clause power. Revelations about contamination of the food supply led to the Food, Drug, and Cosmetics Act of 1938. The technologies of WWII were turned to civilian use by the industrial firms, regulated through the Federal Insecticide, Fungicide, and Rodenticide Act (FIFRA) (1947), among others.[17] But pollution damage was seen as a health and safety issue left to state police powers. By the 1960s, federal pollution laws were focused on incentivizing state law and assisting with research.[18]

With this history, it's clear that "environmental law" was at work long before the first environmental law conference in 1969 and first Earth Day in 1970.[19] Even so, the "environmental decade" of the 1970s was inaugurated with a televised signing ceremony for the National Environmental Policy Act (NEPA) on January 1, 1970.[20] NEPA is a procedural and informational policy tool that requires federal administrative agencies to publicly document significant environmental impacts before major federal actions. NEPA has been described as being both a singular genius of policymaking because citizens can sue the government to enforce its procedural and informational requirements, and yet fatally flawed because an agency is not required to change its actions based on the environmental impacts.[21]

The 1970s environmental era pioneered cooperative federalism through command-and-control policies: pollution limits are set through either public health, technological, or a balancing-based standard; federal and state authority is apportioned based on characteristics of the impacted resource; and adaptive regulatory mechanisms have tightened standards over time while pushing technological progress and reducing the cost of pollution abatement. The laws have become the pillars of U.S. environmental law that we know today: Clean Air Act (1970), Clean Water Act (1972), Endangered Species Act (1973), Energy Policy and Conservation Act (1975), Toxic Substances Control Act (1976), Resource Conservation and Recovery Act (1976). While these laws have significantly reduced pollution burdens from industrial sources, many sources and pollutants are still not effectively controlled, including greenhouse gasses.

The 1970s command-and-control policies also created perverse incentives, leading to illegal dumping of captured pollution, including hazardous waste. Pollution-control laws also elicited complaints about the cost of regulation, which echoed through political circles. In the 1980s, liability-based policy tools made a comeback through the Comprehensive Environmental Response, Compensation, and Liability Act of 1980 (CERCLA, also known as the Superfund). CERCLA applies strict liability for the full environmental damages to anyone who contributed to contamination of natural resources. The Superfund also had a pricing policy—a tax on chemical companies created the fund—although the tax expired and was never re-authorized.

Now the public bears the burden of cleanup through the general tax fund when polluters are not held financially accountable.

Throughout all of the phases of environmental regulation, pricing policy tools in the form of taxes and subsidies have been at work inflating or reducing the prices of products and services. Fossil fuels and nuclear energy have long been subsidized to provide cheap and plentiful energy to grow the economy, despite environmental risks. Now subsidies also support renewable energy and energy efficiency technologies. The government has always put a thumb on the supply and demand for energy and other resources, influencing society's pollution burden.

By the 1980s, two pollution problems caught the public's attention—one regional and one global. Acid rain was killing forests in the northeastern United States, caused by coal-fired power plants in the Midwest. On a global scale, scientists discovered the "hole" in the ozone layer above Antarctica, caused by chlorofluorocarbons (CFCs) such as aerosols and refrigerants, addressed internationally by the Montreal Protocol (1987). The United States tackled both problems through market-based policy tools in the 1992 Clean Air Act Amendments. Rather than specifying the amount of pollution allowed from each particular firm, regulators set an overall cap on pollution for the entire industry. Individual firms then obtain a "right" to emit a particular amount of pollution from the industry-wide allotment. Firms that could abate their pollution more cheaply sold their "rights" to firms with higher abatement costs, all while the total pollution cap decreased over time. The cap and trade programs worked more quickly and cheaply than anticipated: Both the forests of the U.S. Northeast and the "hole" in the ozone layer are healing.[22]

In the 1990s, information policies were enacted to reduce pollution by influencing consumer demand. While the United States already required fuel economy stickers on new cars, the Energy Star program and National Organic Standards were added as government-defined and regulated labels for consumer goods. Consumers now had access to government-regulated information to choose more energy efficient appliances and food grown without synthetic chemicals. Government standards have been updated over time, and consumer demand has pushed the market to react. For example, sales of U.S. Department of Agriculture (USDA)-labeled "organic" products have more than doubled from 2011 to 2020.[23]

Looking back at the history, U.S. governance systems tend to respond to acute harms with identifiable causes. Policy tools work when they are tailored to the scientific, economic, and political nature of an environmental problem. Economic actors are incentivized to develop new technology to control pollution or substitute cleaner goods or services. But when it comes to a systemic, long-term, ubiquitous type of pollution that is fully entwined in the economy and society, such as greenhouse gas emissions, U.S. governance systems have failed to act at the speed and ambition required. No major new environmental law has been enacted since the 1990s. Regulatory advances under existing laws are seen as temporary—they can be rolled back as political administrations change.[24]

With this much environmental law on the books, why is the United States the world's largest historical contributor to climate change damages?[25] The shallow answer is that U.S. public policy has favored plentiful fossil fuels as energy sources to benefit economic growth. Existing environmental laws, such as the Clean Air Act, have not regulated greenhouse gas pollution until recently and were not designed for the task. The deeper answer involves the relationship between the U.S. capitalist economy, its energy system, and its cultural and political values. It is a "wicked problem" because of its multidimensional causes and effects.[26] This raises the question: can existing policy tools be applied in a capitalist economy to create a more sustainable future?

Who Has the Rights, Sir? Rights Frameworks for Environmental Protection

Dr. Seuss published *The Lorax* in 1971. Cultural attention had turned to environmental damage; he kept up with current events. In short, the Once-ler moves into a pristine Truffala Tree forest, using the trees to produce Thneeds in his factory. The Lorax pops out of the stump of a freshly felled tree and demands that the Once-ler stop cutting trees and polluting the air and water. The Once-ler retorts: "Well, I have my rights sir, and I'm telling you, I intend to go on doing just what I do!"[27]

As a strict Seussian textualist, I ask my environmental law students to find the exact language that explains why the Once-ler clear-cuts the Truffula Trees, releasing smogulous smoke, Gluppity-Glupp, and Scholppity-Schlop, driving away the Brown Bar-ba-loots, Swomee Swans, and Humming-Fish. Most students first point to economic forces, such as demand for the Thneeds: "You never can tell what some people will buy." Some point to the profit motive and growth imperative of supply: "[B]usiness is business! And business must grow." The market logic underlying the destruction of the Truffala forest is undeniably a contributing force, but non-capitalist economies seem equally willing to unsustainably exploit natural resources. While capitalism is disastrous for the environment, it is not the fundamental cause of the Truffala forest crisis.

The true underlying cause of environmental harm comes in the Once-ler's response to the repeated complaints from the Lorax: "Well, I have my RIGHTS sir, and I'm telling you, I intend to go on doing just what I do!" (emphasis added). The Lorax disappears from the story, leaving only a stone marker inscribed with "unless."

Unless what—"someone like you cares a whole awful lot" and plants a tree? While an appropriate ending for a children's book, it is not a solution based on Dr. Seuss's diagnosis of the problem. If the Once-ler indeed has the right to cut down trees and pollute the air and water, then re-thinking rights is the ultimate solution. The Lorax "speaks for the trees" but all he can do is "yap yap and say bad bad bad bad," according to the Once-ler. Dr. Seuss shows us that appealing to the morality of the economic actor doesn't work. Only public policy, "collective action in restraint, liberation, and expansion" of economic actors through "the legislative activity of democratic societies" can redefine and enforce rights.[28] "Unless someone like you" votes, organizes, lobbies, passes laws or regulations, thus changing the legal constraints on economic actors, "nothing is going to get better. It's not."[29]

Choosing and designing the right policy tool for the future of environmental law requires us to wrestle with the legal question—who has the rights now? And who should have the rights if we want an environmentally sustainable future? "Is it individuals as autonomous market participants, or is it the community that decides to intervene and alter the market status quo for the greater good?"[30] And is this actually a binary choice? Assigning rights to one party implies responsibilities for others; it shifts the relations between parties and incentives for private decisions and social outcomes. Different rights regimes lead to different allocations of risks, costs, and benefits for social welfare and equitable distribution. The Coase Theorem (1937)—that the assignment of rights is irrelevant to reaching a socially efficient outcome—does not hold in practice because we do not live in a world where property rights are fully enforceable and transferrable, transaction costs are low, and private costs reflect the full social value of resources, a conclusion that Coase came to himself.[31] In the real world, who has the rights matters, and the law defines rights. The road to any sustainable economic system goes through legal institutions.

Right to Pollute

The Once-ler essentially declares a "right to pollute." Is this true? The Western legal tradition has several justifications for property rights claims.[32] People have polluted because the land, water, and air were "attached" to property that they had a right to use. Legal doctrines also recognize the taking of rights by force or occupation, through a Western economic and cultural definition of "beneficial" use.[33] Perhaps the right to pollute is held in common by the public, and some people like the Once-ler just use it more than others. From the pigsty of the 1600s in England[34] to the inconsiderate dog owner of today, we assume that nature will absorb our waste or someone else can deal with it. Whatever the implicit justification—culture, economics, bio-physical—the right to pollute seems to be an implicit personal or property right in the Western legal tradition underpinning capitalist economies. Whether the land is publicly owned and the Once-ler has a lease or easement, or whether the Once-ler claims outright ownership, he certainly acts as if he has property rights.

Right to a Healthy Environment

U.S. constitutional rights are negative rights—they only limit government interference with particular categories of private action. There is no explicit recognition of a right to environmental protection in the U.S. Constitution, and courts have declined or sidestepped the request to declare federal constitutional environmental rights as implicit in the U.S. constitutional structure.[35] Negative rights are also enshrined in the common law tradition, such as the law of nuisance that protects property owners from substantial and unreasonable interference with property rights by other private actors.

Although state constitutions contain some substantive positive rights, such as the right to a free public education, positive rights typically come from legislation.[36] Positive rights can be substantive or procedural. Substantive rights create an individual entitlement or provision of public goods, such as enforceable pollution limits, operation of public water systems, public parks, and others. Procedural rights create a right to be heard, to participate in public decisions, or require government actors to provide particular information to the public. An innovation of U.S. environmental law is the citizen suit, allowing any impacted individual to sue polluters for violating limits in pollution control laws like the Clean Air Act and Clean Water Act. Therefore, limiting the right to pollute creates responsibilities on the polluter, and creates rights for people who are harmed by violations of pollution limits.

Around half of U.S. state constitutions have some mention of natural resources or the environment, and eight to ten states, some other countries, and Indigenous tribal nations have articulated specific environmental rights.[37] However, assigning environmental rights has resulted in limited environmental protection in the United States. Judicial interpretation has limited vague environmental rights to damage caused by government actors, with the most success protecting procedural rights, broad public interests, and human health rather than purely ecosystem health.[38]

Market-based Policy: The Paradoxical Road to Protecting Environmental Sustainability

Law, economics, and human nature seem to beg for the simplicity of clearly defined mutually exclusive rights. This is where strong "rights talk" creates a political and judicial impasse or leads us to dismiss viable policy solutions.[39] In the United States, rights are typically connected to individuals rather than to populations or ecosystems. Legislatures and courts are more comfortable assigning an individual right to pollute because it is measurable and enforceable.

Paradoxically, a public right to a healthy environment can be created and protected by explicitly defining a limited collective right to pollute, then allocating that collective right among individual polluters. The shift in thinking is from unfettered and undefined individual rights creating collective impacts, to shared collective rights protected by limited scarce individual rights with accompanying responsibilities. A shift to a community rights framework can be accomplished through the legal-economic framework of market-based policy or a pricing policy.

Defining a Collective Right to a Healthy Environment

A collective right to a healthy environment would require a government to explicitly define and enforce a public right to a functioning ecosystem, then set community-based pollution limits based on that public right. A persistent problem in environmental law today is the inability to limit overall cumulative pollution and its disproportionate impact on the public, particularly for vulnerable communities and ecosystems. For example, one model for defining and enforcing baseline environmental health is through the Clean Air Act's National Ambient Air Quality standards, limiting criteria pollutants to a level "requisite to protect public health with an adequate margin of safety."[40] The Clean Air Act has been overwhelmingly successful at reducing overall pollution nationwide—criteria pollutants dropped 78 percent from 1970 to 2020 while all economic indicators have grown.[41] But this public health standard has not ensured that every person in the country breathes equally clean air because enforceable pollution limits are based on the technological and economic ability of an industry to control its pollution. Limited individual rights to pollute are necessary but not sufficient for sustainable and equitable environmental outcomes.

Defining collective environmental rights shifts the policy goal and decision standards from pollution control to environmental sustainability and equity. A community-based public health standard is a way to define a collective right to ecosystem function and human health in a specified geographic area, considering the total pollution burden from multiple sources of pollution, weather patterns and risk, existing infrastructure, historical systems of marginalization, socio-economic indicators, and other factors. Public health must be linked to a geographical place where people form community, while considering both immediate and long-term impacts. A community-based public health standard also requires robust public participation so that community members can express their public health needs and hold decision makers accountable.

Allocating Collective Pollution Limits among Individual Polluters

Dr. Seuss was correct that the market system plays a role in environmental damage. Polluting goods and services are valued for their human use, but the pollution they create is a type of market failure in which society bears the cost of pollution damage, disproportionately impacting marginalized communities and ecosystems. While "you never can tell what some people will buy," public policy influences economic decisions whether it targets the supply or demand side, prices or quantity. Environmental law has used a variety of public policy tools to limit pollution over time, including market-based or pricing approaches. Markets are self-organizing systems to allocate anything that should be "scarce," making pollution a perfect candidate.

Environmental law can make pollution scarce by defining and enforcing a pollution limit based on a community-based public health standard. Markets are a system for self-organizing under changing circumstances, such as meeting new legal constraints on pollution. Pollution limits create an incentive to develop new technology, infrastructure, and human behaviors that provide for our needs while limiting our environmental impact. "Economists often model technology as literal manna, coming from nowhere, costing nothing . . . [but] the raw material is the body of understanding people have accumulated . . . the source of variety is human creativity . . . and the selection mechanism can be whatever the market will reward or whatever governments . . . will fund."[42] By using the "visible hand of human agency" to legislate a community-based right to environmental quality, then by allowing the "invisible hand" of a market system to develop new ways of meeting human needs, we reduce pollution associated with the goods and services that society depends on.[43] Community-based pollution rights based on public participation also create more public pressure to reduce pollution. The market will not—indeed cannot—reduce pollution on its own.

Market-based tools, such as a cap and trade program, work from the quantity side: defining and limiting the overall quantity of pollution rights increases the price to pollute for each firm, creating an economic incentive to reduce their own pollution. Firms that can reduce pollution quickly can sell some rights to pollute to other firms, as long as the transaction does not violate a community's right to ecosystem function. Pricing policies such as emissions taxes, fees, or auction of pollution rights transform something that was once "free"—waste disposal by way of pollution—into a cost borne by the firm. Explicit pollution rights also reveal information about the cost of pollution reduction through the actions of firms, allowing regulators to continue to reduce pollution burdens as new technology or human behavior patterns emerge. When overall pollution is limited, individual firms get an economic benefit from reducing their pollution, harnessing the power of markets to secure the right to a healthy environment for the collective.

A market is simply a mechanism for allocating collective rights among individuals or firms. Reclaiming a community-based right to public health and functioning ecosystems requires public policy to explicitly grant a limited right to use ecosystem services—such as waste disposal—to private parties. Reclaiming a community-based right to public health and ecosystem services removes the historical implicit right to pollute.

When Market-based or Pricing Policies Are Appropriate

Many people feel that using private property rights and markets, hallmarks of capitalism, to correct environmental degradation is a fool's errand. Markets may be ethically repugnant to some people and for some situations—markets for drugs, organ transplants, and reproductive services, for example, are legally prohibited in some jurisdictions but not in others.[44] Markets or pricing are not appropriate tools for every problem, and, as with any policy tool, need to be designed to equitably reach policy goals. But if Dr. Seuss's diagnosis is indeed correct and the Once-ler's right to pollute is the root of ecosystem destruction, limiting the implicit right to pollute based on a collective right to a sustainable Truffala forest is a path forward.

Capitalism concerns itself with rights when it is profitable to do so, asserting them to justify means or ends, or to assess liability for damage to the rights of others. Over time, the United States has moved toward a more comprehensive approach to pollution, but that policy evolution is still underway. Liability-based policy through common law torts was prevalent through the 1960s. Policy tools shifted in part because courts began to apply monetary pollution damages rather than injunctions to stop pollution, which a dissenting judge complained was "licensing a continuing wrong."[45] The court's decision emphasizes that legislative action is required to re-define the rights: "A court performs its essential function when it decides the rights of parties before it. . . . This is an area beyond the circumference of one private lawsuit. It is the direct responsibility for government."[46]

Command-and-control policy maintained the pollution-rights status quo through a limiting, but not a shifting, of the right to pollute; pollution standards apply to particular pollutants of a particular quantity from a particular source to a particular place based on polluter profiles, available technology or economic-balancing tests. Firms were allowed to continue to exploit market failures for their own benefit, socializing the costs of pollution, and maintaining asymmetric information by withholding the true costs of pollution control. Command-and-control policy has a place, but excluding market-based policy tools from consideration removes a powerful tool from the policy toolkit, and limits the range of possible options.

Other policy tools can be used in conjunction with market-based or pollution-pricing tools to accelerate pollution reductions or equitably distribute the costs and benefits of market changes. Subsidies are pricing tools that can reduce the cost of "clean" technologies, goods, or services that substitute for higher-priced polluting goods or services. Subsidies can also remedy disproportionate impacts of pollution burden or costs by assisting vulnerable communities or those who have historically been burdened by environmental harms. Information policies alert consumers to pollution and pricing profiles that can help the demand side adjust more quickly. Public management will continue to be appropriate for infrastructure or environmental amenities that deliver public goods.

Market systems are suited to problems like climate change, where the pollution is ubiquitous in the economy and causes globalized harm rather than pollution that causes immediate acute localized harm. The community-based public interest can be defined by the most vulnerable communities, then will benefit all people. The profligate use of fossil fuels has created a Gordian knot that will not be undone by targeting each individual source of greenhouse gas emissions, or supporting each method of carbon sequestration. Instead, the vast number of individuals and firms in our energy system can be simultaneously regulated by targeting their common link: the price of fossil fuels. Market-based or pricing policies should be made at the highest level of government that has legal authority over economic transactions—in the United States, that is the federal government. Market-based policies should be forged in cooperation among sovereigns to cover the world economy, and must touch the essential inputs—such as extraction of fossil fuels—so that the price is transmitted through every subsequent market transaction.

Capitalism has responded to market-based policy to reduce pollution in other settings, such as ending acid rain and healing our global ozone layer, where comprehensive policy was necessary to address all sources of pollution at once. Defining and enforcing market-based property rights to pollute is not "commoditizing" natural systems—it is removing implicitly claimed rights from the private sector and putting natural systems back under public control. The "right" to pollute is then a scarce and limited right, whereas now it is a boundless right only limited by command-and-control regulation that can be manipulated or defied with only a fine paid into government coffers. Democratic governance properly defines collective and individual rights, implemented with public policy tools designed to secure collective and equitable well-being.

Future Governance for Sustainable Capitalism—Lessons and Humility

Our human economic and legal structures are no less complex than the vast ecosystems that support life on earth. The "eco-" in economics and ecosystem comes from the Greek *oikos*, meaning "household" or "home." Ecosystems and economics are interconnected; resources are managed for survival of the community, not only the individual. Markets are a method for allocating resources even in ecosystems, where organisms exchange energy and nutrients in ways that humans are only beginning to realize, both within and across species.[47] If resources are not distributed appropriately, the web of relations will fail, sometimes in unexpected ways.

The ecosystem of human relations is constructed from political, economic, legal, cultural, and scientific realms interacting with the natural world, inextricably intertwined relations exhibiting decentralization, flexibility, and adaptation to changes in any dimension.[48] One redeeming quality about economics is that it acknowledges we cannot perfectly engineer individual or social outcomes that result from human decisions. Instead, economics allows us to set our sights on a desired outcome, then design dynamic policy responses to achieve that outcome. If rights are like the sunlight or shade of the institutional ecosystem, then the dynamic and self-organizing forces of markets will grow toward the rights that we establish and recede from the rights that we limit. When setting a course for a more sustainable future, humility requires that we consider how our systems will dynamically respond to change.

The poster child of a capitalist economy—the United States—has a strong multi-level governance system that touches all aspects of the economy and provision of public goods. The history of environmental law has demonstrated the power of working at multiple levels of government to bring policy to bear on a broad range of problems—from those with localized causes or impacts to those at a national or global scale. History has shown that when we restrict the right to pollute, economic incentives to reduce pollution lead to dynamic technological change, and society changes in response. A policy portfolio that leverages appropriate policy tools at the salient levels of government, crafted from the perspective of broad community rights to environmental protection and equity, is our path forward.[49] If we want to move with speed and ambition to blunt the climate crisis, we must start today and pick up the tools that we have at hand.

To create a sustainable capitalist economy, government must function as more than an administrator and enforcer of capitalism; it must become an "innovator" that spurs the capitalist system to "adapt to a changing economic, technological, and political environment," and critically, a changing natural environment.[50] Capitalism without government constraint leads to concentration of wealth and political power, creating both economic inequality and environmental degradation. By forcing polluters to internalize the costs of pollution that are now borne by society, particularly by the most vulnerable and historically marginalized communities, environmental law is inherently redistributive.[51] As Dr. Seuss knew, the contours of capitalism is a story that we tell. For his audience, caring "a whole awful lot" contributed to cultural change as a part of the United States' collective environmental journey. His articulation of the Once-ler's right to pollute, on the other hand, points to a new way to continue the story. Systems of governance must shift the collective right to community-based human and ecosystem health into the sunlight, letting polluters compete for the limited right to use the commons to dispose of their waste. Aligning economic incentives will allow communities to flourish in the right to a functioning healthy ecosystem.

Notes

1. Elinor Ostrom, "Design Principles of Robust Property-Rights Institutions: What Have We Learned?," in *Property Rights and Land Policies*, ed. Gregory K. Ingram and Yu-Hung Hong (Lincoln Institute of Land Policy, 2009).

2. Bruce R. Scott, *Capitalism: Its Origins and Evolution as a System of Governance* (Springer, 2011), 27.

3. Daniel W. Bromley, *Possessive Individualism: A Crisis of Capitalism* (Oxford University Press, 2019), 184.

4. Jamal K. Greene, *How Rights Went Wrong: Why Our Obsession with Rights Is Tearing America Apart* (Boston: Houghton Mifflin Harcourt, 2021).

5. Yanis Varoufakis, *Talking to My Daughter about the Economy: or, How Capitalism Works—and How It Fails* (MacMillan, 2019).
6. John C. Dernbach, "The Dozen Types of Legal Tools in the Deep Decarbonization Toolbox," *Energy Law Journal* 39 (2018); James Salzman and Barton Thompson, *Environmental Law and Policy* (Foundation Press, 2019).
7. Cheryl I. Harris, "Whiteness as Property," *Harvard Law Review* 106, no. 8 (June 1993).
8. *National Audubon Society v. Superior Court, 658 P.2d 709 (Cal. 1983).*
9. Karl B. Brooks, *Before Earth Day: The Origins of American Environmental Law, 1945–1970* (University Press of Kansas, 2009); Richard J. Lazarus, "Super Wicked Problems and Climate Change: Restraining the Present to Liberate the Future," *Cornell Law Review* 94 (2009).
10. Migratory Bird Treaty Act of 1918, 16 U.S.C. §§ 703–712.
11. Robert V. Percival, et al., *Environmental Regulation: Law, Science, and Policy* (Wolters Kluwer, 2013).
12. Lazarus, "Super Wicked Problems and Climate Change."
13. Percival, et al., *Environmental Regulation: Law, Science, and Policy.*
14. Lazarus, "Super Wicked Problems and Climate Change."
15. Brooks, *Before Earth Day*; Lazarus, "Super Wicked Problems and Climate Change."
16. Brooks, *Before Earth Day.*
17. Brooks, *Before Earth Day.*
18. Brooks, *Before Earth Day*; Lazarus, "Super Wicked Problems and Climate Change."
19. Brooks, *Before Earth Day*; Lazarus, "Super Wicked Problems."
20. Richard Nixon, "Statement about the National Environmental Policy Act of 1969" (statement, January 1, 1970).
21. Bradley C. Karkkainen, "Toward a Smarter NEPA: Monitoring and Managing Government's Environmental Performance," *Columbia Law Review* 102, no. 4 (May 2002).
22. Michael A. Heller and James Salzman, *Mine! How the Hidden Rules of Ownership Control our Lives* (Doubleday, 2021).
23. Organic Trade Association, "U.S. Organic Sales Soar to New High of Nearly $62 Billion in 2020," May 25, 2021.
24. Nadja Popovich, Livia Albeck-Ripka, and Kendra Pierre-Louis, "The Trump Administration Rolled Back More Than 100 Environmental Rules. Here's the Full List," *New York Times*, January 20, 2021.
25. Christopher W. Callahan and Justin S. Mankin, "National Attribution of Historical Climate Damages," *Climatic Change* 172, no. 40 (2022).
26. Lazarus, "Super Wicked Problems and Climate Change."
27. Dr. Seuss, *The Lorax* (Random House, 1971).
28. Bromley, *Possessive Individualism*, 195.
29. Dr. Seuss, *The Lorax.*
30. Greene, *How Rights Went Wrong*, 42.
31. Ronald Coase, "The Problem of Social Cost," *Journal of Law & Economics* 3 (October, 1960).

32. Heller and Salzman, *Mine! How the Hidden Rules of Ownership Control our Lives*.
33. Harris, "Whiteness as Property."
34. Aldred's Case (1610), 77 Eng. Rep. 816 (KB).
35. See *Tanner v. Armco, 340 F.Supp. 532 (S.D. Tex. 1972)* (holding there is no right to healthy environment, no state action); *Juliana v. US, 947 F.3d 1159 (9th Cir. 2020)* (dismissing due to no standing for lack of redressability).
36. Emily Parker, *Constitutional Obligations for Public Education: 50-State Review* (Education Commission of the States, 2016).
37. Jack R. Tuholske, "U.S. State Constitutions and Environmental Protection: Diamonds in the Rough," *Widener Law Review* 21 (2015).
38. Art English and John J. Carroll, "State Constitutions and Environmental Bills of Rights," *The Book of the States* 47 (2015). https://issuu.com/csg .publications/docs/bos2015.
39. Greene, *How Rights Went Wrong*.
40. 42 U.S.C. §7409(b)(1) (1970).
41. Environmental Protection Agency, "Our Nation's Air: Trends through 2020" (May 2021).
42. Donella Meadows, "Leverage Points: Places to Intervene in a System," *Sustainability Institute*, December 1999, 15.
43. Scott, *Capitalism: Its Origins*, 9.
44. Heller and Salzman, *Mine! How the Hidden Rules of Ownership Control our Lives*.
45. *Boomer v. Atlantic, 257 N.E.2d 870 (N.Y. 1970)* (Jansen, J., dissenting).
46. *Boomer v. Atlantic, 257 N.E.2d 870 (N.Y. 1970)*.
47. Suzanne W. Simard, et al., "Net Transfer of Carbon Between Ectomycorrhizal Tree Species in the Field," *Nature* 388 (1997).
48. Scott, *Capitalism: Its Origins*.
49. Dernbach, "The Dozen Types of Legal Tools."
50. Scott, *Capitalism: Its Origins*, 19.
51. Lazarus, "Super Wicked Problems and Climate Change."

Conclusion

Inara Scott

This book began with the fundamental and inescapable conclusion that the world is on an unsustainable trajectory. Most starkly, climate change is already ravaging ecosystems with drought, fire, disease, and flooding, and realistic scenarios are that the world will almost certainly exceed two degrees Celsius—what had previously been touted as the upper limit to global warming necessary to prevent unpredictable tipping points and massive societal disruptions.[1] Drawing a wide definition of sustainability, however, we can point to many other examples of unsustainable conditions as well, including increasing wealth inequality, threats to democracy and rising authoritarianism, racism, and poverty. The question at the heart of this work is whether a more sustainable world can be achieved while capitalism continues to be the defining global economic system.

For the authors of this book, the answer to that question is a qualified yes. Capitalism reflects individual political, social, and cultural realities, and is a system that is subject to almost limitless modification (see Chapter 1). Though often portrayed as a set of rigid characteristics, in fact, capitalism is more of a broad philosophy and flexible socio-political system (see Chapter 2). As discussed in Chapter 4, one key aspect of this philosophic structure that may drive society toward greater sustainability is its ability to nurture and incentivize innovation, which may be the reason we have seen improvement in the living standards for millions as capitalism has spread across the globe.

As discussed across multiple chapters, however, American capitalism is uniquely focused on individualism, wealth maximization, shareholder profits, deregulation, and growth (see Chapters 5–8). Many proponents of American capitalism, particularly those grounded in neoliberal theory, may even suggest that capitalism requires an absence of government regulation, or so-called "free markets," to flourish—a destructive myth taken on directly in Chapters 1 and 14. As American capitalism has had global influence (see Chapter 6), it represents the version of capitalism with which millions of people are most familiar—or which may seem to be the only way capitalism can operate.

In the face of this negative experience of capitalism, the authors of this work have proposed multiple means of restructuring or redesigning capitalism, particularly as experienced in the United States. By comparing the American and European systems and tracing the development of the American system, they provide avenues of distinction. We do not have to ask if capitalism can look different; we can instead point to places where it is different. The authors have also proposed a variety of specific regulatory mechanisms (see Chapters 4, 10, 12–15) that would have significant impacts on the lived experience of capitalism. From changes to the labor system (Chapter 12) to the development of corporate human rights instruments (Chapter 9), we can see the potential for new regulatory structures to have significant impacts on the daily lives of people living in capitalist systems.

It is important to point out, however, that other authors in this volume also express deep concerns about the contrast between changes that can be made on a theoretical basis, and those that can be made in the real world. In Chapter 11, Ryan Katz-Rosene convincingly argues that capitalism may be theoretically decoupled from growth, but in practice, decoupling would require authoritarian regulation and significant limitations on consumer choice, both of which he notes are "anathema to capitalism's espousal of market freedom." On a related but separate note, as Robert Prentice discusses in Chapter 3, capitalism's very production of wealth can create a "vicious downward spiral" in which those who have wealth also gain political power, which then allows them to alter regulatory structures to favor their own interests and thereby create more wealth and more power.

In Chapter 15, Christy Brekken urges us to imagine that capitalism is like an ecosystem, and thus the conditions for sustainability necessarily arise out of complex and interconnected systems of governance, politics, and culture. Using this analogy, I urge the readers of this book not to lose hope—there are many different tipping points to change in an ecosystem, and they may come from small, seemingly powerless players within those systems. Capitalism is not a monolithic structure that is incapable of change, nor is it an independent entity hell-bent on destroying the environment. It is fundamentally a human creation, deeply tied to law and politics, and the evolution of that system must arise out of political and legal structures and policies. It is therefore incumbent on all of those seeking a more sustainable future to continue to advocate for ways to adapt this flexible structure to our will and opportunities to build a better world for ourselves, our children, and all of humanity.

Note

1. J. B. Ruhl and Robin Kundis Craig, "4° Celsius," *Minnesota Law Review* 106, no. 1 (Nov. 2021):197–99.

Bibliography

Abbinnett, Ross. *The Thought of Bernard Stiegler: Capitalism, Technology and the Politics of Spirit*. Oxford: Routledge, 2018.

Adamczyk, Alicia. "Inequality Has Been Building for Decades in the U.S., but Experts Say the Pandemic 'Ripped It Open.'" *CNBC*, October 23, 2020. https://www.cnbc.com/2020/10/23/coronavirus-is-exacerbating-economic-inequality-in-the-us.html.

Albareda, Laura, Josep M. Lozano, and Tamyko Ysa. "Public Policies on Corporate Social Responsibility: The Role of Governments in Europe." *Journal of Business Ethics* 74 (2007): 391–407.

Aldred's Case, 77 Eng. Rep. 816 (KB 1611).

Alexander, Michelle. *The New Jim Crow: Mass Incarceration in the Age of Colorblindness*. New York: The New Press, 2012.

Allison, Graham. *Destined for War: Can America and China Escape Thucydides's Trap?* Boston: Houghton Mifflin Harcourt, 2017.

Alm, James. "Tax Evasion, Technology, and Inequality." *Economics of Governance* 22, no. 4 (December 2021): 321–343.

Alpert, Bill. "With Rare Speed, Gene Editing Emerges as Biotech's New Cutting Edge." *Barron's*, January 14, 2021.

Altvater, Elmar, Eileen C. Crist, Donna J. Haraway, Daniel Hartley, Christian Parenti, and Justin McBrien. *Anthropocene or Capitalocene? Nature, History, and the Crisis of Capitalism*. Edited by Jason W. Moore. Oakland: PM Press, 2016.

Amable, Bruno. *The Diversity of Modern Capitalism*. Oxford University Press, 2003.

Amadeo, Kimberly. "What Is a Mixed Economy?," *The Balance*, October 23, 2021. https://www.thebalance.com/mixed-economy-definition-pros-cons-examples-3305594.

American Hospital Association v. Becerra, 142 S.Ct. 1896 (2022).

The American Presidency Project, UC Santa Barbara. "Richard Nixon, Statement about the National Environmental Policy Act of 1969." https://www.presidency.ucsb.edu/documents/statement-about-the-national-environmental-policy-act-1969.

Anderson, Meg. "Racist Housing Practices from the 1930s Linked To Hotter Neighborhoods Today." *National Public Radio*, January 14, 2020. https://www.npr.org/2020/01/14/795961381/racist-housing-practices-from-the-1930s-linked-to-hotter-neighborhoods-today.

Antia, Murad. "Wealth Inequality Is Far Worse than People Guess." *Tampa Bay Times*, October 2, 2021. https://www.tampabay.com/opinion/2021/10/02/wealth-inequality-is-far-worse-than-people-guess-column/.

Antipode Foundation. *Geographies of Racial Capitalism with Ruth Wilson Gilmore.* Directed by Kenton Card, June 1, 2020. https://antipodeonline.org/geographies-of-racial-capitalism.

Aponte, Claudia Irizarry. "When Private Equity Came Knocking, Bronx Renters Were Given Two Options: Buy or Get Out." *The City*, February 23, 2022. https://www.thecity.nyc/2022/2/23/22947878/when-private-equity-came-knocking-these-bronx-renters-were-given-two-options-buy-or-get-out.

Arno, Peter, and Michael H. Davis. "Why Don't We Enforce Existing Drug Price Controls? The Unrecognized and Unenforced Reasonable Pricing Requirements Imposed upon Patents Deriving in Whole or in Part from Federally Funded Research." *Tulane Law Review* 75, no. 3 (February 2001): 631–94.

Arno, Peter, Dana Neacşu, and Kathryn Ardizzone. "March-In Rights Could Ensure Patient Access by Keeping Drug Prices in Check. They're Under Attack." *Health Affairs*, April 30, 2021. https://www.healthaffairs.org/do/10.1377/hblog20210428.519540/full/.

Aronoff, Kate. *Overheated: How Capitalism Broke the Planet—And How We Fight Back.* New York: Bold Type Books, 2021.

Asante-Muhammed, Dedrick, Chuck Collins, Josh Hoxie, and Emanuel Nieves. *The Ever-Growing Gap: Without Change, African-American and Latino Families Won't Match White Wealth for Centuries.* Institute for Policy Studies, August 2016. https://ips-dc.org/wp-content/uploads/2016/08/The-Ever-Growing-Gap-CFED_IPS-Final-1.pdf.

Aspen Institute. "Idea Lab on Worker Voice in Corporate Governance." 2023: 19. https://www.aspeninstitute.org/programs/business-and-society-program/worker-voice-lab/.

Aspen Institute Business & Society Program. *Worker Voice and the New Corporate Boardroom.* Aspen Institute, 2021. https://www.aspeninstitute.org/wp-content/uploads/2021/08/Worker-Voice-and-the-Corporate-Boardroom.pdf.

Assaf-Zakharov, Katya. "Capitalism against Freedom." *NYU Review of Law & Social Change* 38, no. 2 (2014): 201–68.

Attaran, Amir. "How Do Patents and Economic Policies Affect Access to Essential Medicines in Developing Countries?," *Health Affairs* 23, no. 3 (2004): 155–66.

Ayres, Robert U. *On Capitalism and Inequality: Progress and Poverty Revisited.* Cham, Switzerland: Springer, 2020.

Baccaro, Lucio, and Jonas Pontusson. "Rethinking Comparative Political Economy: The Growth Model Perspective." *Politics & Society* 44, no. 2 (2016): 175–207. https://doi.org/10.1177%2F0032329216638053.

Backhouse, Roger E., and Bradley W. Bateman. "Keynes and Capitalism." *History of Political Economy* 41, no. 4 (2009): 645–671.

Baek, Jieun. *North Korea's Hidden Revolution: How the Information Underground Is Transforming a Closed Society.* New Haven: Yale University Press, 2016.

Baer, Hans. "Global Capitalism and Climate Change: The Need for an Alternative World System." In *Handbook on International Political Economy,* edited by Ralph Pettman, 395–415. Singapore: World Scientific Publishing, 2012.

Bai, Geetha. "Business Schools Should Drive Positive Societal Change, Says AACSB's New CEO." *U2B,* September 7, 2020. https://u2b.com/2020/09/07/business-schools-societal-impact-aacsb-ceo/.

Bailey, Brian. *The Luddite Rebellion.* Stroud: Sutton Publishing Limited, 1998.

Bakan, Joel. *The Corporation: The Pathological Pursuit of Profit and Power.* Free Press: New York, 2004.

Baptist, Edward E. *The Half Has Never Been Told: Slavery and the Making of American Capitalism.* New York: Basic Books, 2016.

Baradaran, Mehrsa. *The Color of Money: Black Banks and the Racial Wealth Gap.* Cambridge: Belknap, 2017.

Barnett, Michael, Benjamin Cashore, Irene Henriques, Bryan W. Husted, Rajat Panwar, and Jonatan Pinkse. "Reorient the Business Case for Corporate Sustainability." *Stanford Social Innovation Review* (Summer 2021): 35–39.

Barnett, Thomas. *The Pentagon's New Map: War and Peace in the Twenty-First Century.* Oakland, CA: Penguin, 2005.

Bartels, Larry M. *Unequal Democracy: The Political Economy of the New Gilded Age.* New York, NY: Russell Sage Foundation, 2008.

Baselli, Valerio. "Mapping ESG Practices and Carbon Risk in 48 Countries' Stock Markets." *Morningstar,* April 12, 2022. https://www.morningstar.com/articles/1095901/mapping-esg-practices-and-carbon-risk-in-48-countries-stock-markets.

Bättig, Michèle, and Thomas Bernauer. "National Institutions and Global Public Goods: Are Democracies More Cooperative in Climate Change Policy?" *International Organization* 63, no. 2 (April 2009): 281–308.

Beck, Naomi. *Hayek and the Evolution of Capitalism.* Chicago: University of Chicago Press, 2018.

Beckert, Sven, and Seth Rockman. *Slavery's Capitalism: A New History of American Economic Development.* Philadelphia: University of Pennsylvania Press, 2016.

Beer, Tommy. "Top 1% Of U.S. Households Hold 15 Times More Wealth Than Bottom 50% Combined." *Forbes*, October 8, 2020. https://www.forbes.com/sites/tommybeer/2020/10/08/top-1-of-us-households-hold-15-times-more-wealth-than-bottom-50-combined/?sh=bofee8e51795.

Bellamy, Richard. "Liberalism: Political Doctrine and Impact on Social Science." In *International Encyclopedia of the Social & Behavioral Sciences*, edited by James D. Wright, 26–31. 2nd ed. Oxford: Elsevier, 2015. https://doi.org/10.1016/B978-0-08-097086-8.93070-8.

Berger, David J. "Expanding Diversity in the Boardroom by Adding Worker Voice." In *Worker Voice and the New Corporate Boardroom*, 2–5. Aspen Institute, 2021. https://www.aspeninstitute.org/wp-content/uploads/2021/08/Worker-Voice-and-the-Corporate-Boardroom.pdf.

Berger-Walliser, Gerlinde, and Inara Scott. "Redefining Corporate Social Responsibility in an Era of Globalization and Regulatory Hardening." *American Business Law Journal* 55, no. 1 (Spring 2018): 167–218. https://doi.org/10.1111/ablj.12119.

Berle, Adolf A., Jr. "Corporate Powers as Powers in Trust." *Harvard Law Review* 44, no. 1049 (1931).

Bernauer, Thomas, and Vally Koubi. "Effects of Political Institutions on Air Quality." *Ecological Economics* 68 (2009): 1355–65.

Bertrand, Marianne, Matilde Bombardini, and Francesco Trebbi. "Is It Whom You Know or What You Know? An Empirical Assessment of the Lobbying Process." *American Economic Review* 104, no. 12 (December 2014): 3885–3920.

Biasucci, Cara, and Robert Prentice. *Behavioral Ethics in Practice: Why We Sometimes Make the Wrong Decisions*. New York, NY: Routledge, 2021.

Bird, Robert C., and Vivek Soundararajan, "From Suspicion to Sustainability in Global Supply Chains." *Texas A&M Law Review* 7, no. 2 (2020): 383–418.

Bishop, Richard C., et al. "Putting a Value on Injuries to Natural Assets: The BP Oil Spill." *Science* 356, no. 6335 (April 21, 2017): 253–54. DOI: 10.1126/science.aam8124.

Blanchette, Jude, and Scott Kennedy. "Chinese State Capitalism: Diagnosis and Prognosis." *Center for Strategic Studies*, October 2021. https://csis-website-prod.s3.amazonaws.com/s3fs-public/publication/211007_Kennedy_Chinese_State_Capitalism.pdf?34C5XDb775Ws8W6TZ6oMGPlWhIY8Z.rf.

Bland, Scott, and Maggie Severns. "Documents Reveal Massive 'Dark-Money' Group Boosted Democrats in 2018." *Politico*, November 19, 2019. https://www.politico.com/news/2019/11/19/dark-money-democrats-midterm-071725.

Block, Fred. "Karl Polanyi and the Writing of 'The Great Transformation.'" *Theory and Society* 32, no. 3 (2003): 275–306.

Blumberg, Alex. "Senator by Day, Telemarketer by Night." *National Public Radio*, March 30, 2012. https://www.npr.org/sections/money/2012/03/30/149648666/senator-by-day-telemarketer-by-night.

Board of Governors of the Federal Reserve System. "Report on the Economic Well-Being of U.S. Households in 2017." *Federal Reserve Board*, 2018. https://www
.federalreserve.gov/publications/files/2017-report-economic-well-being-us
-households-201805.pdf.

Bohrer, Ashley J. *Marxism and Intersectionality: Race, Gender, Class and Sexuality under Contemporary Capitalism*. New York: Columbia University Press, 2019.

Bonica, Adam, Nolan McCarty, Keith T. Poole, and Howard Rosenthal. "Why Hasn't Democracy Slowed Rising Inequality?," *Journal of Economic Perspectives* 27, no. 3 (2013): 103–24.

Booker, Brakkton. "George Floyd and the New Civil Rights Era." *Politico*, May 5, 2021. https://www.politico.com/newsletters/the-recast/2021/05/25/george
-floyd-death-anniversary-civil-rights-492986.

Bork, Robert. *The Antitrust Paradox*. New York: Free Press, 1978.

Bornemann, Basil, Henrike Knappe, and Patrizia Nanz, eds. *The Routledge Handbook of Democracy and Sustainability*. London: Routledge, 2022.

Boucher, Geoff. *Understanding Marxism*. London: Taylor & Francis Group, 2014. https://ebookcentral.proquest.com/lib/osu/detail.action?docID=3061157.

Boushey, Heather, and Helen Knudsen. "The Importance of Competition for the American Economy." The White House, July 9, 2021. https://www.whitehouse
.gov/cea/written-materials/2021/07/09/the-importance-of-competition-for
-the-american-economy/#:~:text=Healthy%20market%20competition%20is
%20fundamental,greater%20variety%2C%20and%20more%20innovation.

Bowen, Howard. *Social Responsibilities of the Businessman*. New York: Harper, 1953.

Boyce, James K. "Inequality and Environmental Protection." In *Inequality, Cooperation, and Environmental Sustainability*, edited by Jean-Marie Baland, Samuel Bowles, and Pranab Bardhan, 314–48. Princeton, N.J.: Princeton University Press, 2018.

Boyce, James K., et al. "Power Distribution, the Environment, and Public Health: A State-Level Analysis." *Ecological Economics* 29 (1999): 127–40.

Braithwaite, John. "Tempered Power, Variegated Capitalism, Law and Society." *Buffalo Law Review* 67, (2019): 527–594.

Bromley, Daniel W. *Possessive Individualism: A Crisis of Capitalism*. Oxford: Oxford University Press, 2019.

Brooks, Karl Boyd. *Before Earth Day: The Origins of American Environmental Law, 1945–1970*. Lawrence, KS: University Press of Kansas, 2009.

Brooks, Megan. "Highly Processed Foods are Bad for Older Brains, Study Says." *WebMD News Brief*, August 15, 2022. https://www.webmd.com/alzheimers/
news/20220815/highly-processed-foods-bad-older-brains-study.

Brown, Jeffrey R., and Jiekun Huang. "All the President's Friends: Political Access and Firm Value." *Journal of Financial Economics* 138 (2020): 415–31.

Buchanan, James M., and Gordon Tullock. *The Calculus of Consent: Logical Foundations of Constitutional Democracy.* Ann Arbor: University of Michigan Press, 1962.

Burch, Audra D.S., Amy Harmon, Sabrina Tavernise, and Emily Badger. "The Death of George Floyd Reignited a Movement. What Happens Now?," *New York Times,* last updated October 5, 2021. "https://www.nytimes.com/2021/04/20/us/george-floyd-protests-police-reform.html.

Burton, Katherine. "George Soros Commits $1 Billion to Start Global University to Fight Climate Change." *Financial Post,* January 23, 2020. https://financialpost.com/personal-finance/high-net-worth/george-soros-commits-1-billion-to-start-global-university-to-fight-climate-change.

Business Roundtable. "Business Roundtable Redefines the Purpose of a Corporation to Promote 'An Economy That Serves All Americans'." *Business Roundtable,* August 19, 2019. https://www.businessroundtable.org/business-roundtable-redefines-the-purpose-of-a-corporation-to-promote-an-economy-that-serves-all-americans.

Business Roundtable. *Statement of Corporate Responsibility,* October 1981.

Business Roundtable. *Statement on Corporate Governance,* 1997.

Business Roundtable. *Statement on the Purpose of a Corporation,* 2019.

Buttenwieser, Peter. "Why I Participate in a Corrupt System." In *Inside the Campaign Finance Battle: Court Testimony on the New Reforms,* edited by Anthony Corrado, Thomas E. Mann, and Trevor Potter, 308–14. Washington, DC: Brookings Institution Press, 2003.

Butz, Christoph, Jürg Liechti, Julia Bodin, and Sarah E. Cornell. "Towards Defining an Environmental Investment Universe within Planetary Boundaries." *Sustainable Science* 13, no. 4 (2018): 1031–44.

Buxbaum, Richard M. "A Legal History of International Reparations." *Berkeley Journal of International Law* 23, no. 2 (2005): 314–46. http://dx.doi.org/10.15779/Z38J936.

Cahn, Naomi R., and Linda C. McClain. "Gendered Complications of COVID-19: Towards a Feminist Recovery Plan." *Georgetown Journal of Gender and the Law* 22, no. 1 (Fall 2020): 1–56.

Callahan, Christopher W., and Justin S. Mankin. "National Attribution of Historical Climate Damages." *Climatic Change* 172, no. 40 (2022). https://doi.org/10.1007/s10584-022-03387-y.

Carey, Charles W., Jr. "Corporations and Big Business." *Nineteenth Century U.S. Newspapers,* 2008. https://www.gale.com/intl/essays/charles-w-carey-jr-corporations-big-business (navigate to "Gale International").

Caron, Paul, and James Repetti. "Occupy the Tax Code: Using the Estate Tax to Reduce Inequality and Spur Economic Growth." *Pepperdine Law Review* 40 (2013): 1255–89.

Case, Anne, and Angus Deaton. *Deaths of Despair and the Future of Capitalism.* Princeton, NJ: Princeton University Press, 2020.

Casey, Christopher A., Cathleen D. Cimino-Isaacs, and Katarina C. O'Regan. *Section 307 and Imports Produced by Foreign Labor.* Washington, DC: Congressional Research Service, 2022.

Chakrabarty, Bidyut. "Universal Benefit: Gandhi's Doctrine of Trusteeship: A Review Article." *Modern Asian Studies* 49, no. 2 (2015): 572–608.

Chakraborty, Sukumar, and Adrian C. Newton. "Climate Change, Plant Diseases and Food Security: An Overview." *Plant Pathology* 60, no. 1 (2011): 2–14.

Chambers, Rachel. "Parent Company Direct Liability for Overseas Human Rights Violations: Lessons from the U.K. Supreme Court." *University of Pennsylvania Journal of International Law* 42, no. 3 (2021): 519–79.

Chambers, Rachel, and Gerlinde Berger-Walliser. "The Future of International Corporate Human Rights Litigation: A Transatlantic Comparison." *American Business Law Journal* 58, no. 3 (2021): 579–642. https://doi.org/10.1111/ablj.12193.

Chandler, Alfred D., Jr. "The Beginnings of the Modern Industrial Corporation." *Proceedings of the American Philosophical Society* 130, no. 4 (December 1986): 382–389.

Chang, Michele, Federico Steinberg, and Francisco Torres, eds. *The Political Economy of Adjustment throughout and beyond the Eurozone Crisis: What Have We Learned?* Oxford: Routledge, 2020.

Chemerinsky, Erwin. *Worse than Nothing: The Dangerous Fallacy of Originalism.* New Haven, CT: Yale University Press, 2022.

Chilton, Adam S., and Galit A. Sarfaty. "The Limitations of Supply Chain Disclosure Regimes." *Stanford Journal of International Law* 53, no. 1 (2017): 1–54.

Cho, Renee. "Leave No One Behind: The Sustainable Development Goals." *State of the Planet,* September 14, 2015. https://news.climate.columbia.edu/2015/09/14/leave-no-one-behind-the-sustainable-development-goals/.

Chung, Emily. "What Really Happens to Plastic Drink Bottles You Toss in Your Recycling Bin." *CBC,* January 7, 2020. https://www.cbc.ca/news/science/bottle-recycling-1.5416614.

Clarke, Linda. *Building Capitalism: Historical Change and the Labour Process in the Production of Built Environment.* New York: Routledge, 1992.

Clift, Ben, and Sean McDaniel. "Capitalist Convergence? European (dis?)Integration and the Post-crash Restructuring of French and European Capitalisms." *New Political Economy* 26, no. 1 (2021): 1–19. https://doi.org/10.1080/13563467.2019.1680963.

Coase, Ronald H. "The Problem of Social Cost." *Journal of Law & Economics* 3, no. 1 (1960): 1–44. DOI:10.1086/466560.

Coates, Ta-Nehisi. "The Case for Reparations." *Atlantic,* June 2014. https://www.theatlantic.com/magazine/archive/2014/06/the-case-for-reparations/361631/.

Cochrane, Emily, and Lisa Friedman. "What's in the Climate, Tax and Health Care Package." *New York Times,* August 7, 2022.

Cohen, Joel E. "Population Growth and Earth's Human Carrying Capacity." *Science* 269, no. 5222 (1995): 341–46.

Cohen, Julie E. *Between Truth and Power: The Legal Constructions of Informational Capitalism.* Oxford: Oxford University Press, 2019.

Collins, Chuck. "U.S. Billionaires Are Now $2.1 Trillion Richer than before the Pandemic." *Nation of Change*, October 23, 2021. https://www.nationofchange .org/2021/10/23/us-billionaires-are-now-2-1-trillion-richer-than-before-the -pandemic/.

Collins, Keith, and Josh Holder. "See How Rich Countries Got to the Front of the Vaccine Line." *New York Times*, March 31, 2021.

Collins, Lindsay J., Anne H Gaglioti, Kristen M. Beyer, Yuhong Zhou, Miranda A. Moore, Rebecca Nash, Jeffery M. Switchenko, et al. "Neighborhood-Level Redlining and Lending Bias Are Associated with Breast Cancer Mortality in a Large and Diverse Metropolitan Area." *Cancer Epidemiology, Biomarkers & Prevention* 30, no. 1 (January 2021): 53–60. https://doi.org/10.1158/1055-9965 .epi-20-1038.

Committee for the Promotion and Advancement of Cooperatives (COPAC). "Cooperative Contributions to SDG 1." In *Transforming Our World: A Cooperative 2030.* January 31, 2018. http://www.copac.coop/wp-content/uploads/2018/02/ COPAC_TransformBrief_SDG1_web.pdf.

Committee for the Promotion and Advancement of Cooperatives. "Cooperative Contributions to SDG 6." In *Transforming Our World: A Cooperative 2030.* May 24, 2018. http://www.copac.coop/wp-content/uploads/2018/05/COPAC _TransformBrief_SDG6.pdf.

Committee for the Promotion and Advancement of Cooperatives. "Cooperative Contributions to SDG 12." In *Transforming Our World: A Cooperative 2030.* June 20, 2018. https://www.ilo.org/wcmsp5/groups/public/---ed_emp/---emp _ent/---coop/documents/publication/wcms_632633.pdf.

Commons, John R., Jeff E. Biddle, and Warren J. Samuels. "Introduction." In *Legal Foundations of Capitalism*, edited by John R. Commons. New York: Routledge, 2007.

Cook, John, Naomi Oreskes, et al. "Consensus on Consensus: A Synthesis of Consensus Estimates on Human-Caused Global Warming." *Environmental Research Letters* 11, no. 4 (2016). https://10.0.4.64/1748-9326/11/4/048002.

Cook, John, Geoffrey Supran, Stephan Lewandowsky, Naomi Oreskes, and Ed Maibach. *America Misled: How the Fossil Fuel Industry Deliberately Misled Americans About Climate Change.* Fairfax, VA: George Mason University Center for Climate Change Communication, 2019.

Cousins, Ian T., Jana H. Johansson, Matthew E. Salter, Bo Sha, and Martin Scheringer. "Outside the Safe Operating Space of a New Planetary Boundary for Per- and Polyfluoroalkyl Substances (PFAS)." *Environmental Science and Technology* 56, no. 16 (2022): 11172–79.

Cowen, Tyler. *The Great Stagnation: How America Ate All the Low-Hanging Fruit of Modern History, Got Sick, and Will (Eventually) Feel Better.* New York: Dutton, 2011.

Cowen, Tyler. "How the United States Funds the Arts." *National Endowment for*

the Arts, October 2004. https://www.americansforthearts.org/sites/default/
files/how_o.pdf.

Coy, Peter. "Wealth Inequality Is the Highest Since World War II." *New York Times*,
February 2, 2022.

Crenshaw, Kimberlé. "Demarginalizing the Intersection of Race and Sex. A Black
Feminist Critique of Antidiscrimination Doctrine, Feminist Theory, and Anti-
Racist Politics." *University of Chicago Legal Reform* 8, no. 1 (1989): 139–67.
https://chicagounbound.uchicago.edu/uclf/vol1989/iss1/8/.

Cross, Frank, and Robert Prentice. *Law and Corporate Finance*. Northampton, MA:
Edward Elgar, 2007.

Cudd, Ann E. "Is Capitalism Good for Women?" *Journal of Business Ethics* 127,
no. 4 (2015): 761–70. https://doi.org/10.1007/s10551-014-2185-9.

Dahl, Robert. *A Preface to Democratic Theory*. Chicago, IL: University of Chicago
Press, 1956.

Dale, Ann, Fiona Duguid, Melissa Garcia Lamarca, Peter Hough, Petronella Tyson,
Rebecca Foon, Robert Newell, and Yuill Herbert. *Co-operatives and Sustainability: An Investigation into the Relationship*. Geneva: International Cooperative Alliance, October 23, 2013.

Dalio, Ray. "Why and How Capitalism Needs to Be Reformed (Parts 1 & 2)."
Linked-In, April 5, 2019. https://www.linkedin.com/pulse/why-how-capitalism
-needs-reformed-parts-1-2-ray-dalio/.

Dallas, Lynne. "Short-Termism, the Financial Crisis, and Corporate Governance."
Journal of Corporate Law 37, no. 2 (2012): 265–364.

Danielson, Dan. "Trade, Distribution and Development Under Supply Chain Capitalism." In *Globalization Reimagined: A Progressive Agenda for World Trade
and Investment*, edited by Alvaro Santos, Chantal Thomas, and David Trubek,
121–30. New York: Anthem Publishing, 2019.

Davenport, Coral, and Eric Lipton. "The Pruitt Emails: E.P.A. Chief Was Arm in Arm
with Industry." *New York Times*, February 22, 2017. https://www.nytimes.com/
2017/02/22/us/politics/scott-pruitt-environmental-protection-agency.html.

Dearing, James W., and Jeffrey G. Cox. "Diffusion of Innovations Theory, Principles, and Practice." *Health Affairs* 37, no. 2 (2018): 183–90.

De Bakker, Frank G.A., et al. "The Elephant in the Room: The Nascent Research
Agenda on Corporations, Social Responsibility, and Capitalism." *Business & Society* 59, no. 7 (2020): 1295–1302. https://doi.org/10.1177/
0007650319898196.

DeFino, Jessica. "How White Supremacy and Capitalism Influence Beauty Standards." *TeenVogue*, October 19, 2020. https://www.teenvogue.com/story/
standard-issues-white-supremacy-capitalism-influence-beauty.

Delgado, Richard. "Rodrigo's Equation: Race, Capitalism, and the Search for
Reform." *Wake Forest Law Review* 49, no. 87 (2014): 87–120. https://
scholarship.law.ua.edu/fac_articles/464/.

Deller, Steven, Ann Hoyt, Brent Hueth, and Reka Sundaram-Stukel. *Research on the Economic Impact of Cooperatives.* Madison: University of Wisconsin Center for Cooperatives, 2009.

Dernbach, John. "The Dozen Types of Legal Tools in the Deep Decarbonization Toolbox." *Energy Law Journal* 39 (2018): 313–52. https://ssrn.com/abstract= 3247105.

DeSilver, Drew. "U.S. Income Inequality, on Rise for Decades, Is Now Highest Since 1928." *Pew Research Center,* December 5, 2013. https://www.pewresearch .org/fact-tank/2013/12/05/u-s-income-inequality-on-rise-for-decades-is-now -highest-since-1928/.

Desmond, Matthew. "To Understand the Brutality of American Capitalism, You Have to Start on the Plantation." *New York Times,* August 14, 2019. https:// www.nytimes.com/interactive/2019/08/14/magazine/slavery-capitalism.html.

Deva, Surya. "Sustainable Good Governance and Corporations: An Analysis of Asymmetries." *Georgetown International Environmental Law Review* 18, no. 4 (2006): 707–50.

Diamandis, Peter H., and Steven Kotler. *Abundance: The Future is Better Than You Think.* New York, NY: Free Press, 2012.

Dionne, E. J., Jr. and William A. Galston. "Socialism: A Short Primer." *Brookings Institute,* May 13, 2019. https://www.brookings.edu/blog/fixgov/2019/05/13/ socialism-a-short-primer/.

Dodd, E. Merrick. "For Whom Are Corporate Managers Trustees?" *Harvard Law Review* 45, no. 1148 (1932).

Donaldson, Thomas. "Values in Tension: Ethics Away from Home." *Harvard Business Review* 74, no. 5 (1996): 48–56.

Draper, John William. *History of the American Civil War.* New York: Harper & Brothers Publishers, 1867.

Dr. Seuss. *The Lorax.* Random House, 1971.

Du Bois, W.E.B. "Negroes and the Crisis of Capitalism in the United States." *Monthly Review* 54, no. 11 (April 2003) (reprinted from *Monthly Review,* April 1953).

Du Bois, W.E.B. *The Souls of Black Folk.* New York: Oxford, 1903 (rev. ed. 2007).

Eastwood, Sam, James Ford, Libby Reynolds, and Malcolm Wu. "Business and Human Rights—The Netherlands to Introduce Mandatory Human Rights Due Diligence Legislation." *Mayer Brown,* December 28, 2021. https://www .eyeonesg.com/2021/12/business-and-human-rights-the-netherlands-to -introduce-mandatory-human-rights-due-diligence-legislation/.

Economic Policy Institute. "Why the U.S. Needs a $15 Minimum Wage," January 26, 2021. https://www.epi.org/publication/why-america-needs-a-15 -minimum-wage/.

Edsall, Thomas. "The Republican Strategists Who Have Carefully Planned all of This." *New York Times,* April 12, 2023.

Ehrlich, Paul R. *The Population Bomb.* New York, NY: Ballentine Books, 1968.

Ekardt, Felix. *Sustainability: Transformation, Governance, Ethics, Law.* Cham, Switzerland: Springer International Publishing, 2020.

Elkjær, Mads Andreas, and Michael Baggesen Klitgaard. "Economic Inequality and Political Responsiveness: A Systematic Review." *Perspectives on Politics* 19 (2021), https://www.cambridge.org/core/journals/perspectives-on-politics/article/economic-inequality-and-political-responsiveness-a-systematic-review/3364318C95A3D608048BA1800013C7E1.

Elliott, Rebecca. "Tesla Surpasses $1 Trillion in Market Value as Hertz Orders 100,000 Vehicles." *Wall Street Journal,* October 25, 2021.

Elnaiem, Mohammed. "Black Conquistadors and Black Maroons." *JSTOR Daily,* April 1, 2021. https://daily.jstor.org/black-conquistadors-and-black-maroons/.

Ely, Gene. "Can Deregulation Fix What's Broken About Radio? That's The Hope." *Forbes,* May 14, 2018. https://www.forbes.com/sites/geneely/2018/05/14/can-deregulation-fix-whats-broken-about-radio-thats-the-hope/?sh=75b0a51d7761.

Emerson, Thomas I., David Haber, and Norman Dorsen. *Political and Civil Rights in the United States: A Collection of Legal and Related Materials.* 3rd ed. Boston: Little, Brown, 1967.

English, Art, and John J. Carroll. "State Constitutions and Environmental Bills of Rights." *The Book of the States* 47 (2015). https://issuu.com/csg.publications/docs/bos2015.

Environmental Protection Agency (EPA). "Our Nation's Air: Trends through 2020." (2021). https://gispub.epa.gov/air/trendsreport/2021/#growth_w_cleaner_air.

Escobari, Marcela, Dhruv Gandhi, and Sebastian Strauss. *How Federal Infrastructure Investment Can Put America to Work.* Washington, DC: Brookings Center for Sustainable Development, March 17, 2021. https://www.brookings.edu/research/how-federal-infrastructure-investment-can-put-america-to-work/.

European Environmental Agency. *Status of the Nine Planetary Boundaries.* European Union. Last modified November 23, 2019. https://www.eea.europa.eu/soer/2020/soer-2020-visuals/status-of-the-nine-planetary-boundaries/view.

Farber, Daniel, and Phillip Frickey. *Law and Public Choice: A Critical Introduction.* Chicago, IL: University of Chicago Press, 1991.

Faria, João R., and Franklin G. Mixon Jr. "Entrepreneurial Philanthropy and University Creation: An Economic Model." *Journal of Knowledge Economy* 9 (2018): 1067–1086.

Feagin, Joe. "Documenting the Costs of Slavery, Segregation, and Contemporary Discrimination: Are Reparations in Order for African Americans?" Center for Social Development Working Paper No. 00-10, St. Louis, MO: Washington University, Center for Social Development (2000): 9–11.

Fifield, Anna. "China Compels Uighurs to Work in Shoe Factory That Supplies Nike." *Washington Post,* February 29, 2020. https://www.washingtonpost.com/world/

asia_pacific/china-compels-uighurs-to-work-in-shoe-factory-that-supplies-nike/
2020/02/28/ebddf5f4-57b2-11ea-8efd-0f904bdd8057_story.html.

Fink, Eric M. "Post-Realism, or the Jurisprudential Logic of Late Capitalism." *Hastings Law Journal* 55, no. 4 (2004): 931–964.

Finley, Allysia. "Capitalism Is What Will Defeat COVID." *Wall Street Journal,* March 19, 2021. https://www.wsj.com/articles/capitalism-is-what-will-defeat-covid-11616192690.

Fisher, Earle J. "Black Liberation Theology and the Movement for Black Lives: A Match Made in Heaven." *Berkley Forum,* January 6, 2022. https://berkleycenter.georgetown.edu/responses/black-liberation-theology-and-the-movement-for-black-lives-a-match-made-in-heaven.

Flanders, Laura. "Solidarity Economics, a Forgotten Practice of the Black Radical Tradition: An Interview with Jessica Gordon Nembhard." *Truthout,* April 9, 2014. https://truthout.org/video/solidarity-economics-a-forgotten-practice-of-the-black-radical-tradition-an-interview-with-author-jessica-gordon-nembhard/.

Foster, John Bellamy. "Marx's Theory of Metabolic Rift: Classical Foundations for Environmental Sociology." *American Journal of Sociology* 105, no. 2 (1999): 366–405.

Fountain, Henry. "The World Can Make More Water from the Sea, but at What Cost?" *New York Times,* October 25, 2019.

Fox, Tom, Halina Ward, and Bruce Howard. *Public Sector Roles in Strengthening Corporate Social Responsibility: A Baseline Study.* Washington, DC: World Bank, 2002.

Freeman, Edward R. *Strategic Management: A Stakeholder Approach.* Boston: Pitman, 1984.

Friedlingstein, Pierre, et al. "Global Carbon Budget 2021." *Earth System Science Data* (November 4, 2021). https://doi.org/10.5194/essd-2021-386.

Friedman, Milton. *Capitalism and Freedom.* Fortieth Anniversay Edition. Chicago: University of Chicago Press, 2002.

Friedman, Milton. *Essays in Positive Economics.* Chicago: University of Chicago Press, 1953.

Friedman, Milton. "The Social Responsibility of Business is to Increase its Profits." *New York Times Magazine,* September 13, 1970.

Friedman, Thomas L. *Hot, Flat, and Crowded: Why We Need a Green Revolution—and How It Can Renew America.* Release 2.0, New York: Picador/Farrar, Strauss and Giroux, 2009.

Friedman, Thomas L. "Want to Save the Earth? We Need a Lot More Elon Musks." *New York Times,* November 16, 2021. https://www.nytimes.com/2021/11/16/opinion/glasgow-climate-change.html.

Friedman, Walter A. *American Business History: A Very Short Introduction.* Oxford University Press, 2020.

Fukuyama, Francis. *Trust: Human Nature and the Reconstitution of Social Order.* New York, NY: Free Press, 1995.

Gallup. *State of the American Workplace.* 2017. https://www.gallup.com/workplace/238085/state-american-workplace-report-2017.aspx.

Gelter, Martin. "Taming or Protecting the Modern Corporation? Shareholder-Stakeholder Debates in a Comparative Light." *New York University Journal of Law & Business* 7, no. 2 (Spring 2011): 641–730. https://ir.lawnet.fordham.edu/faculty_scholarship/899/.

Gerstle, Gary. *The Rise and Fall of the Neoliberal Order: America and the World in the Free Market Era.* New York: Oxford University Press, 2022.

Gevurtz, Franklin A. "Disney in a Comparative Light." *American Journal of Comparative Law* 55, no. 3 (Summer 2007): 453–92. https://doi.org/10.1093/ajcl/55.3.453.

Gilens, Martin. *Affluence & Influence: Economic Inequality and Political Power in America.* New York, NY: Russell Sage Foundation, 2012.

Gilens, Martin, and Benjamin I. Page. "Testing Theories of American Politics: Elites, Interest Groups, and Average Citizens." *Perspectives on Politics* 12, no. 3 (September 2014): 564–81.

Gillis, Justin, and Nadja Popovich. "The U.S. Is the Biggest Carbon Polluter in History. It Just Walked Away From the Paris Climate Deal." *New York Times,* June 1, 2017. https://www.nytimes.com/interactive/2017/06/01/climate/us-biggest-carbon-polluter-in-history-will-it-walk-away-from-the-paris-climate-deal.html.

Glachant, Matthieu, Simone Schucht, Alexandra Bültmann, and Frank Wätzold. "Companies, Participation in EMAS: The Influence of the Public Regulator." *Business Strategy and the Environment* 11, no. 4 (2002): 254–66.

Glasgow Financial Alliance for Net Zero (GFANZ). "Financing Roadmaps: Exploring Investment Opportunity Roadmaps." *Glasgow Financial Alliance for Net Zero (GFANZ),* June 22, 2022. https://www.gfanzero.com/netzerofinancing/.

Glater, Jonathan D. "Enron's Many Strands: Accounting; 4 Audit Firms Are Set to Alter Some Practices." *New York Times,* February 1, 2022.

Glenza, Jessica. "Rosewood Massacre: A Harrowing Tale of Racism and the Road toward Reparations." *Guardian,* January 3, 2016. https://www.theguardian.com/us-news/2016/jan/03/rosewood-florida-massacre-racial-violence-reparations.

Global Reporting Initiative. "About GRI." https://www.globalreporting.org/about-gri/.

Godoy, Maria. "COVID-19 May Have A More Serious Impact On Formerly Redlined Communities." *National Public Radio,* September 18, 2020. https://www.npr.org/2020/09/18/914281550/covid-19-may-have-a-more-serious-impact-on-formerly-redlined-communities.

Gond, Jean-Pascal, Nahee Kang, and Jeremy Moon. "The Government of Self-regulation: On the Comparative Dynamics of Corporate Social Responsibility." *Economy and Society* 40, no. 4 (2011): 640–71.

Goodman, Peter S. "The Nordic Model May Be the Best Cushion Against Capitalism. Can It Survive Immigration?" *New York Times*, July 11, 2019. https://www.nytimes.com/2019/07/11/business/sweden-economy-immigration.html.

Gould, Eric D., and Alexander Hijzen. *Growing Apart, Losing Trust? The Impact of Inequality on Social Capital.* International Monetary Fund, 2016.

Gould, Kenneth Alan, David N. Pellow, and Allan Schnaiberg. *The Treadmill of Production: Injustice and Unsustainability in the Global Economy.* Boulder: Paradigm Publishers, 2008.

Goulder, Robert. "The Capital Gains Tax Break: Great Idea Or Big Mistake?" *Forbes*, November 16, 2021. https://www.forbes.com/sites/taxnotes/2021/11/16/the-capital-gains-tax-break-great-idea-or-big-mistake/?sh=358c793c3a02.

Governance and Accountability Institute. "Sustainability Reporting in Focus." *Governance and Accountability Institute*, November 2021. https://www.ga-institute.com/research/ga-research-directory/sustainability-reporting-trends/2021-sustainability-reporting-in-focus.html.

Graziano Da Silva, Jose. "Feeding the World Sustainably." *UN Chronicle* XLIX, no. 1 & 2 (June 2012). https://www.un.org/en/chronicle/article/feeding-world-sustainably.

Greene, Brian. "How 'Occupy Wall Street' Started and Spread." *U.S. News & World Report*, October 17, 2011. https://www.usnews.com/news/washington-whispers/articles/2011/10/17/how-occupy-wall-street-started-and-spread.

Greene, J. *How Rights Went Wrong: Why Our Obsession with Rights Is Tearing America Apart.* New York: Houghton Mifflin Harcourt, 2021.

Greenfield, Kent. "A New Strategy to Fight Citizens United." *Huffington Post*, September 14, 2012. Updated November 14, 2012. https://www.huffpost.com/entry/a-new-strategy-to-fight-c_b_1882744.

Greider, William. *The Soul of Capitalism: Opening Paths to a Moral Economy.* New York, NY: Simon & Schuster, 2004

Grewal, David Singh. "The Legal Constitution of Capitalism." In *After Piketty: The Agenda for Economics and Inequality*, edited by Heather Boushey, J. Bradford De Long, and Marshall Steinbaum, 471–502. Cambridge: Harvard University Press, 2017.

Gross, Liza. "No Place for Predators?" *PLOS Biology* 6, no. 2 (February 2008). https://doi.org/10.1371/journal.pbio.0060040.

Grundgesetz. Art 20a (Ger.). https://www.gesetze-im-internet.de/gg/art_20a.html.

Hacker, Jacob S., and Paul Pierson. *Off Center: The Republican Revolution and the Erosion of American Democracy.* New Haven, CT: Yale University Press, 2005.

Hacker, Jacob S., and Paul Pierson. *Winner-Take-All Politics: How Washington Made the Rich Richer—And Turned Its Back on the Middle Class.* New York, NY: Simon & Schuster, 2010.

Haggard, Stephan, and Lydia Tiede. "The Rule of Law and Economic Growth: Where Are We?" *World Development* 39, no. 5 (2011).

Hall, Peter, and David Soskice. "An Introduction to the Varieties of Capitalism." In *Varieties of Capitalism: The Institutional Foundations of Comparative Advantage*, edited by Peter Hall and David Soskice, 1–70. Oxford University Press, 2001.

Halloran, Tyler. "A Brief History of the Corporate Form and Why it Matters." *Fordham Journal of Corporate & Financial Law*, November 18, 2018.

Hanauer, Nick. "The Pitchforks are Coming... For Us Plutocrats." *Politico*, July/August 2014. https://www.politico.com/magazine/story/2014/06/the-pitchforks-are-coming-for-us-plutocrats-108014/.

Hanauer, Nick, and David M. Rolf. "The Top 1% of Americans Have Taken $50 Trillion From the Bottom 90%—And That's Made the U.S. Less Secure." *Time*, September 14, 2020. https://time.com/5888024/50-trillion-income-inequality-america/.

Hanlon, Gerard. "Rethinking Corporate Social Responsibility and the Role of the Firm—On the Denial of Politics." In *The Oxford Handbook of Corporate Social Responsibility*, edited by A. Crane, et al., 156–72. UK: Oxford University Press, 2008.

Harcourt, Bernard E. *The Illusion of Free Markets: Punishment and the Myth of Natural Order*. Cambridge: Harvard University Press, 2011.

Hardman, Scott, Amrit Chandan, Gil Tal, and Tom Turrentine. "The Effectiveness of Financial Purchase Incentives for Battery Electric Vehicles—A Review of the Evidence." *Renewable and Sustainable Energy Reviews* 80 (2017): 1100–11.

Harris, Angela P. "Racial Capitalism and Law." In *Histories of Racial Capitalism*, edited by Destin Jenkins and Justin Leroy. New York: Columbia University Press, 2021.

Harris, Cheryl. "Whiteness as Property." *Harvard Law Review* 106, no. 8 (1993).

Hartnett, Lynne. "The Long History of Russian Imperialism Shaping Putin's War." *Washington Post*, March 2, 2022. https://www.washingtonpost.com/outlook/2022/03/02/long-history-russian-imperialism-shaping-putins-war/.

Harvey, David. *A Brief History of Neoliberalism*. Oxford: Oxford University Press, 2005.

Harvey, David. *The Enigma of Capital: And the Crises of Capitalism*. Oxford: Oxford University Press, 2010.

Harvey, David. "The Geography of Capitalist Accumulation: A Reconstruction of the Marxian Theory." *Antipode* 7, no. 2 (September 1975): 9–21.

Hayden, Grant M., and Matthew T. Bodie. "Codetermination in Theory and Practice." *Florida Law Review* 73, no. 2 (March 2021): 321–46.

Hayden, Grant M., and Matthew T. Bodie. "The Corporation Reborn: From Shareholder Primacy to Shared Governance." *Boston College Law Review* 61, no. 7 (2020): 2419–85. https://advance.lexis.com/api/document?collection=analytical-materials&id=urn:contentItem:618M-64K1-F30T-B3RB-00000-00&context=1516831.

Hayden, Grant M., and Matthew Bodie. *Reconstructing the Corporation: From Shareholder Primacy to Shared Governance*. Cambridge: Cambridge University Press, 2021.

Hayek, F. A. *The Constitution of Liberty*. Chicago: University of Chicago Press, 1960.

Hayek, F. A. *The Road to Serfdom*. Chicago: University of Chicago Press, 1944.

Hayes, Adam. "What Are the Most Important Aspects of a Capitalist System?" *Investopedia*, updated June 28, 2022. https://www.investopedia.com/ask/answers/040715/what-are-most-important-aspects-capitalist-system.asp.

He, Chunyang, Zhifeng Liu, Jianguo Wu, Xinhao Pan, Zihang Fang, Jingwei Li, and Brett A. Bryan. "Future Global Urban Water Scarcity and Potential Solutions." *Nature Communications* 12, no. 4667 (2021). https://doi.org/10.1038/s41467-021-25026-3.

Heller, Michael A., and James Salzman. *Mine! How the Hidden Rules of Ownership Control Our Lives*. New York: Doubleday, 2021.

Hellman, Rachel. "Denmark Shines, U.S. Lags in Latest Climate Protection Rankings." *U.S. News & World Report*, February 28, 2022.

Henderson, Rebecca. *Reimagining Capitalism in a World on Fire*. New York: PublicAffairs, 2020.

Henley, Will. "The New Water Technologies that Could Save the Planet." *Guardian*, July 22, 2013. https://www.theguardian.com/sustainable-business/new-water-technologies-save-planet.

Henry, Patrick. "Economic Inequality Has Deepened during the Pandemic. That Doesn't Mean It Can't Be Fixed." World Economic Forum, April 7, 2022. https://www.weforum.org/agenda/2022/04/economic-inequality-wealth-gap-pandemic/.

Heritage Foundation. "2022 Index of Economic Freedom." *Heritage Foundation*, 2022. https://www.heritage.org/index/.

Hess, David. "Combating Corruption in International Business: The Big Questions." *Ohio Northern University Law Review* 41, no. 4 (2015): 676–96.

Hess, David. "Modern Slavery in Global Supply Chains: Towards a Legislative Solution." *Cornell International Law Journal* 54, no. 2 (2021): 245–89.

Hess, David. "The Transparency Trap: Non-Financial Disclosure and the Responsibility of Business to Respect Human Rights." *American Business Law Journal* 56, no. 1 (2019): 5–54.

Hodgson, Geoffrey. "1688 and All That: Property Rights, the Glorious Revolution and the Rise of British Capitalism." *Journal of Institutional Economics* 13, no. 1 (March 2017): 79–108.

HoF's-Den Haag 29 januari 2021, NJ 2021, 77 m.nt. (Milieudefensie/Shell Petroleum N.V.) (Neth.).

Hogeland, Julie A. "The Economic Culture of U.S. Agricultural Cooperatives." *Culture & Agriculture* 28, no. 2 (September 2006): 67–79. https://doi.org/10.1525/cag.2006.28.2.67.

Holcombe, Randall G. "Capitalism, Cronyism, and Inequality." In *Capitalism and Inequality: The Role of State and Market*, edited by G. P. Manish and Stephen C. Miller, 9–24. New York, NY: Routledge, 2020.

Holland, Tim, et al. "A Cross-National Analysis of How Economic Inequality Predicts Biodiversity Loss." *Conservation Biology* 23, no. 5 (2009): 1304–13.

Hong, Sungki, and Hannah Shell. "The Impact of Automation on Inequality." *Economic Synopses*, no. 29 (2018): 1–2. (https://doi.org/10.20955/es.2018.29).

Höpner, Martin, and Armin Schäfer. "A New Phase of European Integration: Organised Capitalisms in Post-Ricardian Europe." *West European Politics* 33, no. 2 (2010): 344–68. https://doi.org/10.1080/01402380903538997.

Huesemann, Michael, and Joyce Huesemann. *Techno-Fix: Why Technology Won't Save Us Or the Environment*. Gabriola Island, Canada: New Society Publishers, 2011.

Hunt, Albert. "Washington's Oldest Contact Sport: Lobbyists Scrum to Dilute or Kill Democrats' Tax Bill." *The Hill*, September 19, 2021. https://thehill.com/opinion/campaign/572906-washingtons-oldest-contact-sport-lobbyists-scrum-to-dilute-or-kill-democrats.

Hunt, E. K. *Property and Prophets: The Evolution of Economic Institutions and Ideologies*. NY: Harper & Row, 1981.

Hunt, E. K., and Mark Lautzenheiser. *History of Economic Thought: A Critical Perspective*. 3rd ed. Oxford: Routledge, 2011.

Iacurci, Greg. "The Legacy of 2020: Riches for the Wealthy, Well Educated and Often White, Financial Pain for Others." *CNBC*, January 1, 2021. https://www.cnbc.com/2021/01/01/the-covid-recession-brought-extreme-inequality-in-2020.html.

Indiviglio, Daniel. "A Free Market Needs Free Contracts." *Atlantic*, January 20, 2010. https://www.theatlantic.com/business/archive/2010/01/a-free-market-needs-free-contracts/33861/.

Intergovernmental Panel on Climate Change (IPCC). "Summary for Policymakers." In *Climate Change 2021: The Physical Science Basis. Contribution of Working Group I to the Sixth Assessment Report of the Intergovernmental Panel on Climate Change*, edited by V. Masson-Delmotte, et al., 3–32. United Kingdom and New York, NY (2021).

International Cooperative Alliance (ICA). "Cooperative Identity, Values & Principles." http://ica.coop/en/whats-co-op/co-operative-identity-values-principles.

"International Covenant on Civil and Political Rights." Adopted December 16, 1966. *United Nations Treaty Series Online*, registration no. I-14668. https://treaties.un.org/doc/publication/unts/volume%20999/volume-999-i-14668-english.pdf.

International Energy Agency (IEA). "About CCUS." *International Energy Agency*, April 2021. https://www.iea.org/reports/about-ccus.

International Energy Agency (IEA). "Direct Air Capture." *International Energy Agency*, November 2021. https://www.iea.org/reports/direct-air-capture.

International Energy Agency (IEA). *Global Energy Review: CO2 Emissions in 2021*. International Energy Agency, March, 2022. https://iea.blob

.core.windows.net/assets/c3086240-732b-4f6a-89d7-db01be018f5e/
GlobalEnergyReviewCO2Emissionsin2021.pdf.

International Energy Agency (IEA). *The Role of Critical Minerals in Clean Energy Transitions*. International Energy Agency, March 2022. https://iea .blob.core.windows.net/assets/ffd2a83b-8c30-4e9d-980a-52b6d9a86fdc/ TheRoleofCriticalMineralsinCleanEnergyTransitions.pdf.

International Labour Organization. "Forced Labour Convention 1930 (No. 29)." Information System on International Labour Standards. https://www.ilo.org/ dyn/normlex/en/f?p=NORMLEXPUB:12100:0::NO::P12100_ILO_CODE:C029.

International Labour Organization. *Profits and Poverty: The Economics of Forced Labour*. Geneva: ILO Publications, 2014. https://www.ilo.org/global/publications/ ilo-bookstore/order-online/books/WCMS_243391/lang--en/index.htm.

International Labour Organization, Organization for Economic Co-operation and Development, International Organization for Migration, and United Nations Children's Fund. *Ending Child Labour, Forced Labour and Human Trafficking in Global Supply Chains*. Geneva: 2019. https://www.ilo.org/ipec/ Informationresources/WCMS_716930/lang--en/index.htm.

International Labour Organization and Walk Free Foundation. *Global Estimates of Modern Slavery: Forced Labour and Forced Marriage*. Geneva: ILO Publications, 2017. https://www.ilo.org/global/publications/books/WCMS_575479/ lang--en/index.htm.

Investopedia Team. "Capitalism." *Investopedia*, Updated July 6, 2022. https://www .investopedia.com/terms/c/capitalism.asp.

Ioannou, Ioannis, and George Serafeim. "The Consequences of Mandatory Corporate Sustainability Reporting." Harvard Business School Research Working Paper No. 11-100 (2017): 11–100.

Ishii, Kazuya. "The Socioeconomic Thoughts of Mahatma Gandhi: As an Origin of Alternative Development." *Review of Social Economy* 59, no. 3 (2001): 297–312.

Islam, S. Nazrul. "Inequality and Environmental Sustainability." United Nations DESA Working Paper No. 145, August 2015. https://www.un.org/esa/desa/ papers/2015/wp145_2015.pdf.

Iversen, Torben, and David Soskice. *Democracy and Prosperity: Reinventing Capitalism through a Turbulent Century*. Princeton: Princeton University Press, 2019.

Jackson, Gregory, and Richard Deeg. "How Many Varieties of Capitalism? Comparing the Comparative Institutional Analyses of Capitalist Diversity. MPIfG Discussion Paper 06/2." *Max-Planck-Institut für Gesellschaftsforschung* (April 2006). https://papers.ssrn.com/sol3/papers.cfm?abstract_id=896384.

Jacobson, Adam. "Deregulation Meltdown: Is More the Answer For Radio?" *Radio+Television Business Report*, September 3, 2021. https://www.rbr.com/ deregulation-meltdown-is-more-the-answer-for-radio/.

Jäger, Simon, Benjamin Schoefer, and Jörg Heining. "Labor in the Boardroom." *National Bureau of Economic Research*, Working Paper 26519, November 2019. Revised August 2020, doi:10.3386/w26519.

Jahan, Sarwat, and Ahmed Saber Mahmud. "What is Capitalism?" *Finance and Development* 52, no. 2 (2015). https://doi.org/10.5089/9781484371220.022.

Janeway, William H. *Doing Capitalism in the Innovation Economy: Reconfiguring the Three-Player Game between Markets, Speculators and the State.* 2nd ed. Cambridge: Cambridge University Press, 2018.

Jayachandran, Seema. "How Economic Development Influences the Environment," *Annual Review of Economics* 14, issue 1 (2022): 229–252. https://doi.org/10.1146/annurev-economics-082321-123803.

Jennings, Marianne M. "A Primer on Enron: Lessons from a Perfect Storm of Financial Reporting, Corporate Governance and Ethical Culture Failures." *California Western Law Review* 39, no. 2 (2003).

Jensen, Carsten Strøby. "Trade Unionism: Differences and Similarities—A Comparative View on Europe, USA and Asia." *Industrial Relations Journal* 48, no. 1 (2006): 59–81. https://doi-org.library.lcproxy.org/10.1177/0022185606059314.

Jensen, Michael C., and William H. Meckling. "Theory of the Firm: Managerial Behavior, Agency Costs and Ownership Structure." *Journal of Financial Economics* 3, no. 4 (1976): 305.

Johnson, Walter. "To Remake the World: Slavery, Racial Capitalism, and Justice." *Boston Review*, February 20, 2018. https://bostonreview.net/forum/walter-johnson-to-remake-the-world/.

Johnson, Walter. *The Broken Heart of America: St. Louis and the Violent History of the United States.* New York: Basic Books, 2020.

Johnson Hess, Abigail. "In 2020, top CEOs earned 351 times more than the typical worker." *CNBC*, September 15, 2021. https://www.cnbc.com/2021/09/15/in-2020-top-ceos-earned-351-times-more-than-the-typical-worker.html.

Johnston, Alison, and Aidan Regan. "Introduction: Is the European Union Capable of Integrating Diverse Models of Capitalism?" *New Political Economy* 23, no. 2 (2018): 145–59. https://doi.org/10.1080/13563467.2017.1370442.

Jones, Alexandra. "Left Unchecked, Capitalism Will Ruin Human Relationships Forever." *Face* 4, no. 3 (March 17, 2020). https://theface.com/society/capitalism-politics-sex-relationships-volume-4-issue-3.

Kaarsholm, Preben. "Marx, Globalisation and the Reserve Army of Labour." In *The Politics of Historical Thinking*, Vol. 2, *What's Left of Marxism*, edited by Benjamin Zachariah, Lutz Raphael and Brigitta Bernet, 309–22. Berlin: De Gruyter Oldenbourg, 2020.

Kagan, Robert. "Our Constitutional Crisis is Already Here." *Washington Post*, September 24, 2021. https://www.washingtonpost.com/opinions/2021/09/23/robert-kagan-constitutional-crisis/.

Kapczynski, Amy. "The Law of Informational Capitalism." *Yale Law Journal* 129, no. 5 (2020): 1460–1515.

Kaplan, Sarah. "Beyond the Business Case for Social Responsibility." *Academy of Management Discoveries* 6, no. 1 (2020): 1–4.

Kareiva, Peter, and Michelle Marvier. "What is Conservation Science?" *BioScience* 62, no. 11 (2012): 962–69.

Karkkainen, Bradley C. "Toward a Smarter NEPA: Monitoring and Managing Government's Environmental Performance." *Columbia Law Review* 102, no. 903 (2002).

Kaswan, Mark J. "Developing Democracy: Cooperatives and Democratic Theory." *International Journal of Urban Sustainable Development* 6, no. 2 (2014): 190–205. https://doi.org/10.1080/19463138.2014.951048.

Kealy, Courtney. "A Decade on, Occupy Wall Street's Legacy on Income Inequality." *Al Jazeera*, September 17, 2021. https://www.aljazeera.com/economy/2021/9/17/a-decade-on-occupy-wall-streets-legacy-on-income-inequality.

Kelley, Robin D.G. "Why Black Marxism, Why Now?" *Boston Review*, February 1, 2021. https://bostonreview.net/articles/robin-d-g-kelley-tk-2/.

Kelly, Kim. "What 'Capitalism' Is and How It Affects People." *TeenVogue*, August 25, 2020. https://www.teenvogue.com/story/what-capitalism-is.

Kenworthy, Lane. *Social Democratic Capitalism*. New York, NY: Oxford University Press, 2020.

Keynes, John Maynard. *A Tract on Monetary Reform*. London: MacMillan & Co., 1923. https://www.gutenberg.org/files/65278/65278-h/65278-h.htm#sec_14.

Kherdeen, Riad. "Democracy Is Incompatible with Capitalism." *Medium*, December 17, 2020. https://medium.com/illumination/democracy-is-incompatible-with-capitalsim-4fcb7576ba6c.

Klein, Ezra. "In the UK's Health System, Rationing Isn't a Dirty Word." *Vox*, January 28, 2020. https://www.vox.com/2020/1/28/21074386/health-care-rationing-britain-nhs-nice-medicare-for-all.

Klein, Naomi. *This Changes Everything: Capitalism vs. the Climate*. New York: Simon & Schuster, 2015.

Kline, Maureen. "How to Build a Sustainable Capitalism." *Inc.*, September 14, 2020. https://www.inc.com/maureen-kline/how-to-build-a-sustainable-capitalism.html.

Klobuchar, Amy. *Antitrust: Taking on Monopoly Power from the Gilded Age to the Digital Age*. New York: Knopf, 2021.

Knudsen, Jette Steen. "Government Regulation of International Corporate Social Responsibility in the US and UK: How Domestic Institutions Shape Mandatory and Supportive Initiatives." *British Journal of Industrial Relations* 56, no. 1 (2018): 164–88.

Knudsen, Jette Steen, Jeremy Moon, and Rieneke Slager. "Government Policies for Corporate Social Responsibility in Europe: A Comparative Analysis of Institutionalization." *Policy & Politics* 43, no. 1 (2015): 81–89.

Kolhatkar, Sheelah. "What Happens when Investment Firms Acquire Trailer Parks." *New Yorker*, March 8, 2021.

Koop, Gary, and Lise Tole. "Deforestation, Distribution, and Development." *Global Environmental Change* 11, no. 3 (2001): 193–202.

Korff, Geoffrey D. "Reviving the Forgotten American Dream." *Penn State Law Review* 113, no. 417 (Fall 2008): 417–60. https://www.pennstatelawreview .org/print-issues/articles/reviving-the-forgotten-american-dream/.

Kramer, Ronald C. *Carbon Criminals, Climate Crimes*. New Brunswick, NJ: Rutgers University Press, 2020.

Krieger, Nancy. "Climate Crisis, Health Equity, and Democratic Governance: The Need to Act Together." *Journal of Public Health Policy* 41 (2020): 4–10.

Krier, James E., and Clayton P. Gillette. "The Un-Easy Case for Technological Optimism." *Michigan Law Review* 84 (1985): 405–29.

Krugman, Paul. "Corporate America Is Lobbying for Climate Disaster." *New York Times*, September 2, 2021. https://www.nytimes.com/2021/09/02/opinion/ corporate-taxes-biden-spending-bill.html.

Kuhner, Timothy K. *Capitalism v. Democracy: Money in Politics and the Free Market Constitution*. Stanford, CA: Stanford University Press, 2014.

Kunzig, Robert. "Here's How a 'Circular Economy' Could Save the World." *National Geographic*, February 18, 2020. https://www.nationalgeographic.com/ magazine/article/how-a-circular-economy-could-save-the-world-feature.

Kuttner, Robert. "Neoliberalism: Political Success, Economic Failure." *American Prospect*, June 25, 2019. https://prospect.org/economy/neoliberalism-political -success-economic-failure/.

Kwate, Naa Oyo A., and Ji Meng Loh. "Separate and Unequal: The Influence of Neighborhood and School Characteristics on Spatial Proximity Between Fast Food and Schools." *Preventive Medicine* 51, (2010).

Labor Network for Sustainability. "Labor, Sustainability and Justice." https://www .labor4sustainability.org/post/labor-sustainability-and-justice/.

Lampe, Joanna. *Congress and Police Reform: Current Law and Recent Proposals*. Washington, DC: Congressional Research Service, 2020.

Landes, William M., and Richard A. Posner. *The Economic Structure of Intellectual Property Law*. Cambridge, MA: Harvard University Press, 2003.

Lane, Sylvan. "Manchin to Oppose Biden Fed Pick over Climate Stances." *The Hill*, March 14, 2022.

Laplume, Andre O., Reginald A. Litz, and Karan Sonpar. "Stakeholder Theory: Reviewing a Theory That Moves Us." *Journal of Management* 34, no. 6 (2008): 1152–89. https://doi.org/10.1177/0149206308324322.

Laster Pirtle, Whitney N. "Racial Capitalism: A Fundamental Cause of Novel Coronavirus (COVID-19) Pandemic Inequities in the United States." *Health Education and Behavior* 47, no. 4 (2020): 504–8.

Lawrence, Mark A, and Phillip I. Baker. "Ultra-Processed Food and Adverse Health Outcomes." *BMJ* 365 (May 29, 2019). https://doi.org/10.1136/bmj.l2289.

Lazarus, Richard J. *The Making of Environmental Law*. Chicago: University of Chicago Press, 2004.

Lazarus, Richard J. "Super Wicked Problems and Climate Change: Restraining the Present to Liberate the Future." *Cornell Law Review* 94, no. 5 (2009): 1153–1234. https://scholarship.law.cornell.edu/clr/vol94/iss5/8

Lederman, Leandra. "The IRS, Politics, and Income Inequality." *Tax Notes* 150, no. 11 (2016): 1329.

Lee, Ian B. "Efficiency and Ethics in the Debate about Shareholder Primacy." *Delaware Journal of Corporate Law* 31, no. 2 (2006): 533–587. https://advance.lexis.com/api/document?collection=analytical-materials&id=urn:contentItem:4KMB-B1M0-00CW-B00C-00000-00&context=1516831.

Lenin, Vladimir. *Imperialism: The Highest Stage of Capitalism.* London: Penguin Books, 2010. First published 1916 by Life and Knowledge Publishers (St. Petersburg).

Leonard, Christopher. *Kochland: The Secret History of Koch Industries and Corporate Power in America.* New York, NY: Simon & Schuster, 2019.

Leong, Nancy. "Racial Capitalism." *Harvard Law Review* 126, no. 2151 (2013).

Leonhardt, David. "America's Cash Glut." *New York Times*, October 18, 2021. https://www.nytimes.com/2021/10/18/briefing/us-economy-cash-glut.html.

Leroy, Justin, and Destin Jenkins. *Histories of Racial Capitalism.* New York: Columbia University Press, 2021.

Leslie, Jacques. "Where Water is Scarce, Communities Turn to Reusing Wastewater." *Yale Environment 360*, May 1, 2018. https://e360.yale.edu/features/instead-of-more-dams-communities-turn-to-reusing-wastewater.

Levi-Faur, David. "The Rise of Regulatory Capitalism: The Global Diffusion of a New Order." *Annals of the American Academy of Political and Social Science* 598, (2005): 12–32.

Levitin, Michael. "The Triumph of Occupy Wall Street." *Atlantic*, June 10, 2015. https://www.theatlantic.com/politics/archive/2015/06/the-triumph-of-occupy-wall-street/395408/.

Li, Minqi. *Profit, Accumulation, and Crisis in Capitalism: Long-Term Trends in the UK, US, Japan, and China, 1855–2018.* Oxford: Routledge, 2020.

Lianzhang, Wang. "Government Orders Chinese Air Quality App to Limit Readings." *Sixth Tone*, January 10, 2017. https://www.sixthtone.com/news/1796/government-orders-chinese-air-quality-app-to-limit-readings.

Liebman, Benjamin L., and Curtis J. Milhaupt. *Regulating the Visible Hand? The Institutional Implications of Chinese State Capitalism.* New York: Oxford University Press, 2015.

Lind, Michael. "Why Big Business Fears the Tea Party." *Politico*, June 15, 2014.

Lindgreen, Adam, and Valérie Swaen. "Corporate Social Responsibility." *International Journal of Management Reviews* 12, no. 1 (2010): 1–7. https://doi.org/10.1111/j.1468-2370.2009.00277.x.

Lobosco, Katie. "The IRS Is Set to Get Billions for Audit Enforcement. Here's What It Means for Taxpayers." *CNN*, August 11, 2022. https://www.cnn.com/2022/08/11/politics/irs-inflation-act-funding-audit-enforcement/index.html.

Loh, Tracy Hadden, Christopher Coes, and Becca Buthe. "Separate and unequal: Persistent residential segregation is sustaining racial and economic injustice in the U.S." *Brookings*, December 16, 2020. https://www.brookings.edu/essay/trend-1-separate-and-unequal-neighborhoods-are-sustaining-racial-and-economic-injustice-in-the-us/.

Lovins, L. Hunter. "Climate Capitalism: The Business Case for Climate Protection." *Pace Environmental Law Review* 27, no. 735 (2010): 774–779. https://doi.org/10.58948/0738-6206.1650.

Lukes, Dylan, and Christopher Cleveland. "The Lingering Legacy of Redlining on School Funding, Diversity, and Performance." EdWorkingPaper: 21-363, Annenberg Institute at Brown University, 2021. https://doi.org/10.26300/qeer-8c25.

Lund, Dorothy S. "Corporate Finance for Social Good." *Columbia Law Review* 121, no. 5 (2021): 1617–58. https://dx.doi.org/10.2139/ssrn.3511631.

Lustgarten, Abrahm, and Ryan Knutson. "Years of Internal BP Probes Warned That Neglect Could Lead to Accidents." *ProPublica*, June 7, 2010. https://www.propublica.org/article/years-of-internal-bp-probes-warned-that-neglect-could-lead-to-accidents.

Mackey, John, and Raj Sisodia. *Conscious Capitalism: Liberating the Heroic Spirit of Business.* Boston, MA: Harvard Business School Publishing Corporation, 2013.

MacLean, Nancy. *Democracy in Chains: The Deep History of the Radical Right's Stealth Plan for America.* New York, NY: Viking Press, 2017.

Magnani, Elisabetta. "The Environmental Kuznets Curve, Environmental Protection Policy and Income Distribution." *Ecological Economics* 32 (2000): 431–43.

Majersik, Cliff, and Alex Dews. "What the Inflation Reduction Act Does and Doesn't Do for Climate Change and Equity." *Institute for Market Transformation*, August 10, 2022. https://www.imt.org/news/what-the-inflation-reduction-act-does-and-doesnt-do-for-climate-and-equity/.

Malhotra, Neil, Benoît Monin, and Michael Tomz. "Does Private Regulation Preempt Public Regulation?" *American Political Science Review* 113, no. 1 (2019), 19–37.

Malthus, Thomas Robert. *An Essay on the Principle of Population.* London, UK: Electronic Scholarly Publication Project, 1798 (republished 1998).

Manjoo, Farhad. "Private Equity Doesn't Want You to Read This." *New York Times*, August 4, 2022. https://www.nytimes.com/2022/08/04/opinion/private-equity-lays-waste.html.

Mann, Charles C. *The Wizard and the Profit: Two Remarkable Scientists and Their Dueling Visions to Shape Tomorrow's World.* New York, NY: Vintage, 2019.

Manyika, James, et al. "The Social Contract in the 21st Century." *McKinsey Global Institute*, February 5, 2020. https://www.mckinsey.com/industries/public-and-social-sector/our-insights/the-social-contract-in-the-21st-century.

Marable, Manning. *How Capitalism Underdeveloped Black America*, 2nd ed. Cambridge: South End Press, 2000.

Martinez, Mark A. *The Myth of the Free Market: The Role of the State in a Capitalist Society*. Boulder, CO: Kumarian Press, 2009.

Marx, Karl. *Capital*. Everyman's Library, No. 848, 849. London: J. M. Dent & Sons, 1967.

Marx, Karl. *Capital: A Critique of Political Economy*. Vol. 1. Translated by Samuel Moore and Edward Aveling. Edited by Frederick Engels. Moscow: Progress Publishers, 1887. Reprint, New York: International Publishers, 1967.

Marx, Karl. *Critique of the Gotha Programme*. London: Electric Book Co. ProQuest Ebook Central, 2001.

Marx, Karl. *Das Kapital*. Edited by Friedrich Engels. Washington, DC: Regnery Publishing, 1996.

Marx, Karl. *Economic and Philosophic Manuscripts of 1844*. Translated by Martin Milligan. Moscow: Progress Publishers, 1959.

Marx, Karl, and Friedrich Engels. *The Communist Manifesto*. London: Workers' Educational Association, 1908.

Marx, Karl, and Friedrich Engels. *The German Ideology*. Translated by Tim Delaney and Bob Schwartz. Moscow: Progress Publishers, 1968. https://www.marxists.org/archive/marx/works/download/Marx_The_German_Ideology.pdf..

Mason, Whit, ed. *The Rule of Law in Afghanistan: Missing in Inaction*. Cambridge: Cambridge University Press, 2011.

Maurice, Marc, François Sellier, and Jean-Jacques Silvestre. *The Social Foundations of Industrial Power: A Comparison of France and Germany*. Cambridge, MA: MIT Press, 1986.

Max [@deepfates]. "Status May 23, 2022, at 8:43 AM." Twitter post, May 23, 2022. https://twitter.com/deepfates/status/152876365844395212.

Mayer, Colin. *Prosperity: Better Business Makes the Greater Good*. Oxford University Press, 2018.

Mayer, Jane. "The Big Money Behind the Big Lie." *New Yorker*, August 9, 2021. https://www.newyorker.com/magazine/2021/08/09/the-big-money-behind-the-big-lie.

Mayer, Jane. *Dark Money: The Hidden History of the Billionaires Behind the Rise of the Radical Right*. New York, NY: Doubleday, 2016.

Mazzucato, Mariana. "We Socialize Bailouts. We Should Socialize Successes, Too." *New York Times*, July 1, 2020. https://www.nytimes.com/2020/07/01/opinion/inequality-goverment-bailout.html.

McAfee, Andrew. *More from Less: The Surprising Story of How We Learned to Prosper Using Few Resources—and What Happens Next*. New York: Scribner's, 2019.

McCann, Duncan, and Christine Berry. *Shareholder Capitalism—A System in Crisis*. New Economics Foundation, 2017.

McCloskey, Deirdre Nansen. "Sweden is Capitalist." *National Review*, May 2, 2019. https://www.nationalreview.com/magazine/2019/05/20/sweden-is-capitalist/.

McDermott, Amy. "Climate Change Hastens Disease Spread Across the Globe." *PNAS* 119, no. 7 (February 9, 2022). https://doi.org/10.1073/pnas.2200481119.

McDonnell, Gary. "What Caused Airline Deregulation: Economists or Economics?" *Independent Review* 19, no. 3 (Winter 2015): 379–95.

McIntosh, Kriston, et al. "Examining the Black-White Wealth Gap." *The Brookings Institute*, February 27, 2020. https://www.brookings.edu/blog/up-front/2020/02/27/examining-the-black-white-wealth-gap/.

Mead, Walter Russell. *Special Providence: American Foreign Policy and How It Changed the World.* New York: Random House, 2001.

Meadows, Donella. "Leverage Points: Places to Intervene in a System." *Sustainability Institute* (1999). https://donellameadows.org/wp-content/userfiles/Leverage_Points.pdf.

Melamed, Jodi. "Racial Capitalism." *Critical Ethnic Studies* 1, no. 1 (Spring 2015): 76–85. https://doi.org/10.5749/jcritethnstud.1.1.0076.

Merkel, Wolfgang. "Is Capitalism Compatible With Democracy?" *Zeitschrift für Vergleichende Politikwissenschaft* 8, no. 2 (July 26, 2014): 110–128. https://doi.org/10.1007/s12286-014-0199-4.

Mervosh, Sarah. "How Much Wealthier are White School Districts than Nonwhite Ones? $23 Billion, Report Says." *New York Times*, February 27, 2019. https://www.nytimes.com/2019/02/27/education/school-districts-funding-white-minorities.html.

Michaels, David. *The Triumph of Doubt: Dark Money and the Science of Deception.* New York, NY: Oxford University Press, 2020.

Migratory Bird Treaty Act of 1918, 16 U.S.C. §§703–712. https://fws.gov/birds/policies-and-regulations/laws-legislations/migratory-bird-treaty-act.php.

Mikkelson, Gregory, et al. "Economic Inequality Predicts Biodiversity Loss." *PLOS One* 2, no. 5 (2007): e444.

Milberg, William, and Deborah Winkler. "Globalization, Offshoring, and Economic Insecurity in Industrialized Countries." UN Department of Economic and Social Affairs Working Paper 87, New York: UN Department of Economic & Social Affairs, 2009.

Milhaupt, Curtis J., and Katharina Pistor. *Law and Capitalism: What Corporate Crises Reveal about Legal Systems and Economic Development around the World.* Chicago: University of Chicago Press, 2008.

Mills, Cliff, and Will Davies. *Blueprint for a Co-operative Decade.* Geneva: International Co-operative Alliance, 2013. https://www.ica.coop/sites/default/files/2021-11/Blueprint%20for%20a%20Co-operative%20Decade%20-%20English.Blueprint%20for%20a%20Co-operative%20Decade%20-%20English.

Milman, Oliver. "'He's a Villain': Joe Manchin Attracts Global Anger over Climate Crisis." *Guardian*, January 26, 2022.

Milman, Oliver, and Fiona Harvey. "John Kerry Commits US to Climate Crisis Fight but Warns World Is Way off Pace." *Guardian*, January 21, 2021. https://www.theguardian.com/us-news/2021/jan/21/john-kerry-climate-crisis-joe-biden-envoy.

Mitbestimmungsgesetz [MitbestG] [Co-determination Act]. May 4, 1976. BGBl. I at
    1153. Last amended by Artikel 17 des Gesetzes. August 7, 2021. BGBl. I at 3311
    (Ger.). https://www.gesetze-im-internet.de/mitbestg/BJNR011530976.html.
Monbiot, George. "Capitalism Is Killing the Planet—It's Time to Stop Buying into
    Our Own Destruction." *Guardian*, October 30, 2021. https://www.theguardian
    .com/environment/2021/oct/30/capitalism-is-killing-the-planet-its-time-to
    -stop-buying-into-our-own-destruction.
Monbiot, George. "Neoliberalism—The Ideology at the Root of All Our Problems."
    Guardian, April 15, 2016. https://www.theguardian.com/books/2016/apr/15/
    neoliberalism-ideology-problem-george-monbiot.
Monroe, Robert. "Earth Has Crossed Several 'Planetary Boundaries,' Threshold
    of Human-Induced Environmental Changes." *Scripps Institution of Ocean-
    ography*, January 15, 2015. https://scripps.ucsd.edu/news/earth-has-crossed
    -several-planetary-boundaries-thresholds-human-induced-environmental
    -changes.
Mooney, Chris. *The Republican War on Science.* New York, NY: Basic Books, 2005.
Moore, Adrian. "California: How Not to Deregulate Electricity." *reason Founda-
    tion*, January 7, 2001. https://reason.org/commentary/california-how-not-to
    -deregula/.
Moore, Julia Robinson. "The Black Church and the Black Radical Tradition."
    Berkley Forum, January 26, 2022. https://berkleycenter.georgetown.edu/
    responses/the-black-church-and-the-black-radical-tradition.
Moore, Stephen, and Tyler Grimm. "An Economy in Crisis: Law, Policy, and Moral-
    ity During the Recession: Straw Man Capitalism and a New Path to Prosper-
    ity." *Harvard Journal of Law and Public Policy* 33, (2010): 475–487.
Mosbergen, Dominique. "Why Southeast Asia Is Flooded with Trash from
    America and Other Wealthy Nations." *Huffington Post*, March 8,
    2019. https://www.huffpost.com/entry/malaysia-plastic-recycling_n
    _5c7f64a9e4b020b54d7ffdee.
Movement for Black Lives (M4BL). *Reparations Now Toolkit.* 2019. https://m4bl
    .org/wp-content/uploads/2021/06/Reparations-Now-Toolkit-FINAL.pdf.
Mowery, David C., Richard R. Nelson, Bhaven N. Sampat, and Arvids A. Ziedonis.
    Ivory Tower and Industrial Innovation. Redwood City, CA: Stanford University
    Press, 2004.
Murray, Fiona. "Evaluating the Role of Science Philanthropy in American
    Research Universities." *Innovation Policy and the Economy* 13, (2013): 23–59.
Mutschler, Phyllis, ed. *Women and Caregiving: Facts and Figures.* San Francisco:
    Family Caregiver Alliance, 2003. Accessed February 20, 2022. https://www
    .caregiver.org/resource/women-and-caregiving-facts-and-figures/.
Mutschler-Supplee, Andre J. "The Caregiving Burden on the Caregivers of Aged
    Loved Ones: Qualitative Interviews of Female Caregivers with Male Siblings."
    Professional Psychology Dissertations (2019). https://ir.stthomas.edu/caps
    _gradpsych_docdiss/59.

Nagy, Donna M. "Playing Peekaboo with Constitutional Law: The PCAOB and Its Public/Private Status." *Notre Dame Law Review* 80, no. 975 (2005).

Nardone, Anthony, Joan A. Casey, Rachel Morello-Frosch, Mahasin Mujahid, John R. Balmes, and Neeta Thakur. "Associations between historical residential redlining and current age-adjusted rates of emergency department visits due to asthma across eight cities in California: an ecological study." *Lancet Planetary Health* 4, no. 1 (January 2020): E24–E31. https://doi.org/10.1016/S2542 -5196(19)30241-4.

National Academies of Sciences, Engineering, and Medicine (NAS). *Reflecting Sunlight: Recommendations for Solar Geoengineering Research and Research Governance*. Washington, DC: The National Academies Press, 2021.

National Academies of Sciences, Engineering, and Medicine (NAS). *A Research Strategy for Ocean-based Carbon Dioxide Removal and Sequestration*. Washington, DC: The National Academies Press, 2022.

National Aeronautics and Space Administration (NASA), Goddard Institute for Space Studies. "GISS Surface Temperature Analysis (GISTEMP v4)." *NASA*, June 23, 2023. https://data.giss.nasa.gov/gistemp/.

National Partnership for Women & Families. *Sexual Harassment and the Gender Wage Gap Fact Sheet*. March 2021. https://www.nationalpartnership.org/ our-work/resources/economic-justice/fair-pay/sexual-harassment-and-the -gender-wage-gap.pdf.

National Renewable Energy Laboratory (NREL). "Life Cycle Assessment Harmonization." *National Renewable Energy Laboratory*, June 20, 2022. https://www .nrel.gov/analysis/life-cycle-assessment.html.

National Research Council (NRC). *Review of the Desalination and Water Purification Technology Roadmap*. Washington, DC: The National Academies Press, 2004.

National Rural Electric Cooperative Association. "Co-op 101 Electric Co-op Facts & Figures." Last Modified October 22, 2021. https://www.electric.coop/electric -cooperative-fact-sheet.

National Science Foundation (NSF), National Center for Science and Engineering Statistics. "U.S. R&D Increased by $62 Billion in 2019 to $667 Billion." *National Center for Science and Engineering Statistics*, June 1, 2022. https:// ncses.nsf.gov/pubs/nsf22330.

Neacşu, Dana. "The Aesthetic Ideology of *Juliana v. United States* and Its Impact on Environmentally Engaged Citizenship." *Journal of Environmental Studies and Sciences* 12, no. 1 (Spring 2022): 28–42. https://doi.org/10.1007/s13412-021-00731-z.

Neacşu, Dana. *The Bourgeois Charm of Karl Marx & the Ideological Irony of American Jurisprudence*. Leiden; Boston: Brill, 2020.

Neal, Larry, and Jeffrey G. Williamson. *The Cambridge History of Capitalism: Volume 1, The Rise of Capitalism: From Ancient Origins to 1848*. Cambridge: Cambridge University Press, 2015.

Nellis, Ashley. *The Color of Justice: Racial and Ethnic Disparity in State Prisons*. The Sentencing Project, 2021.

Nelson, Anne. *Shadow Network: Media, Money, and the Secret Hub of the Radical Right.* New York, NY: Bloomsbury Publishing, 2019.

Nesbit, Jeff. *Poison Tea: How Big Oil and Big Tobacco Invented the Tea Party and Captured the GOP.* New York, NY: St. Martin's Press, 2016.

Net Zero Tracker. "Companies." *Net Zero Tracker.* Accessed August 24, 2022. https://zerotracker.net.

Neumayer, Eric. "Sustainability and Inequality in Human Development." *UNDP Human Development Report Office Occasional Papers,* No. 2011/04, November 2011. https://www.researchgate.net/publication/228264939_Sustainability _and_Inequality_in_Human_Development.

Newell, Peter, Freddie Daley, and Michelle Twena. "Changing Our Ways? Behaviour Change and the Climate Crisis." Brighton, UK: Cambridge Sustainability Commissions, 2021.

Newell, Peter, and Matthew Paterson. *Climate Capitalism.* Cambridge, UK: Cambridge University Press, 2010.

Nixon, Rob. "Naomi Klein's 'This Changes Everything.'" *New York Times,* November 6, 2014. https://www.nytimes.com/2014/11/09/books/review/naomi-klein -this-changes-everything-review.html.

Njuki, Eric. "A Look at Agricultural Productivity Growth in the United States, 1948–2017." United States Department of Agriculture (USDA), March 5, 2020. https://www.usda.gov/media/blog/2020/03/05/look-agricultural-productivity -growth-united-states-1948-2017.

Noble, Safiya Umoja. *Algorithms of Oppression: How Search Engines Reinforce Racism.* New York: New York University Press, 2018.

Nölke, Andreas. "Economic Causes of the Eurozone Crisis: The Analytical Contribution of Comparative Capitalism." *Socio-Economic Review* 14, no. 1 (2016): 141–61. https://doi.org/10.1093/ser/mwv031.

Nordhaus, William D. "After Kyoto: Alternative Mechanisms to Control Global Warming." *American Economic Review* 96, no. 2 (May 2006): 31–34. https:// doi.org/10.1257/000282806777211964.

Nwoke, Uchechukwu. "Corporations and Development: The Barriers to Effective Corporate Social Responsibility (CSR) in a Neoliberal Age." *International Journal of Law and Management* 59, no. 1 (2017): 122–46.

O'Connor, James. "Capitalism, Nature, Socialism: A Theoretical Introduction." *Capitalism Nature Socialism* 1, no. 1 (1988): 11–38. DOI: 10.1080/10455758809358356.

Offe, Claus. "The European Model of 'Social' Capitalism: Can It Survive European Integration?" *Journal of Political Philosophy* 11, no. 4 (2003): 437–69. https:// doi.org/10.1046/j.1467-9760.2003.00185.x.

Office of Senator Tammy Baldwin. *Reward Work Not Wealth.* 2019. https://www .baldwin.senate.gov/imo/media/doc/Reward%20Work%20Not%20Wealth %20Baldwin%20Staff%20Report%203.26.19.pdf.

Oishi, Shigehiro, Kostadin Kushlev, and Ulrich Schimmack. "Progressive Taxation, Income Inequality, and Happiness." *American Psychologist* 73, no. 2 (2018): 157–68.

O'Mara, Margaret. "The Church of Techno-Optimism." *New York Times*, September 28, 2019.

O'Neil, Cathy. *Weapons of Math Destruction: How Big Data Increases Inequality and Threatens Democracy*. New York: Broadway Books, 2016.

Open-ended Intergovernmental Working Group on Transnational Corporations and Other Business Enterprises with Respect to Human Rights (OEIGWG). *Legally Binding Instrument to Regulate, In International Human Rights Law, the Activities of Transnational Corporations and other Business Enterprises*. OEIGWG Chairmanship Third Revised Draft, August 17, 2021. https://www.ohchr.org/en/hrbodies/hrc/wgtranscorp/pages/igwgontnc.aspx.

OpenSecrets.Org. "Top Individual Contributors: All Federal Contributions." *OpenSecrets*, 2019–2020. https://www.opensecrets.org/elections-overview/biggest-donors?cycle=2020&view=fc.

Organic Trade Association. "U.S. Organic Sales Soar to New High of Nearly $62 Billion in 2020." (May 25, 2021). https://ota.com/news/press-releases/21755.

Organization for Economic Cooperation and Development. *In it Together: Why Less Inequality Benefits All*. Paris: OECD, 2015.

Ossewaarde, Marinus, and Wessel Reijers. "The Illusion of the Digital Commons: 'False Consciousness' in Online Alternative Economies." *Organization* 24, no. 5 (2017): 609–28.

Ostrom, E. "Design Principles of Robust Property-Rights Institutions: What Have We Learned." Presented at the conference on *Land Policies and Property Rights*, Lincoln Institute of Land Policy, Cambridge, MA, June 2–3, 2008. https://dlc.dlib.indiana.edu/dlc/bitstream/handle/10535/3785/W08-19_Ostrom_DLC.pdf?sequence=1&isAllowed=y.

Ostrom, Elinor. *Governing the Commons: The Evolution of Institutions for Collective Action*. Cambridge: Cambridge University Press, 1990.

Osugi, Kenichi. "What is Converging? Rules on Hostile Takeovers in Japan and the Convergence Debate." *Asian-Pacific Law & Policy Journal* 9, no. 1 (Winter 2007): 143–62. https://manoa.hawaii.edu/aplpj/wp-content/uploads/sites/120/2011/11/APLPJ_09.1_osugi.pdf.

Otto, Shawn. *The War on Science: Who's Waging It, Why It Matters, What We Can Do about It*. Minneapolis, MN: Milkweed Press, 2016.

Page, Benjamin I., and Martin Gilens. *Democracy in America? What Has Gone Wrong and What We Can Do About It*. Chicago, IL: University of Chicago Press, 2017.

Paludan, Phillip Shaw. *Victims: A True Story of the Civil War*. Knoxville: University of Tennessee Press, 2004.

Panwar, Rajat, Shweta Nawani, and Vivek Pandey. "Legislated CSR: A Brief

Introduction." In *Corporate Social Responsibility*, edited by David Crowther and Shahla Seifi, 133–46. *Business and Society 360*, vol. 2 (2018).

Panwar, Rajat, Vivek Pandey, Roy Suddaby, and Natalia G. Vidal. "Did India's CSR Mandate, Enhance or Diminish Firm Value?" *Business & Society* 62, no. 2 (2022). https://doi.org/10.1177/00076503221085962.

Panwar, Rajat, Tomi Rinne, Eric Hansen, and Heikki Juslin. "Corporate Responsibility: Balancing Economic, Environmental and Social Issues in the Forest Products Industry." *Forest Products Journal* 56, no. 2 (2006): 4–12.

Pappas, Michael, and Victor Byers Flatt. "Climate Changes Property: Disasters, Decommodification, and Retreat." *Ohio State Law Journal* 82, no. 331 (2021).

Parker, Emily. *Constitutional Obligations for Public Education: 50-State Review*. Education Commission of the States, March 2016. https://www.ecs.org/wp-content/uploads/2016-Constitutional-obligations-for-public-education-1.pdf.

Parshina-Kottis, Yuliya, Anjali Singhvi, Audra D.S. Burch, Troy Griggs, Mika Gröndahl, Lingdong Huang, Tim Wallace, Jeremy White, and Josh Williams. "What the Tulsa Race Massacre Destroyed." *New York Times*, May 24, 2021. https://www.nytimes.com/interactive/2021/05/24/us/tulsa-race-massacre.html.

Partnoy, Frank. "Why Markets Crash and What Law Can Do about It." *University of Pittsburg Law Review* 61, no. 3 (2000): 741.

Payne, Rodger. "Freedom and the Environment." *Journal of Democracy* 6, no. 3 (1995): 41–55.

Pearlstein, Steven. *Can American Capitalism Survive? Why Greed Is Not Good, Opportunity Is Not Equal, and Fairness Won't Make Us Poor*. New York, NY: St. Martin's Press, 2018.

Pearlstein, Steven. "Social Capital, Corporate Purpose and the Revival of American Capitalism." *Brookings Institution*, January, 2014. https://www.brookings.edu/research/social-capital-corporate-purpose-and-the-revival-of-american-capitalism/.

Peck, Jamie, and Adam Tickell. "Conceptualizing Neoliberalism, Thinking Thatcherism." In *Contesting Neoliberalism: Urban Frontiers*, edited by Helga Leitner, Jamie Peck, and Eric Sheppard, 26–50. New York: The Guilford Press, 2007.

Percival, Robert V., et al. *Environmental Regulation: Law, Science, and Policy*. 4th ed. New York: Aspen Publishers, 2003.

Perls, Hannah. "Deconstructing Environmental Deregulation Under the Trump Administration." *Vermont Law Review* 45, no. 591 (2021).

Pfeffer, Fabian T., and Robert F. Schoeni. "How Wealth Inequality Shapes Our Future." *Russell Sage Foundation Journal of the Social Sciences* 2, no. 6 (2016): 2–22.

Phelps, Edmund S. *Capitalism and Keynes: From the Treatise on Probability to the General Theory*. 2007. https://doi.org/10.7916/D86D65GN.

Philippon, Thomas. *The Great Reversal: How America Gave Up on Free Markets*. Cambridge, MA: Harvard University Press, 2019.

Phillips, Kevin. *Wealth and Democracy: A Political History of the American Rich*. New York, NY: Broadway Books, 2002.

Piketty, Thomas. *Capital in the Twenty-First Century.* Cambridge, MA: Harvard University Press, 2014.

Pinker, Steven. *Enlightenment Now: The Case for Reason, Science, Humanism and Progress.* New York, NY: Viking, 2018.

Pirgmaier, Elke. "Consumption Corridors, Capitalism, and Social Change." *Sustainability: Science, Practice, and Policy* 16, no. 1 (2020): 274–285. https://doi.org/10.1080/15487733.2020.1829846.

Pistor, Katharina. *The Code of Capital: How the Law Creates Wealth and Inequality.* Princeton: Princeton University Press, 2019.

Plumer, Brad. "You've Heard of Outsourced Jobs, but Outsourced Pollution? It's Real, and Tough to Tally Up." *New York Times,* September 4, 2018. https://www.nytimes.com/2018/09/04/climate/outsourcing-carbon-emissions.html.

Polanyi, Karl. *The Great Transformation: The Political and Economic Origins of Our Time.* 2nd ed. Boston: Beacon Press, 2001.

Polk, Sam. "What's Wrong With Wall Street? A Culture That Breeds Greed." *PBS,* August 23, 2016. https://www.pbs.org/newshour/economy/whats-wrong-wall-street-culture-breeds-greed.

Pollock, Lauren. "How Capitalism Is a Driving Force of Climate Change." *The People, Ideas, and Things Journal, Special Issue: Pandemic and Politics* (2020). https://pitjournal.unc.edu/content/how-capitalism-driving-force-climate-change#:~:text=Global%20capitalist%20economies%20are%20a,120%20years%20into%20the%20future.

Pond Cummings, André D. "Ain't No Glory in Pain": How the 1994 Republican Revolution and the Private Securities Litigation Reform Act Contributed to the Collapse of the United States Capital Markets." *Nebraska Law Review* 83, no. 979 (2004).

Popovich, Nadja, Livia Albeck-Ripka, and Kendra Pierre-Louis. "The Trump Administration Rolled Back More Than 100 Environmental Rules. Here's the Full List." *New York Times,* January 20, 2021. https://www.nytimes.com/interactive/2020/climate/trump-environment-rollbacks-list.html.

Powell, Michael. "Bank Accused of Pushing Mortgage Deals on Blacks." *New York Times,* June 6, 2009. https://www.nytimes.com/2009/06/07/us/07baltimore.html.

Prell, Christina. "Wealth and Pollution Inequalities of Global Trade." *Social Science Journal* 53, issue 1 (2016): 111–121. https://doi.org/10.1016/j.soscij.2015.08.003.

"Proposition 22: Exempts App-Based Transportation and Delivery Companies from Providing Employee Benefits to Certain Drivers." California General Election, 2020. https://web.archive.org/web/20201030082907/https://voterguide.sos.ca.gov/propositions/22/.

Pulido, Laura. "Flint, Environmental Racism, and Racial Capitalism." *Capitalism, Nature, Socialism* 27, no. 3 (2016): 1–16. https://doi.org/10.1080/10455752.2016.1213013.

Pulido, Laura, and Juan de Lara. "Reimagining 'Justice' in Environmental Justice: Radical Ecologies, Decolonial Thought, and the Black Radical Tradition." *Environment and Planning E: Nature and Space* 1, no. 1 (2018): 1–23. https://doi.org/10.1177%2F2514848618770363.

Quigley, William P. "The Continuing Significance of Race: Official Legislative Racial Discrimination in Louisiana 1861 to 1974." *Southern University Law Review* 47, no. 1 (2019): 1–65. https://papers.ssrn.com/sol3/papers.cfm?abstract_id=3575898.

Rajan, Raghuram G., and Luigi Zingales. *Saving Capitalism from the Capitalists: Unleashing the Power of Financial Markets to Create Wealth and Spread Opportunity.* New York, NY: Crown Business, 2003.

Rasnic, Carol Daugherty. "Die Kundigung, Licenciement, Recesso Dal Contrato, 'Firing', or 'Sacking': Comparing European and American Laws on Management Prerogatives and Discretion in Termination Decisions." *Indiana International and Comparative Law Review* 18, no. 1 (2008): 19–87.

Raworth, Kate. *Doughnut Economics: Seven Ways to Think Like a 21st-Century Economist.* New York: Random House, 2017.

Ray, Deepak K., Paul C. West, Michael Clark, James S. Gerber, Alexander V. Prishchepov, and Snigdhansu Chatterjee. "Climate Change Has Likely Already Affected Global Food Production." *PLoS ONE* 14, no. 5 (May 31, 2019). https://doi.org/10.1371/journal.pone.0217148.

Ray, Michael. "Tea Party movement." *Encyclopedia Britannica.* Updated May 5, 2023. https://www.britannica.com/topic/Tea-Party-movement.

Rees, William. *Our Ecological Footprint: Reducing Human Impact on the Earth.* Philadelphia: New Society Publishers, 1996.

Reich, Robert. "How Capitalism Is Killing Democracy." *Foreign Policy*, October 12, 2009. https://foreignpolicy.com/2009/10/12/how-capitalism-is-killing-democracy/.

Reich, Robert. *Supercapitalism.* New York: Vintage Publishing, 2008.

Reich, Robert. *The System: Who Rigged It and How We Fix It.* New York, NY: Vintage Press, 2020.

Reier, Sharon. "5 Years Later, Greenspan's 'Irrational Exuberance' Alert Rings True." *New York Times*, December 1, 2001. https://www.nytimes.com/2001/12/01/your-money/IHT-5-years-later-greenspans-irrational-exuberance-alert-rings.html.

Reimann, Mathias. "The Good, the Bad, and the Ugly: The Reform of the German Law of Obligations." *Tulane Law Review* 83, no. 4 (2009): 877–918. https://www.tulanelawreview.org/pub/volume83/issue4/the-good-the-bad-and-the-ugly.

Reinke, Benedikt, and Peter C. Zumbansen. "Transnational Liability Regimes in Contract, Tort and Corporate Law: Comparative Observations on 'Global Supply Chain Liability.'" King's College London Law School Legal Studies

Research Paper No. 2019-18, July 29, 2019. https://papers.ssrn.com/sol3/papers.cfm?abstract_id=3312916.

Rekenthaler, John. "Why the Rich Have Become Richer." *Morningstar*, July 26, 2021. https://www.morningstar.com/articles/1049439/why-the-rich-have-become-richer.

Rennert, Kevin, et al. "Comprehensive Evidence Implies a Higher Social Cost of CO_2." *Nature* 610 (September 1, 2022).

Rhee, Robert J. "A Legal Theory of Shareholder Primacy." *Minnesota Law Review* 102, no. 5 (May 2018): 1951–2017. https://advance.lexis.com/api/document?collection=analytical-materials&id=urn:contentItem:5SPF-G2B0-00CW-82FD-00000-00&context=1516831.

Ricardo, David. *On the Principles of Political Economy, and Taxation.* London: John Murray, 1817.

Rikap, Cecilia. *Capitalism, Power and Innovation: Intellectual Monopoly Capitalism Uncovered.* Oxford: Routledge, 2022.

Rikap, Cecilia, and Bengt-Åke Lundvall. "Big Tech, Knowledge Predation and the Implications for Development." *Innovation and Development* 12 (December 2020): 389–416. https://doi.org/10.1080/2157930X.2020.1855825.

Ritchie, Hannah, and Max Roser. "China: Energy Country Profile." *Our World in Data.* Accessed February 10, 2022. https://ourworldindata.org/energy/country/china.

Robertson, Darryl. "The Black Panther Party and the Free Breakfast for Children Program." *Black Perspectives*, February 26, 2016. https://www.aaihs.org/the-black-panther-party/.

Robinson, Cedric. *Black Marxism: The Making of the Black Radical Tradition*, London: Zed Books, 1983.

Rock, Edward, Hideki Kanda, and Reinier Kraakman. "Significant Corporate Actions." In *The Anatomy of Corporate Law, A Comparative and Functional Approach*, edited by Reinier Kraakman, Paul Davies, Henry Hansmann, Gerard Hertig, Klaus Hopt, Heideki Kanda, and Edward Rock, 131–56. Oxford: Oxford University Press, 2004.

Roe, Mark J. "The Shareholder Wealth Maximization Norm and Industrial Organization." *University of Pennsylvania Law Review* 149, no. 6 (2011): 2063–82. https://dx.doi.org/10.2139/ssrn.282703.

Rogerson, Michael, Andrew Crane, Vivek Soundararajan, Johanne Gosvold, and Charles H. Cho. "Organisational Responses to Mandatory Modern Slavery Disclosure Legislation: A Failure of Experimentalist Governance?" *Accounting, Auditing & Accountability Journal*, 33 no. 7 (2020): 1505–34.

Rosenthal, Caitlin. *Accounting for Slavery: Masters and Management.* Cambridge: Harvard University Press, 2018.

Rosenthal, Caitlin. "Capitalism when Labor was Capital: Slavery, Power, and Price in Antebellum America." *Capitalism: A Journal of History and Economics* 1, (2020): 296.

Rosner, David. "The Inflation Reduction Act's Climate Provisions: A Pleasant Surprise." *Milbank Quarterly*, August 25, 2022.

Rothstein, Bo. "Social Capital in the Social Democratic Welfare State." *Politics & Society* 29, no. 2 (June 2001): 207–41.

Rothstein, Richard. *The Color of Law: A Forgotten History of How Our Government Segregated America*. New York: Liveright, 2017.

Rotman, David. "Are you Ready to be a Techno-Optimist Again?" *MIT Technology Review*, February 24, 2021.

Rowley, Charles K., and Bin Wu. *Britannia 1066–1884: From Medieval Absolutism to the Birth of Freedom under Constitutional Monarchy, Limited Suffrage, and the Rule of Law*. Cham, Switzerland: Springer International Publishing, 2014.

Ruef, Martin. *Between Slavery and Capitalism: The Legacy of Emancipation in the American South*. Princeton: Princeton University Press, 2014.

Ruggie, John Gerard. "International Regimes, Transactions, and Change: Embedded Liberalism in the Postwar Economic Order." *International Organization* 36, no. 2 (Spring 1982): 379–415.

Ruggie, John. *Just Business: Multinational Corporations and Human Rights*. New York: W.W. Norton & Company, 2013.

Ruhl, J.B., and Robin Craig. "4° Celsius." *Minnesota Law Review* 106, no. 1 (2021): 191–282.

Sachs, Jeffrey. "6 Ways America Can Get Back on Track with the UN Sustainable Development Goals." *State of the Planet*, September 21, 2018. https://news .climate.columbia.edu/2018/09/21/america-sustainable-development-goals/.

Saez, Emmanuel, and Gabriel Zucman. "The Rise of Income and Wealth Inequality in America: Evidence from Distributional Macroeconomic Accounts." *Journal of Economic Perspectives* 34, no. 4 (2020): 3–26.

Salzman, James, and Barton Thompson. *Environmental Law and Policy*. 5th ed. St. Paul, MN: Foundation Press, 2019.

Sanandaji, Nima. "Nordic Countries Aren't Actually Socialist." *Foreign Policy*, October 27, 2021. https://foreignpolicy.com/2021/10/27/nordic-countries-not -socialist-denmark-norway-sweden-centrist/.

Saunders, Harry. "Does Capitalism Require Endless Growth? Marx and Malthus Reconsidered." *Breakthrough Institute*, June 21, 2016. https:// thebreakthrough.org/journal/issue-6/does-capitalism-require-endless-growth #:~:text=In%20the%20pages%20that%20follow,global%20population %20have%20been%20satisfied.

Saz-Gil, Isabel, Ignacio Bretos, and Millán Díaz-Foncea. "Cooperatives and Social Capital: A Narrative Literature Review and Directions for Future Research." *Sustainability* 13, no. 2 (2021): 534–51. https://doi.org/10.3390/su13020534.

Schaeffer, Katherine. "6 Facts about Economic Inequality in the U.S." *Pew Research Center*, February 7, 2020. https://www.pewresearch.org/fact-tank/ 2020/02/07/6-facts-about-economic-inequality-in-the-u-s/.

Schatzinger, Henrik M., and Steven E. Martin. *Game Changers: How Dark Money and Super PACS Are Transforming U.S. Campaigns.* Lanham, MD: Rowman & Littlefield, 2019.

Scherer, Frederic M. "The Dynamics of Capitalism." HKS Working Paper no. RWP10-001, December 15, 2009. http://dx.doi.org/10.2139/ssrn.1523309.

Schmalensee, Richard, and Robert N. Stavins. "The SO2 Allowance Trading System: The Ironic History of a Grand Policy Experiment." *Journal of Economic Perspectives* 27, no. 1 (2013): 102–22.

Schneider, Sabrina, and Thomas Clauß. "Business Models for Sustainability: Choices and Consequences." *Organization & Environment,* 33, no. 3 (2019): 384–407.

Schuman, Michael. "The Electric-Car Lesson that China is Serving Up for America." *Atlantic,* May 21, 2021.

Scotchmer, Suzanne. *Innovation and Incentives.* Cambridge, MA: MIT Press, 2004.

Scott, Bruce R. *Capitalism: Its Origins and Evolution as a System of Governance.* New York: Springer, 2011.

Scott, Inara. "Antitrust and Socially Responsible Collaboration: A Chilling Combination?" *American Business Law Journal* 53, (2016): 97–144. https://doi.org/10.1111/ablj.12073.

Searchinger, Tim, Richard Waite, Craig Hanson, Janet Ranganathan, and Emily Matthews. *Creating a Sustainable Food Future.* World Resources Institute (WRI), July 2019. https://www.wri.org/publication/creating-sustainable-food-future.

Seelkopf, Laura, and Hanna Lierse. "Democracy and the Global Spread of Progressive Taxation." *Global Social Policy* 20, no. 2 (2020): 165–91.

Selman, Paul. "Social Capital, Sustainability and Environmental Planning." *Planning Theory & Practice* 2, no. 1 (2001): 13–30. https://doi.org/10.1080/14649350122850.

Sentencing Project. *Report to the United Nations on Racial Disparities in the U.S. Criminal Justice System.* April 19, 2018. https://www.sentencingproject.org/publications/un-report-on-racial-disparities/.

Setälä, Maija. "Inclusion, Participation and Future Generations." In *The Routledge Handbook of Democracy and Sustainability,* edited by Basil Bornemann, Henrike Knappe, and Patrizia Nanz, 69–82. London: Routledge, 2022.

Sewell, William H. "Connecting Capitalism to the French Revolution: The Parisian Promenade and the Origins of Civic Equality in Eighteenth-Century France." *Critical Historical Studies* 1, no. 1 (March 2014): 5–46.

Silva, Christianna. "Food Insecurity in the U.S. by the Numbers." *National Public Radio,* September 27, 2020. https://www.npr.org/2020/09/27/912486921/food-insecurity-in-the-u-s-by-the-numbers.

Silver, Caleb. "The Top 25 Economies in the World." *Investopedia,* February 2022. https://www.investopedia.com/insights/worlds-top-economies/.

Simard, Suzanne W., David A. Perry, Melanie D. Jones, David D. Myrold, Daniel M. Durall, and Randy Molina. "Net Transfer of Carbon between Ectomycorrhizal

Tree Species in the Field." *Nature* 388 (1997): 579–82. https://doi.org/10.1038/41557.

Simon, Paul E. "How the Senate Was Corrupted by Soft Money." In *Inside the Campaign Finance Battle: Court Testimony on the New Reforms*, edited by Anthony Corrado, Thomas E. Mann, and Trevor Potter, 317–18. Washington, DC: Brookings Institution Press, 2003.

Sligh, Michael, and Thomas Cierpka. "Organic Values." In *Organic Farming: An International History*, edited by William Lockeretz, 30–39. Oxfordshire: CAB International, 2007.

Smil, Vaclav. *Energy and Civilization: A History*. Cambridge, MA; London: The MIT Press, 2018.

Smith, Adam. *An Inquiry into the Nature and Causes of the Wealth of Nations*. Indianapolis: Liberty Classics, 1976.

Smith, Adam. *The Wealth of Nations*. London: J. M. Dent, 1958.

Smith, Noah. "The Metaverse and (near-)Infinite Economic Growth." *Noahpinion* (blog). *Substack*, November 9, 2021. https://noahpinion.substack.com/p/the-metaverse-and-near-infinite-economic.

Solongo, Dolgor. *Russian Capitalism and Money-Laundering*. New York: United Nations, 2001. https://www.imolin.org/pdf/imolin/rc84066e.pdf.

Solow, Robert M. "Technical Change and the Aggregate Production Function." *Review of Economics and Statistics* 39, no. 3 (1957): 312–20.

Sorkin, Andrew Ross, et al. "A Free Market Manifesto That Changed the World, Reconsidered." *New York Times*, September 11, 2020, https://www.nytimes.com/2020/09/11/business/dealbook/milton-friedman-doctrine-social-responsibility-of-business.html.

Sprinkle, Geoffrey B., and Laureen A. Maines. "The Benefits and Costs of Corporate Social Responsibility." *Business Horizons* 53, no. 5 (2010): 445–53.

Starr, Evan. "Are Noncompetes Holding Down Wages?" In *Inequality and the Labor Market: The Case for Greater Competition*, edited by Sharon Block and Benjamin Harris. Washington, DC: Brookings Institution Press, 2021.

Statista Metals & Electronics. "Passenger and Commercial Vehicle Sales in China from 2009 to 2020." *Statista*, February 1, 2022. https://www.statista.com/statistics/233743/vehicle-sales-in-china/.

Statista Transportation and Logistics. "Light Vehicle Retail Sales in the United States from 1976 to 2021." *Statista*, January 13, 2022. https://www.statista.com/statistics/199983/us-vehicle-sales-since-1951/.

Statista Transportation and Logistics. "Vehicles and Road Traffic." *Statista*. Accessed February 10, 2022. https://www.statista.com/markets/419/topic/487/vehicles-road-traffic/#overview.

Stein, Gertrude. *Geography and Plays*. Boston: Four Seas Company, 1922.

Stern, D. I. "The Rise and Fall of the Environmental Kuznets Curve." *World Development* 32, no. 8 (August 2004): 1419–39.

Sternlight, Jean R. "Mandatory Arbitration Stymies Progress Towards Justice in Employment Law: Where to, #MeToo?" *Harvard Civil Rights-Civil Liberties Law Review* 54, no. 1 (Winter 2019): 155–210.

Stewart, Frances. "Sustainability and Inequality." *Development* 57, no. 3–4 (2015): 344–61.

Stiglitz, Joseph. "The American Economy Is Rigged." *Scientific American*, November 1, 2018. https://www.scientificamerican.com/article/the-american -economy-is-rigged/.

Stiglitz, Joseph. *People, Power and Profits: Progressive Capitalism for an Age of Discontent.* New York, NY: W.W. Norton, 2019.

Stiglitz, Joseph. *The Price of Inequality.* New York, NY: W. W. Norton, 2012.

Stiglitz, Joseph. "Roaring Nineties." *Atlantic*, October 2002. https://www.theatlantic .com/magazine/archive/2002/10/the-roaring-nineties/302604/.

Stockholm Resilience Centre. "The Nine Planetary Boundaries." Last visited October 10, 2022. https://www.stockholmresilience.org/research/planetary -boundaries/the-nine-planetary-boundaries.html.

Stone, Katherine V. W., and Alexander J. S. Colvin. *The Arbitration Epidemic: Mandatory Arbitration Deprives Workers and Consumers of Their Rights.* Washington, DC: Economic Policy Institute, 2015. https://files.epi.org/2015/arbitration -epidemic.pdf.

Stout, Lynn. *Cultivating Conscience: How Good Laws Make Good People.* Princeton: Princeton University Press, 2011.

Strozewski, Zoe. "10 Percent of Americans Don't Believe in Climate Change, 15 Percent Unsure: Poll." *Newsweek*, October 26, 2021.

Stucke, Maurice E. "Is Competition Always Good?" *Journal of Antitrust Enforcement* 1, no. 1 (April 2013): 162–197. https://doi.org/10.1093/jaenfo/jns008.

Suddaby, Roy, and Rajat Panwar. "On the Complexity of Managing Transparency." *California Management Review* 65, no. 1 (2022). https://doi.org/10.1177/ 00081256221128766.

Swanson, Ana. "Nike and Coca-Cola Lobby Against Xinjiang Forced Labor Bill." *New York Times*, January 20, 2021. https://www.nytimes.com/2020/11/29/ business/economy/nike-coca-cola-xinjiang-forced-labor-bill.html.

Sweeney, Shauna J. "Gendering Racial Capitalism and the Black Heretical Tradition." In *Histories of Racial Capitalism*, edited by Destin Jenkins and Justin Leroy. New York: Columbia University Press, 2021. https://doi.org/10.7312/ jenk19074-004.

Tabuchi, Hiroko, and Nadja Popovich. "People of Color Breathe More Hazardous Air. The Sources Are Everywhere." *New York Times*, April 28, 2021. https:// www.nytimes.com/2021/04/28/climate/air-pollution-minorities.html.

Taheri, Shahrad, et al. "Effect of intensive lifestyle intervention on bodyweight and glycaemia in early type 2 diabetes (DIADEM-I): an open-label, parallel-group, randomized controlled trial." *Lancet Diabetes & Endocrinology* 8 (2020): 477–89.

Talmazan, Yuliya. "China's Coronavirus Hospital Built in 10 Days Opens Its Doors, State Media Says." *NBC News,* February 3, 2020. https://www.nbcnews.com/ news/world/china-s-coronavirus-hospital-built-10-days-opens-its-doors -n1128531.

Taylor, Bron. "Religion and Environmentalism in America and Beyond." In *The Oxford Handbook of Religion and Ecology,* edited by Roger S. Gottlieb. Oxford, UK: Oxford University Press, 2006.

Thomas, Dominique, and Tabbye Chavous. "The Black Radical Tradition of Resistance: A Series on Black Social Movements." *Medium,* February 6, 2019. https://medium.com/national-center-for-institutional-diversity/the-black -radical-tradition-of-resistance-7277f09ef396.

Thrush, Glenn, and Lisa Friedman. "Justice Dept. Tries to Shift Environmental Justice Efforts From Symbolic to Substantive." *New York Times,* May 12, 2022. https://www.nytimes.com/2022/05/12/us/politics/justice-department -environmental-justice.html/.

Tigar, Michael E. *Law and the Rise of Capitalism.* New York: Monthly Review Press, 2000.

Timberg, Scott. "Book Publishing in Crisis: Capitalism Kills Culture." *Salon,* November 10, 2012. https://www.salon.com/2012/11/10/book_publishing _crisis_capitalism_kills_culture/.

Tollefson, Jeff. "Why Deforestation and Extinctions Make Pandemics More Likely." *Nature* 584 (August 7, 2020): 175–76.

Torres-Spelliscy, Ciara. "Does 'We the People' Include Corporations?" American Bar Association. *Human Rights Magazine* 4, no. 2 (January 2018).

Tsing, Anna. "Supply Chains and the Human Condition." *Rethinking Marxism* 21, no. 2 (2009): 148–76.

Tsing, Anna. "What Is Emerging? Supply Chains and the Remaking of Asia." *Professional Geographer* 68, no. 2 (2015): 148.

Tuholske, Jack B. "U.S. State Constitutions and Environmental Protection: Diamonds in the Rough." *Widener Law Review* 21 (2015): 239–55.

Tyson, Alec. "On Climate Change, Republicans Are Open to Some Policy Approaches, Even as They Assign the Issue Low Priority." *Pew Research Center,* 2021. https://www.pewresearch.org/fact-tank/2021/07/23/on-climate -change-republicans-are-open-to-some-policy-approaches-even-as-they -assign-the-issue-low-priority/.

Tyson, Alec, and Brian Kennedy. "Two-Thirds of Americans Think Government Should Do More on Climate." *Pew Research Center,* 2020. https://www.pewre search.org/science/2020/06/23/two-thirds-of-americans-think-government -should-do-more-on-climate/.

Ueda, Ryoko. "How Is Corporate Governance in Japan Changing? Developments in Listed Companies and Roles of Institutional Investors." OECD Corporate Governance Working Papers, no. 17. Paris: OECD Publishing, August 7, 2015. https://doi.org/10.1787/5jrw7j3s37hh-en.

Union of Concerned Scientists. "Each Country's Share of CO2 Emissions." Last updated January 14, 2022. https://www.ucsusa.org/resources/each-countrys -share-co2-emissions.

United Nations. "2012—International Year of Cooperatives." Accessed March 18, 2022. https://www.un.org/en/events/coopsyear/.

United Nations. "Decent Work and Economic Growth." United Nations Sustainable Development Goals. Accessed April 21, 2022. https://www.un.org/ sustainabledevelopment/economic-growth/.

United Nations. "International Day for the Abolition of Slavery." Accessed April 22, 2022. https://www.un.org/en/observances/slavery-abolition-day.

United Nations. "Population." *United Nations*, June 23, 2022. https://www.un.org/ en/global-issues/population.

United Nations Conference on Trade and Development. *World Investment Report 2021*. New York: United Nations Publications, 2021.

United Nations Department of Economic and Social Affairs. *Global Sustainable Development Report 2019*. United Nations, 2019. https://movendi.ngo/wp -content/uploads/2019/09/Global-Sustainable-Development-Report-2019.pdf.

United Nations Food and Agriculture Organization (FAO). *The Future of Food and Agriculture—Trends and Challenges*. United Nations Food and Agriculture Organization, 2017. http://www.fao.org/3/a-i6583e.pdf.

United Nations Food and Agriculture Organization (FAO). *The Importance of Ukraine and the Russian Federation for Global Agricultural Markets and the Risks Associated with the Current Conflict*. United Nations Food and Agriculture Organization, March 25, 2022. https://www.fao.org/3/ cb9236en/cb9236en.pdf.

United Nations Food and Agriculture Organization (FAO). *The state of the world's land and water resources for food and agriculture—Systems at breaking point*. United Nations Food and Agriculture Organization, 2021. https://doi.org/10 .4060/cb7654en.

United Nations Framework Convention on Climate Change (UNFCCC). *Glasgow Climate Pact*. United Nations, November 13, 2021. https://unfccc.int/sites/ default/files/resource/cop26_auv_2f_cover_decision.pdf.

United Nations Human Rights: Office of the Commissioner. "Mandatory Human Rights Due Diligence (mHRDD)." Accessed April 22, 2022. https://www.ohchr .org/en/special-procedures/wg-business/mandatory-human-rights-due -diligence-mhrdd.

United Nations Secretary General (UNSG). *Synthesis Report: The Road to Dignity by 2030: Ending Poverty, Transforming All Lives and Protecting the Planet*. United Nations, December 4, 2014.

United Nations Secretary-General's High-Level Panel on Access to Medicines
(USG-HLP). *Promoting Innovation and Access to Health Technologies.* United
Nations, September 14, 2016. http://www.unsgaccessmeds.org/s/UNSG-HLP
-Report-FINAL-12-Sept-2016.pdf.

United Nations World Commission on Environment and Development. *Report
of the World Commission on Environment and Development: Our Common
Future.* Oxford University Press, 1987. https://sustainabledevelopment.un
.org/content/documents/5987our-common-future.pdf.

United States Department of Energy (DOE). "The History of the Electric Car."
ENERGY.GOV, September 15, 2014. https://www.energy.gov/articles/history
-electric-car.

United States Energy Information Administration. *Country Analysis Executive
Summary: China.* US Department of Energy. September 30, 2020. https://www
.eia.gov/international/analysis/country/CHN.

United States Energy Information Administration. "Energy Explained: Electricity in the United States." Updated March 18, 2021. https://www.eia.gov/
energyexplained/electricity/electricity-in-the-us.php.

United States Energy Information Administration. *U.S. Energy-Related Carbon
Dioxide Emissions, 2020.* U.S. Department of Energy, December 2021. https://
www.eia.gov/environment/emissions/carbon/pdf/2020_co2analysis.pdf.

United States Environmental Protection Agency (EPA). "EPA Report Shows Disproportionate Impacts of Climate Change on Socially Vulnerable Populations in
the United States." (September 2, 2021). https://www.epa.gov/newsreleases/epa
-report-shows-disproportionate-impacts-climate-change-socially-vulnerable.

United States Environmental Protection Agency (EPA). "Water Management
Plans and Best Practices at the EPA." *United States Environmental Protection
Agency,* June 15, 2021. https://www.epa.gov/greeningepa/water-management
-plans-and-best-practices-epa.

Usman, Maham. "Breaking Up Big Tech: Lessons from AT&T." *University of Pennsylvania Law Review* 170, no. 523 (2021).

U.S. Bureau of Labor Statistics. "Education Pays." Modified April 21, 2021. https://
www.bls.gov/emp/chart-unemployment-earnings-education.htm.

U.S. Department of Justice Office of Public Affairs. "Justice Department Reaches
Settlement with Wells Fargo Resulting in More Than $175 Million in Relief
for Homeowners to Resolve Fair Lending Claims." Press release, July 12,
2012. https://www.justice.gov/opa/pr/justice-department-reaches-settlement
-wells-fargo-resulting-more-175-million-relief.

U.S. Department of Labor: Bureau of International Labor Affairs. "List of Goods
Produced by Child Labor or Forced Labor." Accessed April 21, 2022. https://
www.dol.gov/agencies/ilab/reports/child-labor/list-of-goods#:~:text=The
%20most%20common%20agricultural%20goods,and%20diamonds%20are
%20most%20common.

U.S. Department of State: Office to Monitor and Combat Trafficking in Persons. "What is Modern Slavery?" Accessed April 21, 2022. https://www.state.gov/ what-is-modern-slavery/.

U.S. Department of the Treasury. "Freedman's Bank Demise." Last visited July 15, 2022. https://home.treasury.gov/about/history/freedmans-bank-building/ freedmans-bank-demise.

U.S. Government Accountability Office, *Forced Labor: CBP Should Improve Communication to Strengthen Trade Enforcement*. GAO-21-259. March 1, 2021. https://www.gao.gov/assets/gao-21-259.pdf.

"U.S. Senator Tammy Baldwin Reintroduces Legislation to Rein in Stock Buybacks and Give Workers a Voice on Corporate Boards." Office of Senator Tammy Baldwin. Updated March 27, 2019. https://www.baldwin.senate.gov/press -releases/reward-work-act-2019.

U.S. War Department. Special Field Orders, No. 15, Headquarters Military Division of the Mississippi, January 16, 1865. Orders & Circulars, series 44, Adjutant General's Office, Record Group 94, National Archives. http://www.freedmen .umd.edu/sfo15.htm.

Valkila, Joni. "Fair Trade Organic Coffee Production in Nicaragua—Sustainable Development or a Poverty Trap?" *Ecological Economics* 68, no. 12 (October 2009): 3018–25. https://doi.org/https://doi.org/10.1016/j.ecolecon.2009.07.002.

Varoufakis, Yanis. *Talking to My Daughter about the Economy: or, How Capitalism Works—and How It Fails*. Translated by Jacob T. Moe. New York: Farrar, Straus and Giroux, 2017.

Vasapollo, Luciano. *Crisis of Capitalism: Compendium of Applied Economics (Global Capitalism)*. Vol. 34. Translated by Barbato Alessandra. Studies in Critical Social Sciences, Leiden, Netherlands: Brill, 2012.

Ventola, C. Lee. "The Antibiotic Resistance Crisis." *Pharmacy and Therapeutics (P&T)* 40, no. 4 (April 2015): 277–83.

Vermeule, Adrian. "The Invisible Hand in Legal and Political Theory." *Virginia Law Review* 96, no. 1417 (2010).

Villarosa, Linda. "Why America's Black Mothers and Babies Are in a Life-or-Death Crisis." *New York Times*, April 11, 2018. https://www.nytimes.com/2018/04/ 11/magazine/black-mothers-babies-death-maternal-mortality.html?smid=fb -nytimes&smtyp=cur.

Viscusi, W. Kip. "The Fatal Failure of the Regulatory State." *William & Mary Law Review* 60, no. 589 (2018).

Vogel, Kenneth, and Shane Goldmacher. "Democrats Decried Dark Money. Then They Won with It in 2020." *New York Times*, January 29, 2022.

Von der Leyen, Ursula. "State of the Union 2021." *European Commission*, September 15, 2021. Video, 59:43. https://ec.europa.eu/info/strategy/strategic -planning/state-union-addresses/state-union-2021_en.

Vornovytskyy, Marina, and James Boyce. "Economic Inequality and

Environmental Quality: Evidence of Pollution in Russia." PERI Working Paper Series, No. 217, 2010.

Waagstein, Patricia Rinwigati. "The Mandatory Corporate Social Responsibility in Indonesia: Problems and Implications." *Journal of Business Ethics* 98, no. 3 (2011): 455–66.

Wall, Derek. *Elinor Ostrom's Rules for Radicals: Cooperative Alternatives beyond Markets and States*. London: Pluto Press, 2017.

Wallison, Peter. "Only the Supreme Court Can Effectively Restrain the Administrative State." *National Review*, December 1, 2020.

Wang, Qian, Junsheng Dou, and Shenghua Jia. "A Meta-analytic Review of Corporate Social Responsibility and Corporate Financial Performance: The Moderating Effect of Contextual Factors." *Business & Society* 55, no. 8 (2016): 1083–1121.

Ward, James D., Paul C. Sutton, Adrian D. Werner, Robert Costanza, Steve H. Mohr, and Craig T. Simmons. "Is Decoupling GDP Growth from Environmental Impact Possible?" *PLoS One* 11, no. 10 (October 2016). https://doi.org/10.1371/journal.pone.0164733.

Watts, Lynelle, and David Hodgson. "Capitalism and Neoliberalism." In *Social Justice Theory and Practice for Social Work*, 59–80. Springer, (2019). https://doi.org/10.1007/978-981-13-3621-8.

Wells, Harwell. "The Modernization of Corporation Law 1920–1940." *University of Pennsylvania Journal of Business Law* 11, no. 573 (2009): 573–630. https://scholarship.law.upenn.edu/jbl/vol11/iss3/2/.

White House. "The American Jobs Plan Will Support Women's Employment." Modified April 21, 2021. https://www.whitehouse.gov/briefing-room/statements-releases/2021/04/21/fact-sheet-the-american-jobs-plan-will-support-womens-employment/.

Wiese, Andrew. *Places of Their Own: African American Suburbanization in the Twentieth Century*. Chicago: University of Chicago, 2004.

Wilkerson, Isabel. *Caste: The Origins of Our Discontents*. New York: Random House, 2020.

Wilkie, Christina. "Lobbyists Shielded Carried Interest from Biden's Tax Hikes, Top White House Economist Says." *CNBC*, September 30, 2021. https://www.cnbc.com/2021/09/30/lobbying-kept-carried-interest-out-of-bidens-tax-plan-bernstein-says.html.

Williams, Cynthia A., and John M. Conley. "An Emerging Third Way? The Erosion of the Anglo-American Shareholder Value Construct." *Cornell International Law Journal* 38, no. 2 (2005): 493–552. https://scholarship.law.cornell.edu/cgi/viewcontent.cgi?article=1645&context=cilj.

Williams, Eric, and Colin A. Palmer. *Capitalism and Slavery*. Chapel Hill: University of North Carolina Press, 1944.

Wolcher, Louis E. "The End of Technology: A Polemic." *Washington Law Review* 79, no. 1 (2004): 331–88.

Wolf, Naomi. *This Changes Everything: Capitalism v. the Climate*. New York: Simon & Schuster, 2015.

Woll, Lisa, and Judy Mares. "The Department of Labor Is Attacking Sustainable Investments—And Harming Plan Participants." *Institutional Investor*, August 25, 2020. https://www.institutionalinvestor.com/article/b1n2lp9y127bwk/The-Department-of-Labor-Is-Attacking-Sustainable-Investments-And-Harming-Plan-Participants.

Wood, Donna J. "Corporate Social Performance Revisited." *Academy of Management Review* 16, no. 4 (1991): 691–718.

Wood, Ellen Meiksins. *The Origin of Capitalism: A Longer View*. London: Monthly Review Press, 1999.

Wootton, David. *The Invention of Science: A New History of the Scientific Revolution*. New York, NY: Harper Perennial, 2016.

Worland, Justin. "The Reason Fossil Fuel Companies Are Finally Reckoning with Climate Change." *Time*, January 16, 2020.

World Bank. "GDP (Current US$)—China." Accessed February 10, 2022. https://data.worldbank.org/indicator/NY.GDP.MKTP.CD?locations=CN.

World Bank. "GDP Growth (Annual %)—China." Accessed February 10, 2022. https://data.worldbank.org/indicator/NY.GDP.MKTP.KD.ZG?locations=CN.

World Health Organization (WHO). *World Health Statistics 2022: Monitoring Health for the SDGs, Sustainable Development Goals*. Geneva: World Health Organization, 2022.

World Justice Report. *WJP Rule of Law Index 2020*. https://worldjusticeproject.org/our-work/research-and-data/wjp-rule-law-index-2020.

Worstall, Tim. "Peak Stuff has Been and Gone." Adam Smith Institute Blog, November 6, 2011. https://www.adamsmith.org/blog/energy-environment/peak-stuff-has-been-and-gone.

Wronski, Laura. "Axios | Momentive Poll: Capitalism and Socialism." *SurveyMonkey*. https://www.surveymonkey.com/curiosity/axios-capitalism-update/.

Yale Center for Environmental Policy & Law. "About the EPI." *Environmental Performance Index*. Accessed June 27, 2022. https://epi.yale.edu/about-epi.

Yergin, Daniel. *The New Map: Energy, Climate, and the Clash of Nations*. New York: Penguin Press, 2020.

Zall, Paul M., ed. "Becoming a Lawyer: 1735–1758." In *Adams on Adams*, 1–14. Lexington: University Press of Kentucky, 2004.

Zeballos-Roig, Joseph. "How the Koch Brothers Used Their Massive Fortune to Power a Conservative Crusade that Reshaped American Politics." *Insider*, November 13, 2020. https://www.businessinsider.com/koch-brothers-fortune-power-conservative-crusade-american-politics-2019-8.

Zeira, Anna. "Mental Health Challenges Related to Neoliberal Capitalism in the United States." *Community Mental Health Journal* 58, no. 2 (2022): 205–212. https://doi.org/10.1007/s10597-021-00840-7.

Zingales, Luigi. "Toward a Political Theory of the Firm." *Journal of Economic Perspectives* 38, no. 3 (2017): 113–30.

Zitelmann, Rainer. "The Driving Force Of Capitalism Is Empathy, Not Greed." *Forbes*, September 2, 2019. https://www.forbes.com/sites/rainerzitelmann/2019/09/02/the-driving-force-of-capitalism-is-empathy-not-greed/?sh=1253a21767aa.

Zuboff, Shoshana. *The Age of Surveillance Capitalism: The Fight for a Human Future at the New Frontier of Power.* New York: PublicAffairs, 2019.

Zucman, Gabriel. "Global Wealth Inequality." *Annual Review of Economics* 11 (2019): 109–38.

Contributors

Gerlinde Berger-Walliser teaches in the School of Business at the University of Connecticut. She is inaugural co-Director of EUROBIZ, a dual-degree program in Business and German Studies. Prior to joining UConn, she held academic positions in France and Germany and was a member of the German Bar.

David Bernell is an associate professor of political science in the School of Public Policy at Oregon State University. He is the author of *The Energy Security Dilemma: US Policy and Practice*, and *Constructing US Foreign Policy: The Curious Case of Cuba*. Prior to coming to OSU, he served as a political appointee in the Clinton Administration with the U.S. Office of Management and Budget, and with the U.S. Department of the Interior.

Christy Anderson Brekken is a senior instructor in the department of applied economics at Oregon State University, Corvallis. She has published research on governance, sustainability, and scale in the context of human-environment systems such as agriculture and land tenure.

Liz Brown is a professor of law and the Wilder Professor of Teaching Excellence at Bentley University in Waltham, Massachusetts. Before joining the Bentley faculty, she represented Fortune 100 companies as a litigator for over a decade in London, San Francisco, and Boston. She is also the author of *Life After Law: How to Find Work You Love with the J.D. You Have* and the co-author, with Amy Impellizzeri, of *How to Leave the Law*.

Daniel R. Cahoy is a professor of business law and the former research director for the Center for the Business of Sustainability at Penn State's Smeal College of Business. He was a member of the editorial board of the peer-reviewed *American Business Law Journal* from 2005–2010 and served as the editor in chief from 2009–2010. He was the Visiting Fulbright Chair in International Humanitarian Law at the University of Ottawa in 2009.

Victor B. Flatt is the Coleman P. Burke Chair in Environmental Law and the associate director of the Burke Center for Environmental Law at Case Western University School of Law. He also holds an appointment as an Energy Fellow at the University of Houston. He was previously the inaugural O'Quinn Chair in Environmental Law at UHLC from 2002–2009, and the Dwight Olds Chair in Law at UHLC from 2017–2023. He was also the inaugural Taft Distinguished Professor in Environmental Law and the director of the Center for Climate, Energy, Environment, and Economics (CE3) at UNC Chapel Hill School of Law.

David Hess is a professor of business law and business ethics at the Ross School of Business at the University of Michigan. He is the Law, Public Policy, and Business Ethics section editor for the *Journal of Business Ethics*, and serves on the editorial boards of the *American Business Law Journal, Business Ethics Quarterly*, and the *Business and Human Rights Journal*. He is currently serving as a co-President of the Global Business and Human Rights Scholars Association.

Ellen Alexandra Holtmaat is a postdoctoral researcher at Oregon State University. Her research on the diffusion of private governance and the impact of environmental disasters has appeared in *World Development* (2019) and *PLoS ONE* (2022). Previously she was a teaching fellow at the London School of Economics.

Ruth Jebe is an associate professor of legal studies in business and the Hansberger Endowed Chair in Business Ethics in the College of Business & Economics at Boise State University. She is currently a member of the editorial board for the *American Business Law Journal*.

Mark J. Kaswan is a professor of political science at the University of Texas Rio Grande Valley. He works at the intersection of political theory and social change, working to expand our understanding of politics and democracy and to find ways to make democracy meaningful for people in their daily lives.

Ryan Katz-Rosene is an associate professor at the University of Ottawa, where he specializes in climate policy debates and environmental political economy. He is the former president of the Environmental Studies Association of Canada, and currently serves as an editor for *Studies in Political Economy.* He is the co-author (with Matthew Paterson) of *Thinking Ecologically about the Global Political Economy,* and co-editor (with Sarah Martin) of *Green Meat?*

Elizabeth J. Kennedy is a professor of law and social responsibility in the Sellinger School of Business at Loyola University Maryland. Prior to joining Loyola, she practiced law with Fried, Frank, Harris, Shriver & Jacobson LLP; served as labor and employment counsel to Senator Edward M. Kennedy on the Senate Health, Education, Labor & Pensions Committee; and organized workers for AFSCME Local 3299 and UNITE!

Dana Neacşu is an associate professor of legal research skills and Director of the Center of Legal Information at Duquesne Kline School of Law, where she teaches an experiential seminar in doctrinal Climate Change Law and Policy combined with Legal Research and Writing. She is also a political science lecturer at Columbia University, and adjunct faculty at Barnard College, where she teaches a course on environmental law, policy, research, and decision making.

Rajat Panwar is an associate professor of responsible and sustainable business at Oregon State University. He has edited two books and has published his work in *Business and Society, Business Strategy and the Environment, California Management Review,* and the *Journal of Business Ethics, Organization and Environment,* among others. He is a deputy editor for *Business and Society.*

Robert Prentice is the Ed and Molly Smith Professor of Business Law at the McCombs School of Business, University of Texas at Austin. He is the faculty director of Ethics Unwrapped, an ethics education video program housed in the Center for Leadership and Ethics. He has co-authored multiple textbooks and academic books and published more than 60 law review articles in such journals as the *Duke Law Journal, Northwestern University Law Review, Cornell Law Review, Georgetown Law Journal,* and the *American Business Law Journal.*

Inara Scott is the Gomo Family Professor and Senior Associate Dean in the College of Business at Oregon State University (OSU). Her research has appeared in numerous premier outlets, including the *American Business Law Journal, Harvard Environmental Law Review,* and the *University of Pennsylvania Journal of Constitutional Law.* She is the editor in chief of the *American Business Law Journal*. Prior to arriving at OSU, she practiced law for almost a decade, both in private practice and as corporate counsel.

Natalia Vidal is an associate professor at the Anderson School of Management, University of New Mexico. Her research focuses on the diffusion of corporate sustainability practices through business collective action for sustainability, socially and environmentally sustainable supply chain practices, and stakeholder engagement.

Index

Please note that *italicized* page numbers in this index indicate illustrations.